SUCCESSFUL GARDENING

A-Z of ANNUALS, BIENNIALS & BULBS

Published by The Reader's Digest Association Limited.

First Edition Copyright © 1993
The Reader's Digest Association Limited,
Berkeley Square House, Berkeley Square, London W1X 6AB

Copyright © 1993
The Reader's Digest Association Far East Limited
Philippines Copyright 1993
The Reader's Digest Association Far East Limited

Originally published as a partwork.
Successful Gardening
Copyright © 1990
Eaglemoss Publications Ltd.

Consultant editor: Lizzie Boyd

Typeset by SX Composing Limited in Century Schoolbook

PRINTED IN SPAIN

ISBN 0 276 42089 6

Opposite: Summer colours spill from baskets of trailing nasturtiums,
lobelias and petunias.

Overleaf: Early spring bulbs defy all weathers, miniature narcissi keeping
company with wood anemones.

Pages 6-7: Bedding tulips raise their straight-stemmed golden bowls
above a carpet of purple, dark-eyed pansies.

PUBLISHED BY THE READER'S DIGEST ASSOCIATION LIMITED
LONDON NEW YORK MONTREAL SYDNEY CAPE TOWN

Originally published in partwork form
by Eaglemoss Publications Limited

SUCCESSFUL GARDENING

A-Z of ANNUALS, BIENNIALS & BULBS

CONTENTS

SPECIAL FEATURES

A-Z OF ANNUALS AND BIENNIALS

A-Z OF BULBS AND CORMS

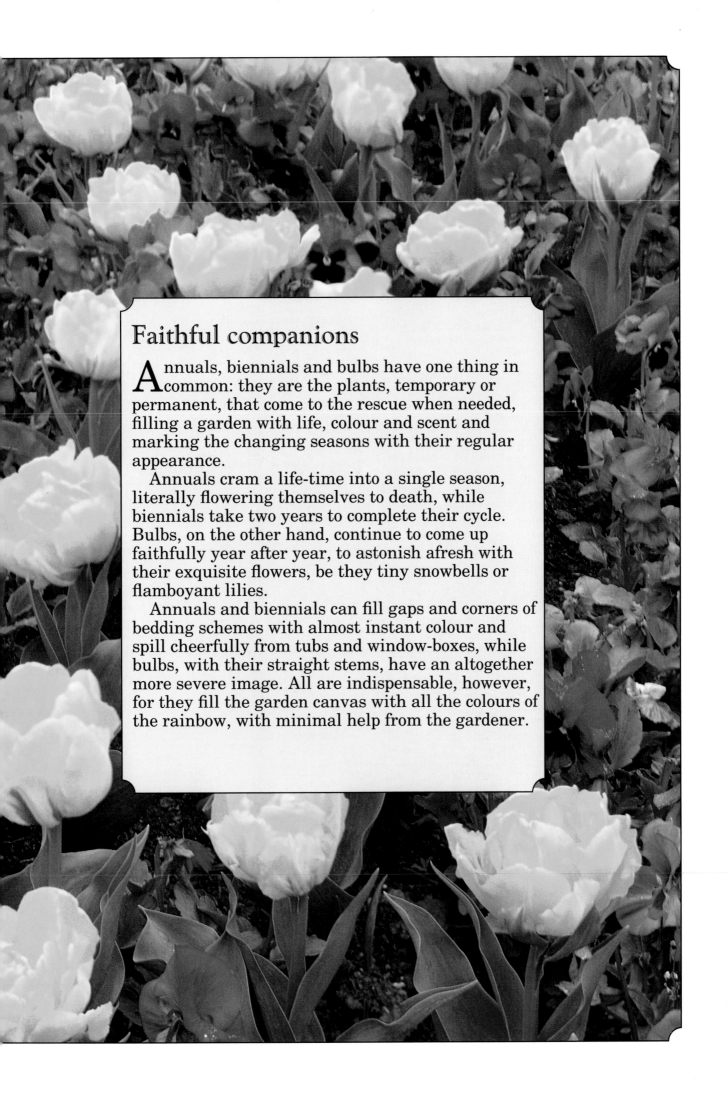

Faithful companions

Annuals, biennials and bulbs have one thing in common: they are the plants, temporary or permanent, that come to the rescue when needed, filling a garden with life, colour and scent and marking the changing seasons with their regular appearance.

Annuals cram a life-time into a single season, literally flowering themselves to death, while biennials take two years to complete their cycle. Bulbs, on the other hand, continue to come up faithfully year after year, to astonish afresh with their exquisite flowers, be they tiny snowbells or flamboyant lilies.

Annuals and biennials can fill gaps and corners of bedding schemes with almost instant colour and spill cheerfully from tubs and window-boxes, while bulbs, with their straight stems, have an altogether more severe image. All are indispensable, however, for they fill the garden canvas with all the colours of the rainbow, with minimal help from the gardener.

Half-hardy annuals Petunias and pelargoniums revel in sunny sheltered spots.

A-Z of annuals and biennials

Annuals and biennials flower just once, yet their ability to grow quickly from seed and their magnificent array of bright colours have earned them an affectionate place in every gardener's heart. Many of our most popular annuals (including petunias, begonias, marigolds and asters) come from the tropics. These annuals are half-hardy in Britain and cannot be moved outdoors until all danger of frost has passed. Sterile compost and heat are a must if seeds are to germinate or the seedlings to make steady growth. The extra attention is repaid, however, by long-lasting shows of flowers in the most brilliant colours.

Hardy annuals, such as pot marigolds, Californian poppies and sweet peas, are much less trouble, sprouting readily from seed. They ask little more than decent soil, a sunny or lightly shaded position, weed-free surroundings and sufficient water.

Whether hardy or half-hardy, annuals are the faithful standbys of many gardeners, filling gaps in beds and borders, providing cut flowers for the house and dying away without fuss at the end of the season.

Biennials, too, flower only once, but in their first year of growth, tucked away in a spare piece of land, they develop only roots and leaves, deferring the flowers until the second year. Like annuals, biennials are an essential element of the flower garden – wallflowers, forget-me-nots and polyanthus primroses in spring, and in summer such all-time favourites as Canterbury bells, hollyhocks and foxgloves.

ANNUAL EVENTS

**Easy to grow from seed, annuals
in all colours and sizes offer a chance to
try new partnerships every year.**

There are so many annuals with so many different habits and such a range of size that their uses are limited only by the imagination. Choose from the true annuals – there is everything from the 2.4m (8ft) tall sunflower to the sweet alyssum, at only 7.5cm (3in) – the sturdy biennials and the tender perennials treated as annuals.

Popular annuals, such as marigolds, lobelias and ageratums are widely used in summer bedding schemes, or containers and window-boxes. They can be bought in trays or strips but seed is much cheaper than plants and the sweeping range available encourages experimentation.

There are dozens of annuals suitable for the less formal mixed border. Sow them in gaps between perennials or in the spaces left by spring bulbs. Treat them as temporary features, useful until their partners have reached maturity, or resow them yearly to become part of the overall scheme.

Hardy favourites – corncockle, cornflower, corn marigold and field poppy – once common growing wild in cornfields, are worth sowing together for their nostalgic associations and their simple, enduring charm.

Annual climbers, such as sweet peas, morning glory, and nasturtiums (*Trapaeolum peregrinum*) provide quick and cheap decoration for fences and walls.

For tropical foliage colour effects, sow castor-oil plant (*Ricinus*), coleus, kochia and *Zea mays* 'Gracillima Variegata'.

▲ **Cottage garden favourite** The biennial Canterbury bell (*Campanula medium*) raises its bells over a pale blue sea of love-in-a-mist (*Nigella damascena*). Summer-flowering, both self-seed readily for future years.

▼ **Late-summer border** Dainty-leaved pink and white cosmos and sweet-scented nicotianas dominate a border fronted with bedding dahlias and perennial cerise-scarlet *Sedum spectabile* and silvery *Artemisia*.

◀ **Subtle companionship** The amiable nasturtium (*Tropaeolum majus*) is one of our easiest annuals. It is a well-known fact that it bears the best and most profuse flowers in poor ground. In rich soils, it tends to produce fewer blooms and more of its characteristic pale green rounded leaves – a good foil for the bright scarlet snapdragon spikes (*Antirrhinum majus*) that can so easily overwhelm a summer bedding scheme.

▼ **Summer riot** Annuals may have one flowering season only, but they more than compensate for their short life with a kaleidoscope of colours. It is impossible to ignore the impact of this carefully planned study in red, all achieved from dormant seeds in less than four months. Towering above the group, love-lies-bleeding (*Amaranthus caudatus*) droops its long wine-red flower tassels over spikes of carmine-pink, double-flowered clarkias and clumps of scarlet flax (*Linum grandiflorum*).

At their feet, nasturtiums (*Tropaeolum majus*) spread an orange-red carpet of spurred trumpet flowers.

▲ **Blue daisies** The kingfisher daisy (*Felicia bergeriana*) is aptly named for its flowers are indeed steel-blue, and borne in such profusion throughout summer as to smother the dwarf plants. South African in origin, it revels in a hot and sunny spot, spilling over the edge of border, raised bed or window-box, perhaps combined with fragrant, white-flowered sweet alyssum.

◄ Summer brightness
The pale green feathery lushness of summer cypress (*Kochia scoparia*) gives no indication of its rich autumn dress of crimson-purple. In high summer, carefully placed hummocks give substance to the floating blue flowers of love-in-a-mist (*Nigella damascena*) and the sprawling golden flowered *Mentzelia lindleyi.*

▼ Harmony in blue Half-hardy by nature, these two annuals revel in sun and each other's company. The multiflora petunia varieties are more weather-resistant than their larger-flowered counterparts, their elegant trumpets shielding tight clusters of lavender-blue *Ageratum houstonianum.*

▶ **Annual grasses** The misty froth of grasses such as *Agrostis nebulosa* (cloud grass) brings an aura of tranquillity to the vibrant tones of many annuals. They also add height to a low-growing composition, and in addition, the branched flower clusters of cloud grass retain their grace and charm if cut and dried for winter arrangements.

▶ **Wild-flower meadow** You don't need acres of garden to create a corner of nature — and conserve the native flowers that are fast disappearing from the countryside. Most seedsmen sell wild-flower mixtures, to be scattered in a sunny corner where they will form swathes of colour from, for example, yellow marigolds (*Chrysanthemum segetum*) and delicate-looking but tough poppies (*Papaver rhoeas*). Most seed selections also include blue cornflowers (*Centaurea*).

Adonis

pheasant's eye

Adonis aestivalis

□ Height 30-45cm (12-18in)
□ Planting distance 30cm (12in)
□ Flowers early and mid summer
□ Sunny or partially shaded site
□ Any humus-rich soil
□ Hardy annual

Pheasant's eye (*Adonis aestivalis*) is the only member of this small genus grown as an annual. The cup-shaped flowers, which appear in early to mid summer, have deep crimson petals and near-black stamens. The plants grow 30-45cm (12-18in) high, accompanied by fine green fern-like leaves.

For best effect, plant in drifts at the front of a border with other annuals and biennials. It also grows well in containers.

Cultivation

For early flowers, sow the seeds in a seed bed in their final position in autumn. After germination, thin the seedlings to 15cm (6in) apart and then, the following spring, to 30cm (12in).

Alternatively sow the seeds in trays under glass in spring and transplant to the final position in late spring, setting the seedlings 30cm (12in) apart. You can also sow the seeds directly in the final flowering position in spring and thin out the seedlings, but flowering will be slightly later.

Pests and diseases Watch out for slugs.

AFRICAN DAISY – see *Arctotis*
AFRICAN MARIGOLD – see *Tagetes*

Ageratum

floss flower

Ageratum houstonianum 'Blue Champion'

□ Height 12-30cm (5-12in)
□ Planting distance for dwarf varieties 23cm (9in); for taller varieties 30cm (12in)
□ Flowers early summer till first severe frost
□ Any moisture-retentive soil
□ Sheltered sunny or lightly shaded site
□ Half-hardy annual

Their abundance of flowers, and their long season – from early summer until the first severe frost – make *Ageratum* a popular bedding plant. Its low, compact habit and powder-puff flowers look most effective edging formal beds, filling gaps in borders of low-growing plants or brightening up window boxes and containers. Some of the taller varieties are useful for flower arranging, associating well with many other garden plants.

The original blue-flowered species, *Ageratum houstonianum*, has largely been replaced by garden varieties. These come in blue, pink, mauve and white.

The F1 hybrids – first generation plants obtained by crossing two varieties known for their ability to produce consistently similar offspring – are particularly vigorous and have the largest flower heads, but you do pay a little more for the seeds.

Popular varieties

'**Adriatic**', an F1 hybrid, has a neat compact habit, reaching 15-20cm (6-8in), and mid-blue flowers.

'**Blue Bouquet**' is a giant, reaching 45cm (18in) high, with lavender-blue flowers, good for cutting.

'**Blue Champion**', a vigorous but compact F1 hybrid, has dark green leaves and large clusters of mid-blue flowers. It grows 15cm (6in) high.

'**Blue Danube**' reaches 15-20cm (6-8in) high and has lavender-blue blooms. It is one of the best early-flowering F1 varieties.

'**Blue Horizon**' is a tall-growing F1 hybrid, to 60cm (2ft) and good for cutting. Small purple-blue flowers are borne in clusters.

'**Blue Mink**' is a compact plant reaching 23-30cm (9-12in) high with powder-blue flowers.

'**Blue Ribbon**', an F1 hybrid, is smothered in bright mid-blue flowers from early summer on. It grows 15-20cm (6-8in) high.

'**Blue Swords**' forms a sturdy and bushy plant, 20cm (8in) tall. It bears dense clusters of mid-blue flowers. Good weather resistance.

'**Capri**' bears rich deep blue flowers on compact plants, 20-30cm (8-12in) high.

'**Highness**' is another tall F1 hybrid, growing up to 60cm (2ft) high. It has clusters of white to pale pink flowers on long stems.

'**North Sea**', an F1 hybrid reach-

Agrostemma
corncockle

Agrostis
cloud grass

Agrostemma githago 'Milas'

Agrostis nebulosa

□ Height 60-120cm (2-4ft)
□ Planting distance 15cm (6in)
□ Flowers mid summer
□ Ordinary or poor garden soil
□ Open sunny site
□ Hardy annual

□ Height 30-45cm (12-18in)
□ Planting distance 15cm (6in)
□ Flowers early to late summer
□ Any well-drained soil
□ Full sun
□ Hardy annual grass

ing 15-20cm (6-8in) high, has deep blue or red flowers that continue until late autumn.
'Pacific', an F1 hybrid, grows 20cm (8in) high and forms a tight dome of deep mauve flowers on fast-growing plants.
'Pinky Improved Selection' is a new hybrid variety of bushy plants, 15-20cm (6-8in) tall. The flowers are dusty pink.
'Southern Cross' grows 20-30cm (8-12in) high and is suitable for bedding, containers and as cut flowers. The flower clusters are bi-coloured in pale blue and white.
'Summer Snow' is an F1 hybrid, 15-20cm (6-8in) tall, with pure white, fluffy flower heads.
'Swing Mixed' is an F1 hybrid mixture, with flowers in soft shades of blue, purple, rose and pink. The plants grow to 20cm (8in) high.

Cultivation
Sow under glass in early spring. Harden off in a cold frame, then plant out seedlings or bought bedding strips in late spring to early summer, setting the dwarf varieties 23cm (9in) apart, and the taller varieties 30cm (12in) apart. They need a sheltered sunny site and moisture-retentive soil. Dead-head regularly to prolong the flowering season.
Pests and diseases Foot and root rot sometimes cause the plants to collapse.

Corncockle has a delicate appearance that belies its hardy constitution as a tough cornfield weed. Two varieties have been developed from the now uncommon weed *Agrostemma githago* – 'Milas' and 'Milas Cerise'.

Tolerating poor soil, they both make excellent cottage garden plants, with their large lilac-pink flowers on tall slender stems. The leaves are long and narrow so it is best to grow corncockles en masse among other annuals and biennials. They are good for cutting and poisonous in all their parts.

Popular varieties
'Milas' has delicate pink flowers deepening in colour towards the edge. The flowers are 5cm (2in) or more wide. The plants reach 90-120cm (3-4ft) high.
'Milas Cerise' is a striking cherry-red strain of 'Milas', reaching 60-90cm (2-3ft) high.

Cultivation
Sow the seeds in their flowering position in spring or autumn in ordinary or even poor soil. Thin to 15cm (6in) apart when the seedlings are strong enough. Give them an open sunny site. In the summer dead-head to prevent less vigorous self-sown seedlings growing. Don't disturb roots.
Pests and diseases Trouble free.

Cloud grass is a pale-branched and graceful grass that serves as a good foil for brightly coloured perennials and annuals in beds and borders. It belongs to the bent grass family, several species of which are used in lawn seed mixtures. However, cloud grass itself is an ornamental grass. Its branched clusters of small white flowers have an airy charm. The flower panicles are suitable for cutting and for drying, if cut before the flowers are fully mature.

Cultivation
Sow seeds in early spring where the plants are to grow; thin the seedlings to 15cm (6in) apart when they are large enough to handle. Cloud grass will grow in any soil, even a poor but well-drained one, and does best in full sun.
Pests and diseases Generally trouble free.

Alonsoa

mask flower

Alonsoa warscewiczii 'Compacta'

☐ Height 30-60cm (1-2ft)
☐ Planting distance 38cm (15in)
☐ Flowers mid summer to mid autumn
☐ Rich well-drained soil
☐ Sunny site
☐ Half-hardy annual

Alonsoa warscewiczii is the only member of this Peruvian genus grown in Britain, though several varieties have been developed from it. A compact bushy plant reaching 30-60cm (12-24in) high, it has glossy dark green oval leaves and red stems. The brilliant scarlet flowers with their yellow centres appear from mid summer till mid autumn, adding colour to formal beds, borders and containers. The plants are half-hardy perennials, but flower in their first year from seed.

Popular varieties
'Compacta' has scarlet blooms and reaches 45-60cm (1½-2ft) high.
'Firestone Jewels Mixed' grows to 30cm (12in) and comes in mixed colours of pink, red, amber and pure white. Excellent for cutting.

Cultivation
Sow seeds in covered seed trays in late winter and early spring, keeping them at a temperature of 15°C (59°F). Prick out, and harden off in a cold frame before planting out in late spring. Set the plants 38cm (15in) apart in rich well-drained soil in a sunny position.
 When the plants are 5-7.5cm (2-3in) high pinch out the growing tips to encourage bushy growth.
Pests and diseases Aphids may infest the stems and leaves.

Althaea

hollyhock

Althaea rosea 'Chater's Double'

☐ Height 60cm-2.4m (2-8ft)
☐ Planting distance 23-60cm (9-24in)
☐ Flowers mid summer to autumn
☐ Heavy rich soil
☐ Sunny site
☐ Hardy biennials and annuals

Hollyhocks (*Althaea* species and now classified as *Alcea*) are old-fashioned garden favourites, their towering spikes of large pink, red, dark crimson, yellow or white flowers, single or double, making a strong impact wherever they are grown. They are well suited to cottage gardens, or the back of annual and herbaceous borders, ideally growing behind much shorter plants so their stately magnificence – reaching 2.4m (8ft) – can be fully appreciated. The large, light green leaves are lobed, rough and hairy.

Popular varieties
The true species hollyhock (*A. rosea*) has been superseded by named varieties bearing single or double flowers in mixed or single colours.
'Chater's Double' is a mixture with peony-shaped, double flowers in a variety of colours.
'Majorette' is a dwarf variety reaching 60-75cm (24-30in) high with double fringed flowers in a mixture of pastel shades.
'Nigra' has single, rich chocolate-maroon flowers and stands 1.5m (5ft) high.
'Pinafore Mixed' has semi-double and single fringed flowers in pink, carmine, rose, yellow and white. It reaches 90-100cm (36-40in) high.
'Powder Puffs' has double red, pink, rose, white and yellow flowers, and reaches 1.8-2.4m (6-8ft) high.
'Summer Carnival' has fully double blooms covering the full length of the 1.5-1.8m (5-6ft) high stems. They come in a wide range

Althaea rosea (single yellow)

of colours. It is an annual so seeds sown in spring produce flowering plants that summer.

Cultivation

Hollyhocks like a heavy rich soil and, preferably, a sheltered site. For biennial plants, sow seeds outdoors in early and mid summer, 23cm (9in) apart. Thin the seedlings to 60cm (2ft) apart in early to mid autumn.

For annual plants, sow under glass in late winter, for planting out in mid spring, or sow directly in the final position in mid spring, and thin to 38cm (15in) apart.

Water freely during dry weather, and stake tall varieties in exposed positions. For perennial growth, cut the plants to 15cm (6in) above ground in autumn.

Pests and diseases Rust, which affects the leaves and stems, is often a problem with older plants – a reason why hollyhocks are best grown as annuals or biennials.

Alyssum

sweet alyssum

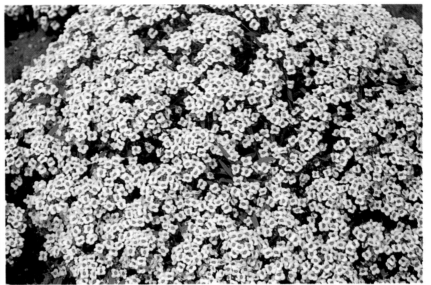

Alyssum maritimum 'Carpet of Snow'

☐ Height 7.5-15cm (3-6in)
☐ Planting distance 23cm (9in)
☐ Flowers early summer to early autumn
☐ Any well-drained soil
☐ Full sun
☐ Hardy annual

Sweet alyssum (*Alyssum maritimum*, or correctly *Lobularia maritima*) is the only annual species – all others are perennials. It forms low, dense cushions invaluable for edging beds, filling cracks between paving stones and bringing colour to rockeries and containers. From early summer till early autumn, sprays of tiny flowers appear in great profusion, their colours ranging from white to pink, lilac, purple and red.

It is an easy annual to grow, tolerating any ordinary garden soil, including poor ones.

Popular varieties

The species itself is rarely grown, but is represented by readily available varieties.

'**Carpet of Snow**' bears clusters of white flowers and reaches 7.5cm (3in) high.

'**Easter Bonnet**' is a mixture of colours in shades of pink, purple, mauve, lavender and white on 12cm (5in) plants.

'**Minimum**' has white flowers which form a low carpet just 7.5cm (3in) high.

'**Oriental Night**' has deep purple flowers on 10cm (4in) high plants.

'**Pastel Carpet**' grows 12cm (5in) high and comes in a mixture of pastel shades – white, cream, pink and pale violet.

'**Rosie O'Day**' has early-flowering rose-coloured blooms and reaches 7.5-10cm (3-4in) high.

'**Royal Carpet**' has scented, lilac-purple flowers and reaches 7.5-10cm (3-4in) high.

'**Snow Crystals**' grows to 10cm (4in) tall and bears large clusters of pure white flowers on compact plants.

'**Trailing Rosy Red**' bears pink flowers along its trailing stems. Suitable for hanging baskets.

'**Wonderland Red**' has deep red flowers which last well. It reaches 7.5-10cm (3-4in) high.

Cultivation

Sweet alyssum needs a sunny position and grows in any well-drained garden soil provided it isn't too rich.

Sow the seeds thinly in the flowering site from early to mid spring. Thin the seedlings to 23cm (9in) apart, when they are strong enough to handle.

For early flowering, sow seeds in seed boxes in late winter or early spring, and maintain a temperature of 10-13°C (50-55°F). Prick out into boxes of potting compost and then harden off, before planting out in mid spring.

Dead-head regularly by trimming lightly with a pair of scissors to encourage a longer flowering season.

Pests and diseases Slugs may eat young plants.

Amaranthus

amaranthus

Amaranthus caudatus

Amaranthus tricolor 'Flaming Fountain'

☐ Height 60cm-1.5m (2-5ft)
☐ Planting distance 30-90cm (1-3ft)
☐ Flowers mid summer to mid autumn
☐ Deep rich soil
☐ Full sun
☐ Half-hardy annual

These tall dramatic plants, some with long drooping crimson flower tassels and others with brilliantly coloured foliage, deserve to be grown as focal points in formal beds of annuals. They can also be grown as pot plants in the greenhouse. The flowers are long-lasting when cut and can also be dried.

Popular species and varieties
Amaranthus caudatus, commonly known as love-lies-bleeding, is the most popular species. Its 45cm (18in) long plumes of blood-red flowers appear from late summer to mid autumn on 90cm-1.2m (3-4ft) high plants. Space the plants 45cm (18in) apart. The variety 'Pigmy Torch' grows only to 60cm (2ft) and has deep maroon, upright flower spikes. 'Viridis' has pale green flowers, popular for flower arranging.
Amaranthus hypochondriachus, also known as prince's feather, has

erect plumes of bright red flowers 15cm (6in) long. These appear from mid summer to mid autumn. The plants reach 1.2-1.5m (4-5ft) high and have bronze-tinted leaves. Space the plants 90cm (3ft) apart. Varieties developed from this species include 'Green Thumb' (vivid green spikes on 60cm (2ft) tall plants) and 'Red

Amaranthus caudatus 'Viridis'

Fox' (tall maroon spikes).
Amaranthus tricolor is chiefly grown for its spectacular foliage: scarlet oval-shaped leaves, overlaid with yellow, bronze and green. The plants reach 60-90cm (2-3ft) high and should be set 30-45cm (12-18in) apart. Varieties of this species include 'Flaming Fountain' (crimson, willow-like leaves), 'Illumination' (scarlet, orange, yellow, green and bronze leaves all on one plant), and 'Joseph's Coat' (a vigorous variety with leaves similar to those of the species). All make good pot plants.

Cultivation
Sow seeds under glass in early spring and keep them at a temperature of 15°C (59°F). Prick out the seedlings into pots, and harden them off in a cold frame, before planting outdoors in late spring. Seeds can be sown directly in the flowering site in late spring, and then thinned out to the required planting distance (see individual species entries above).

A. *caudatus* and its varieties will tolerate poor soil but the other species and their varieties prefer soil enriched with manure. All need a sunny location.
Pests and diseases Aphids sometimes infest the plants.

Anagallis
scarlet pimpernel

Anagallis arvensis 'Caerulea'

☐ Height 2.5-5cm (1-2in)
☐ Planting distance 15cm (6in)
☐ Flowers mid summer to mid autumn
☐ Ordinary well-drained soil
☐ Full sun
☐ Hardy annual

Scarlet pimpernel (*Anagallis arvensis*), with its small scarlet flowers, is a familiar weed in fields. Its cultivated varieties, however, are well worth growing in the garden.

The plants reach only 2.5-5cm (1-2in) high, and form thick bushy clumps with a spread of 15cm (6in) – excellent for edging borders or growing in rockeries. The popular 'Caerulea' variety produces a mass of rich gentian-blue, star-like flowers from mid summer to mid autumn; mixed seed packs will also include red flowered plants.

Cultivation
Sow seeds in the flowering position in early to mid spring. The plants grow in ordinary well-drained garden soil but must have full sun. Thin out to 15cm (6in) apart when the seedlings are strong enough to handle.
Pests and diseases Trouble free.

Anchusa
anchusa

Anchusa capensis 'Blue Angel'

☐ Height 23-45cm (9-18in)
☐ Planting distance 23cm (9in)
☐ Flowers mid to late summer
☐ Ordinary garden soil
☐ Sunny open position
☐ Hardy annual

The bright blue blooms of *Anchusa capensis* (the only annual in this genus of predominantly perennial species) are among the few truly blue flowers. Like the forget-me-not which it closely resembles, it produces flowers over a long season, through mid and late summer. Only at the end of the season do the spent flowers so greatly outnumber the new ones that the plants begin to look bedraggled.

The plants form compact domes of narrow, pointed, mid green leaves, making them suitable for growing at the front of a border; the dwarf variety 'Blue Angel' is also useful for window-boxes.

Popular varieties
Several striking varieties have been developed from *Anchusa capensis*.

'**Blue Angel**' has ultramarine-blue flowers and forms domes 23cm (9in) high.

'**Blue Bird**' has vivid indigo blue flowers and reaches 45cm (18in).

'**Dawn**' grows 23cm (9in) tall and comes as a mixture of white, pink, pale and deep blue, star-like flowers.

Cultivation
Sow in mid spring where the plants are to flower, and thin to 23cm (9in) apart. Any well-cultivated soil is suitable, and the site should be open and in full sun. The plants are best grown in groups.

In summer, remove faded flower stems to encourage more blooms. Water well.
Pests and diseases Cucumber mosaic virus may cause yellow spots on the leaves. Pests are usually not a problem.

ANGEL'S TRUMPET – see *Datura*

Antirrhinum

snapdragon

Antirrhinum majus 'Princess'

- ☐ Height 15cm-1.2m (6-48in)
- ☐ Planting distance 15-45cm (6-18in)
- ☐ Flowers mid summer until first frost
- ☐ Well-drained soil enriched with manure
- ☐ Full sun or light shade
- ☐ Hardy annual

Snapdragons are one of our most ancient garden plants and, if they were not so susceptible to rust, would still be one of the most popular. Coming in an enormous range of colours, and a variety of sizes, they make excellent plants for mixed borders and formal beds throughout the summer. The taller varieties can form a spectacular display along the back of a herbaceous border, medium-sized varieties are useful for formal and informal bedding schemes, while dwarf varieties are ideal as edging and carpeting or for rockeries.

Popular varieties

Snapdragons grown in gardens have all been developed from *Antirrhinum majus*. They are classified in three groups according to plant size. Some come as single colours, others as mixed colours. Below is a selection of readily available varieties.

TALL VARIETIES reach 90cm-1.2m (3-4ft) high and are good as cut flowers.

'**Giant Forerunner**' has densely clustered flowers in a wide range of mixed colours.

Antirrhinum majus 'Coronette'

'**Liberty Mixed**' are sturdy plants, thick-stemmed and with long flower spikes in a range of colours. Early flowering.

'**Madame Butterfly**' has double blooms resembling azaleas in mixed colours.

'**Ruffled Super Tetra**' has large ruffled, veined flowers in mixed colours.

INTERMEDIATE VARIETIES are the most popular group. They reach 38-45cm (15-18in) high.

'**Black Prince**' is a compact plant with deep crimson flowers and bronze foliage.

'**Bright Eyes**' is an F1 hybrid with bright yellow flowers marked with red in the centre.

'**Cinderella**' forms bushy plants with dense flower spikes in a range of colours.

'**Cheerio**' has large bright flowers in mixed colours.

'**Coral Monarch**' has warm coral-pink flowers and is resistant to rust.

'**Coronette**' is a neat plant with flowers in mixed colours. It is both rust and weather resistant.

'**Crimson Monarch**' has crimson flowers and is rust resistant.

'**Forest Fire**' has bright scarlet flower spikes that fade to orange as they age.

'**Lavender Monarch**' has lilac-blue flowers and strong resistance to rust.

'**Monarch Mixed**' include white, yellow, coral, scarlet and crimson. Like other 'Monarch' strains, they are bred to be resistant to rust.

'**Popette**' is an F2 hybrid, with uniform, early and long-lasting flowers that are bicoloured white and purple-rose.

'**Princess**' has a profusion of long-lasting flowers in a wide range of mixed colours.

'**Rembrandt**' has orange flowers with yellow tips to the petals.

'**Sawyers Mixed**' is a rust-resistant mixture in a range of strong colours.

'**Vanity Fair**' produces strong, branching plants, densely set with flowers in white, yellow, pink, salmon, scarlet and near bronze.

Antirrhinum majus 'Yellow Monarch'

'White Monarch' has white flowers and strong rust resistance. **'Yellow Monarch'** has clear yellow flowers and strong rust resistance.
DWARF VARIETIES reach only 15cm (6in) high, and have a compact bushy habit.
'Dwarf Bedding' is a mixed variety coming in an enormous range of colours.
'Floral Carpet' has a profusion of large flowers in mixed colours.
'Little Darling' is early flowering and comes in mixed colours. It is rust resistant.
'Magic Carpet' is of trailing habit and available in mixed colours.
'Pixie' has open-petalled, butterfly-like flowers early in the season. It is free-flowering and comes in crimsons, reds, oranges, yellows and whites.
'Royal Carpet' is one of the best carpeting varieties, being vigorous, long-lasting, and rust resistant. It can be bought in mixed colours, in just orange (**'Royal Carpet Orange'**), or in just pink (**'Royal Carpet Pink'**).
'Sweetheart' has small double azalea-type flowers in red, bronze, pink, yellow or white. It is rust resistant.
'Tahiti' mixtures are compact plants, closely packed with flowers in pure clear colours as well as some bicolours.
'Tom Thumb' is a neat plant bearing flowers in bright mixed colours.
'Trumpet Serenade' has open

Antirrhinum majus 'Dwarf Bedding'

petalled, freesia-like flowers that are long-lasting and come in mixed colours. Height up to 30cm (12in).

Cultivation
Sow the seeds in trays under glass in late winter to early spring and keep at a temperature of 16-18°C (61-64°F). Water seeds gently with a fine spray. After they germinate, water with diluted liquid feed.

When the seedlings are large enough to handle, prick them out into boxes of potting compost. Harden off in a cold frame before planting out in late spring or grow on as pot plants in the greenhouse.

For early flowering snapdragons, sow seeds in early and mid summer, and pot them in early autumn; if you have a warm sheltered site, they can be planted outdoors in autumn.

In the garden, set tall varieties 45cm (18in) apart, intermediate varieties 25cm (10in) apart and dwarf varieties 20cm (8in) apart.

For the best results plant snapdragons in well-drained light to medium soil enriched with rotted manure, though any well-cultivated garden soil is suitable. The site should be in sun or light shade.

When the plants reach 7.5-10cm (3-4in) high, pinch out the growing tips to encourage bushy growth. Dead-head to prolong the flowering season and stake tall varieties in exposed positions.
Pests and diseases Rust is the disease usually associated with snapdragons. If your garden is troubled by this disease, grow only rust-resistant varieties. Damping-off may affect seedlings, and mildew can be a problem with young plants. Look out for aphids on young growth in summer.

APPLE OF PERU – see *Nicandra*

Arctotis
African daisy

Arctotis hybrids

- ☐ Height 15-60cm (6-24in)
- ☐ Planting distance 30cm (12in)
- ☐ Flowers mid summer until the first frosts
- ☐ Ordinary garden soil
- ☐ Open sunny site
- ☐ Half-hardy annual

Bold, brightly coloured daisy-like flowers and woolly silver-grey leaves make this a striking plant to grow in borders and containers. Though tempting to cut for flower arranging, the blooms last only a short while in water.

In the garden, the flower heads tend to close in the afternoon or during dull, overcast weather, so position them where they will receive plenty of light – and can be appreciated in the morning.

Popular species and hybrids
Arctotis acaulis has orange to deep red flowers, 8.5cm (3½in) wide, in mid and late summer. It is a dwarf species (15-23cm/6-9in high), suitable for edging borders or growing in window-boxes.

Arctotis venusta 'Grandis' has large white to primrose-yellow flowers with blue centres and pale lavender reverse. They appear from mid summer until the first frost. The plant grows 60cm (24in) high.

Hybrids come in brilliant shades of red, yellow, apricot, orange, carmine, cream and white. They reach 30-60cm (1-2ft) high, making them popular for borders and bedding schemes. The long-stemmed flowers last longer than the species in water.

Cultivation
Sow seeds directly in the flowering site in mid to late spring and thin out to 30cm (12in) apart.

For earlier flowers, sow seeds indoors, in boxes or trays of seed compost in early spring. Keep at a temperature of 18°C (64°F). Prick out the seedlings into boxes and harden off in a cold frame, before planting out in late spring.

African daisies grow in most soils, but they need a sunny site. When the plants are 10-12cm (4-5in) high, pinch out the grow-

Arctotis venusta 'Grandis'

ing tips to encourage bushy growth. Support the tall varieties with twiggy sticks, and dead-head to extend the flowering season.
Pests and diseases Aphids may infest young growth, and grey mould can sometimes be a problem in wet weather.

Argemone
prickly poppy

Argemone mexicana

☐ Height 60cm (2ft)
☐ Planting distance 30cm (1ft)
☐ Flowers early to late summer
☐ Light well-drained soil
☐ Sunny position
☐ Hardy annual

The prickly poppy (*Argemone mexicana*) from Central America has majestic orange and yellow flowers from early to late summer. With their sweet scent, they are attractive to bees and other insects. The flowers are carried 60cm (2ft) above ground on sprawling prickly stems accompanied by grey-blue, thistle-like leaves. The flowers can reach up to 10cm (4in) across.

Grow them in informal planting schemes in borders, preferably where they can be left alone to scatter their seeds.

Cultivation
Prickly poppies grow best in light well-drained soil in a sunny border. Sow directly in the flowering site in mid spring, and thin out to 30cm (1ft) apart when seedlings are large enough to handle.

Staking is not a good idea as it may damage the succulent stems. Dead-head to encourage a longer flowering season.

For flowers in early summer, sow seeds in trays under glass in early spring. Keep them at 18°C (64°F). Prick out seedlings into small pots, harden off and plant out in late spring.
Pests and diseases Trouble free.

Asperula
annual woodruff

Asperula orientalis

☐ Height 30cm (1ft)
☐ Planting distance 7.5-10cm (3-4in)
☐ Flowers in mid summer
☐ Ordinary moist soil
☐ Partial shade
☐ Hardy annual

Annual woodruff (*Asperula orientalis*) is the only hardy annual in this genus of 200 species – all other woodruffs are perennials. Its strongly scented pale blue flowers appear in mid summer on top of 30cm (1ft) tall stems clothed with narrow green lance-shaped leaves. These are arranged in attractive whorls up the stems.

It is useful for garden decoration as, unlike most annuals, it tolerates partial shade and likes moist soil. With its compact habit, it is also suitable for rock gardens. The flowers are also good for cutting.

Cultivation
Scatter seeds over the flowering site in mid spring, and rake them gently into the soil. When the seedlings are strong enough to handle, thin them to 7.5-10cm (3-4in) apart.
Pests and diseases Trouble free.

Atriplex
purple orach

Atriplex hortensis

☐ Height 90cm-1.2m (3-4ft)
☐ Planting distance 40cm (16in)
☐ Foliage plant
☐ Well-drained good garden soil
☐ Open sunny site
☐ Hardy annual

The varieties of *Atriplex hortensis* are grown for their fine foliage – deep crimson-purple leaves covered, when young, with fine glistening white powder. The flowers are insignificant. The variety 'Cupreata' has bright beetroot-red foliage.

On rich soil, purple orach grows rapidly to reach 90cm-1.2m (3-4ft) high, so use it as an instant hedge, to cover up a screen, or simply to fill an awkward gap at the back of an ornamental border.

Cultivation
Sow the seeds under glass in early spring and transplant outdoors in late spring. Alternatively sow them straight in the ground in late spring. Thin the seedlings to 40cm (16in) apart.

Any good, well-drained soil is suitable, in full sun. The plants are wind resistant and flourish in an open site and in coastal gardens.
Pests and diseases Trouble free.

BABY BLUE EYES – see
Nemophila
BABY'S BREATH – see
Gypsophila
BASIL – see *Ocimum*

Begonia

wax begonia

Begonia semperflorens 'Lucia'

- ☐ Height 15-23cm (6-9in)
- ☐ Planting distance 20-25cm (8-10in)
- ☐ Flowers early summer to mid autumn or first frost
- ☐ Rich, moist, well-drained soil
- ☐ Sunny or lightly shaded site
- ☐ Half-hardy annual

Wax begonia (*Begonia semperflorens*) and its varieties are grown as annuals for summer bedding and pot plants.

The plants, which generally reach 15-23cm (6-9in) high, are smothered with small white, pink, or red flowers from early summer till early autumn. The foliage, too, is attractive: succulent and glossy, pale or dark green, purple or coppery-brown. Fill containers with them to cheer up a patio, window-box or hanging basket, or use them in formal bedding schemes. In autumn you can lift wax begonias and take them indoors as winter pot plants – flowering will continue if the room is well lit.

Popular varieties

Begonia semperflorens is now re-presented by an increasing number of varieties.

'Cocktail' has white, pink, rose, salmon, and red flowers with glossy deep bronze foliage.

'Coco Mixed' comes in mixed colours and has bronze foliage.

'Danica Red' has brick-red flowers and glossy bronze leaves.

'Danica Scarlet' has large scarlet-red flowers and bronze foliage.

'Devon Gems' has red, pink and white flowers with glossy brown, bronze or green leaves.

'Frilly Dilly' has scarlet and pink flowers with frilled petals. The foliage is green.

'Lucifer' has large, bright scarlet flowers and green leaves.

'New Generation' is a mixture of compact plants with shiny rose, salmon, pink, scarlet or white flowers; green or bronzy foliage.

'Olympia' is exceptionally large-flowered, with pink, white, red or bicoloured flowers.

'Options' has green or bronze foliage and pink, carmine or white flowers, often picoteed.

'Organdy' comes in a wide range of flower colours and has green and bronze foliage. The plants are very compact.

'Pink Avalanche' has delicate pink flowers and green foliage.

'Stara' has a branching or cascading habit, with bright green leaves and masses of white, pink or rose-red flowers.

'Viva' has pure white blooms and dark green leaves.

Cultivation

Sow seeds in trays of seed compost in late winter to early spring under glass at 16°C (61°F). Prick them out into boxes of potting compost when the first true leaf appears. Harden off and then plant out in beds or containers in late spring, setting them 20-25cm (8-10in) apart. The soil should be rich and moist but well-drained – and the site should be in sun or light shade.

Pests and diseases Powdery mildew shows as a white coating on leaves and stems.

Bellis
daisy

Bellis perennis 'Bright Carpet'

- ☐ Height 10-20cm (4-8in)
- ☐ Planting distance 20-25cm (8-10in)
- ☐ Flowers late spring to mid summer
- ☐ Ordinary garden soil
- ☐ Sun or partial shade
- ☐ Hardy biennial

From the familiar wild daisy come several bigger, brighter garden varieties which are ideal for edging flower beds or mixing with other plants in window-boxes and containers. They have white, pink and red mop-like flowers borne in profusion from late spring to mid summer on 10-20cm (4-8in) high stems. The loose rosettes of evergreen leaves form a dense carpet on the ground.

Bellis perennis 'Spring Star'

Popular varieties
The following varieties are all developed from *Bellis perennis*.
'Bright Carpet' has small double red, white and rose blooms.
'Goliath' has large double blooms in shades of red, salmon-pink, pink and white.
'Pomponette' produces a mass of very small double flowers in reds, pinks and whites.
'Spring Star' has large, fully double flowers in white, red or rose, carried well above the foliage.

Cultivation
Sow the seeds in early summer in shallow drills in an outdoor seed bed. Thin, then transplant to the flowering site in early autumn, setting the plants 15-23cm (6-9in) apart. Ordinary garden soil, in sun or partial shade is suitable. Dead-head to prevent seeding.
Pests and diseases Trouble free.

BELLS OF IRELAND – see *Molucella*
BLACK-EYED SUSAN – see *Rudbeckia*
BLANKET FLOWER – see *Gaillardia*
BLESSED THISTLE – see *Silybum*
BLUE LACE FLOWER – see *Trachymene*

Brachycome
Swan River daisy

Brachycome iberidifolia

- ☐ Height 15-30cm (6-12in)
- ☐ Planting distance 23cm (9in)
- ☐ Flowers early summer to early autumn
- ☐ Rich soil
- ☐ Sunny, sheltered site
- ☐ Half-hardy annual

The little Swan River daisy (*Brachycome iberidifolia*) is smothered with sweetly scented daisy flowers throughout the summer and into early autumn. They are set on slender stems carrying pale green filigree leaves on compact plants. These are ideal for low summer bedding and in pots, window-boxes and other containers.

Seeds are available in mixtures, producing white, pink, lavender and blue flowers, or as single colours, such as 'Purple Splendour' and 'White Splendour'. The flowers of 'Blue Star' are almost quill-like.

Cultivation
Sow seeds in early spring under glass at a temperature of 18°C (64°F). Prick off the seedlings when large enough to handle and maintain a temperature of 16°C (61°F) until they are growing strongly. Harden the young plants off in a cold frame and transplant to the flowering positions in late spring.

Swan River daisies thrive in rich, moisture-retentive soil and need full sun, preferably with some shelter.
Pests and diseases Trouble free.

Brassica

ornamental cabbage

Brassica oleracea

☐ Height 23-45cm (9-18in)
☐ Planting distance 36-40cm (14-16in)
☐ Any well-drained soil
☐ Sunny position
☐ Hardy annual foliage plant

Ornamental cabbages (*Brassica oleracea*) are foliage plants and popular in summer bedding schemes for their brilliantly coloured leaves. The foliage, which opens out from the centre, is frilled or deeply wavy, varying from palest to deepest green with the midribs often in contrasting colours. The centres, which look like full-blown flowers, are creamy-white, pink or carmine. Ornamental cabbages usually grow about 23cm (9in) tall, while ornamental kale is twice that height, with colourful and feathery centres rising above the foliage. Seeds are available in mixed colours.

Autumn and winter-growing ornamental cabbages, suitable for container growing, come in single colours or in mixtures.

Cultivation
Sow seeds under glass in early spring, or outdoors in a seed bed. When the seedlings are large enough to handle, transplant them to their growing positions, spacing them 36cm (14in) apart, in any good garden soil and in full sun for the colours to develop properly. Another sowing in early summer will produce autumn cabbages and for container-grown winter plants sow in late summer.
Pests and diseases Cabbage aphids and caterpillars may attack the leaves.

Briza

pearl grass

Briza maxima

☐ Height 45cm (18in)
☐ Planting distance 15-23cm (6-9in)
☐ Flowers late spring to mid summer
☐ Ordinary well-drained garden soil
☐ Sunny position
☐ Hardy annual grass

Pearl grass (*Briza maxima*), with its silvery-green spikelets dancing and rustling on slender 45cm (18in) high stems, is deservedly the most popular ornamental grass. The spikelets appear from late spring to mid summer, forming upright tufts with their bright green, narrow, pointed leaves.

Grow pearl grass in large drifts in borders with flowering plants. When the flower heads are well formed, the stems can be cut and dried for indoor flower arrangements.

Cultivation
Sow the seeds thinly in their flowering position in early autumn or in early to mid spring. Any well-drained soil is suitable and the site should be sunny. When the seedlings are large enough to handle, thin to 15-23cm (6-9in) apart.

Cut the flower stems for drying in sunny weather, when the spikelets are fully developed but before they set seeds. Hang up to dry in a cool place.
Pests and diseases Trouble free.

Browallia

browallia

Browallia speciosa 'Blue Bells'

☐ Height 20-30cm (8-12in)
☐ Planting distance 20cm (8in)
☐ Flowers early summer to early autumn
☐ Any good garden soil
☐ Sunny position
☐ Half-hardy annual

This South American plant (*Browallia speciosa*) is a popular greenhouse and house plant, but it can also be grown outdoors as summer bedding. It is prized for its profusion of violet-shaped white-eyed flowers, up to 5cm (2in) wide, handsomely offset by bright green, slender and pointed leaves.

Hybrid varieties are more often seen than the species and include dwarf types for growing in window boxes, pots and hanging baskets. 'Blue Bells' has violet-blue flowers with prominent white centres; 'Blue Troll' is bright blue, and 'White Bells' is pure white.

Cultivation
Sow seeds under glass at a temperature of 18°C (64°F) in early spring. Prick out the seedlings into pots. For outdoor plants, harden them off in a cold frame before setting them out in their flowering positions when all danger of frost is past. Browallias thrive in loamy soil, but will grow in well-drained, even poor soil. They need full sun.
Pests and diseases Trouble free.

Calceolaria

slipper flower

Calceolaria integrifolia

□ Height 30-38cm (12-15in)
□ Planting 30-38cm (12-15in)
□ Flowers early summer to early autumn
□ Light, acid soil
□ Sheltered sunny or partially shaded site
□ Half-hardy annual

The curious kidney-shaped blooms of the slipper flower were favourites for formal bedding schemes in Victorian gardens. *Calceolaria integrifolia* and its varieties can be grown outdoors, but they must be given a warm sheltered spot, preferably at the base of a wall. Here their brightly coloured flowers, coming in various yellows, either plain or blotched, make a cheerful display among their pale fresh green wrinkled leaves. The flowers are borne in succession from early summer until mid autumn.

Popular varieties

Most of the popular varieties have been bred specifically for summer bedding and include:
'Little Sweeties' a seed mixture producing plants up to 38cm (15in) tall with an abundance of small pouch-shaped flowers of pale yellow, orange, pink and scarlet often with contrasting speckles. They will grow in full shade.
'Midas' has golden-yellow blooms, renowned for their long flowering season. The neat, bushy and branching plants reach 20-38cm (10-15in) high.
'Sunshine' is a free-flowering hybrid, bearing bright yellow flowers throughout the summer. It reaches 20-25cm (8-10in) high and has a bushy, compact habit.

Cultivation

Sow the tiny seeds under glass in late winter – they require careful handling. Prick the seedlings off into boxes when they are large enough to handle. In late spring harden off in a cold frame, and then plant outdoors.

They will grow in ordinary garden soil, though the best results are achieved in well-drained acid, rich soil. The site must be sheltered, in sun or partial shade.
Pests and diseases Aphids and slugs are sometimes troublesome.

Calendula

pot marigold

Calendula officinalis 'Fiesta Gitana'

□ Height 30-60cm (1-2ft)
□ Planting distance 30-38cm (12-15in)
□ Flowers late spring till first frosts
□ Any well-drained garden
□ Hardy annual

The pot marigold is one of the easiest hardy annuals to grow and, with its glowing orange or yellow daisy-like flowers, one of the brightest. The flowers and light green lance-shaped leaves were formerly used in cookery, hence the name pot marigold.

Most varieties grow 45-60cm (18-24in) tall, and several 30cm (1ft) high dwarf varieties are also available. Pot marigolds are excellent for growing in borders with poor soil. The long-stemmed varieties make good cut flowers and last well in water.

Popular varieties

All garden varieties are developed from *Calendula officinalis*. This grows 60cm (2ft) high and bears a profusion of single daisy flowers, up to 10cm (4in) wide, in shades of bright orange or yellow. Named varieties, usually with double flowers, include:
TALL VARIETIES
'Art Shades' is a mixture, 60cm (2ft) tall, coming in apricots, oranges, pale yellows and creams. The flowers are large and graceful.
'Geisha Girl' has large orange chrysanthemum-like flowers with incurved petals.
'Indian Prince' has semi-double, dark orange flowers with mahogany brown centres. It grows 45-50cm (18-20in) tall.

Calendula officinalis 'Geisha Girl'

Calendula officinalis

'Kablouna Gold', 50cm (20in) tall, has bright yellow flowers with chocolate brown centres.

'Lemon Queen' has double, clear lemon-yellow flowers on 60cm (2ft) high plants.

'Pacific Apricot', 60cm (2ft) high, has large double, soft apricot flowers with dark brown centres and orange tips to the petals.

'Pacific Beauty' is a mixture, 60cm (2ft) or more tall, with double flowers in shades of orange, apricot, yellow and primrose. Some flowers are bicoloured. All are carried on long stems.

'Pacific Cream Beauty' has cream-yellow flowers with dark brown centres.

Pacific Lemon Beauty' has lemon-yellow blooms with dark brown centres.

'Radio', 45-60cm (18-24in) tall, has orange blooms resembling those of cactus dahlias. Excellent for cutting.

DWARF VARIETIES

'Apricot Bon Bon' grows 30-38cm (12-15in) high and bears double, warm apricot flowers.

'Baby Gold', 30-38cm (12-15in) high, has long-lasting double, golden-yellow flowers carried on long stems on compact plants.

'Double Lemon Coronet' has large grapefruit-yellow flowers on 30cm (12in) high plants.

'Fiesta Gitana' comes in mixed colours – oranges, yellows and creams. It grows 30cm (12in) high and as much across and bears masses of double flowers with dark centres.

Cultivation

Pot marigolds thrive with little attention and in the poorest soil. For the best results, however, grow them in well-drained good garden soil.

Sow the seeds in their flowering site in early spring for summer flowering, or in early autumn for late spring flowering. Cover with 1cm (½in) of soil. Thin out to 30-38cm (12-15in) apart.

Dead-head to prolong the flowering season and prevent self-seeding.

Pests and diseases Mildew and rust may develop on the leaves. In wet weather watch out for smut – dark irregular spots on the leaves. Caterpillars can be a nuisance.

CALIFORNIAN POPPY – see *Eschscholzia*

Calendula officinalis 'Kablouna Gold'

Callistephus

China aster

Callistephus chinensis 'Milady'

Callistephus chinensis 'Nova'

□ Height 15-75cm (6-30in)
□ Planting distance 30-45cm (12-18in)
□ Flowers mid summer till first frosts
□ Well-drained garden soil
□ Open sunny position
□ Half-hardy annual

Just one species, *Callistephus chinensis*, is responsible for the many varieties of China asters on the market – tall and dwarf, single-flowered and double-flowered, mixed colours or one colour. The flowers look like a cross between a daisy and a chrysanthemum and come in shades of pink, red, mauve, blue, cream and white. Flowering from mid summer till the first frosts, they are excellent for providing colour in borders and containers and as they last well in water, they are also suitable for cutting.

Popular varieties

The tall varieties of Chinese aster reach 50-75cm (20-30in) high, the dwarf varieties 15-30cm (6-12in). Single blooms have a clearly vis-ible central disc while double blooms have more petals which conceal the centre.

TALL VARIETIES

'**All Change**' has double pompon-like flowers bicoloured red and white or blue and white.
'**Andrella**' has single, many-petalled flowers in white, rose, scarlet, lavender or blue with prominent yellow centres.
'**Devon Riviera**' is a colour mixture of double, chrysanthemum-like blooms.
'**Duchess**' is late-flowering, good for cutting and with flowers like incurved chrysanthemums in shades of rose-pink, yellow, crimson, blue and pure white.
'**Florette Champagne**' has quilled flowers of soft creamy-pink on sturdy stems.
'**Germannia**' grows up to 75cm (2½ft), with fully double flowers as much as 12.5cm (5in) across, in white, yellow, pink, cerise, mid and dark blue.
'**Gusford Supreme**', 38cm (15in) tall, is wilt-resistant, with scarlet white-centred flowers.
'**Nova**' bears elegant double flowers of slender, needle-like petals in shades of yellow, scarlet, mauve and pink.
'**Operetta**' is a colour mixture of large, double chrysanthemum-like flowers with incurved petals.
'**Ostrich Plume**' has double flowers with curled and feathery petals in a range of colours.
'**Pastel**' is a wilt-resistant mixture with double flowers in soft pastel shades.
'**Powderpuffs**' produces upright, compact plants with an abundance of tightly double flowers in shades of pink, blue and purple as well as white.
'**Super Princess Symphonie**' is a colour mixture with large flowers that have tightly quilled petals.

DWARF VARIETIES

'**Blue Skies**' grows only about 15cm (6in) high but is almost smothered with a mass of double, pale lavender-blue flowers.
'**Carpet Ball**' has tightly packed, double flowers in a good colour range.
'**Comet**' is an early-flowering mixture, with double flowers in white and shades of blue and red.
'**Crimson Sunset**' bears double, deep red flowers.
'**Lilliput Duet**' has small pompon-like flowers in rose, carmine, pink and blue.
'**Milady**' has large double incurved chrysanthemum-like flowers in a range of rich colours; long-lasting and especially weather-resistant.
'**Pink Bedder**' has double, bright rose-coloured blooms.

Callistephus chinensis 'Comet'

'Pinocchio' is a compact seed mixture, bearing a mass of small, double, ball-shaped blooms.

'Teisa Stars' bears large double flowers with long quilled petals in a range of colours; 23cm (10in) tall and good for cutting.

'White Bedder' has pure white, double flowers on 15cm (6in) high, compact plants.

Cultivation

Sow the seeds under glass in early spring at 16°C (61°F). Harden off before planting out in late spring. Alternatively sow directly in the flowering site in mid spring and thin tall varieties to 38-45cm (15-18in) apart, and dwarf varieties to 30cm (12in) apart.

Choose an open sunny site with shelter from wind for the taller varieties. A medium loam is best, though ordinary garden soil still gives good results.

Remove the first dead flowers to encourage blooms on the side shoots.

Pests and diseases Callistephus wilt may attack plants as they are about to flower – avoid using the same bed two years running to deter this disease. Foot and root rot may cause the seedlings or mature plants to collapse. Caterpillars and aphids can be a problem.

Campanula
Canterbury bell

Campanula medium

☐ Height 30-90cm (1-3ft)
☐ Planting distance 30cm (1ft)
☐ Flowers late spring to mid summer
☐ Ordinary well-drained garden soil ·
☐ Sunny or lightly shaded site
☐ Hardy biennial

The Canterbury bell (*Campanula medium*) is a typical cottage garden plant – easily grown, showy in flower for part of the summer, but contributing nothing at other times. It is best planted in small groups where it will not leave large gaps when it has finished blooming.

Popular varieties

Several varieties of Canterbury bell are widely available.

Campanula medium 'Cup and Saucer Mixed'

'Cup and Saucer Mixed' is the traditional Canterbury bell variety. The flowers are delicate shades of pink, blue and white.

'Double Mixed' has a compact habit and reaches 75cm (2½ft) high. The single flowers come in rose-pink, deep blue, white and violet.

'Russian Pink', a recent introduction, grows 38cm (15in) high and has delicate pink bell flowers.

Cultivation

Sow the seed outside in a seed bed in late spring or early summer. Move to the flowering site in autumn, or the following spring, setting the plants 30cm (1ft) apart. Any ordinary well-drained soil is suitable, in sun or light shade.

Pests and diseases Slugs and snails may damage the leaves.

CAMPION – see *Silene*
CANDYTUFT – see *Iberis*
CAPE MARIGOLD – see *Dimorphotheca*
CAPER SPURGE – see *Euphorbia*
CASTER OIL PLANT – see *Ricinus*
CATCHFLY – see *Silene*
CATHEDRAL BELL – see *Cobaea*

Celosia

cockscomb, Prince of Wales' feathers

Celosia 'Apricot Brandy'

Celosia 'Dwarf Fairy Fountains'

- ☐ Height 10-60cm (4-24in)
- ☐ Planting distance 23-30cm (9-12in)
- ☐ Flowers mid summer to early autumn
- ☐ Rich well-drained soil
- ☐ Sheltered sunny site
- ☐ Half-hardy annual

Celosia has large, bright, crested or plumed flowers in reds, oranges and yellows. The varieties with crested flowers are commonly called cockscomb, the plumed ones Prince of Wales' feathers. Both types make excellent bedding or pot plants.

Popular varieties

All garden varieties have been developed from *C. argentea* var. *cristata* or *C.a.* var. *plumosa*.
'Apricot Brandy' has deep orange plumed flowers on branching plants 50cm (20in) high.
'Dwarf Fairy Fountains' has plumed flowers in pastel shades. The plants are 30-38cm (12-15in) high.
'Flamingo Feather' grows to 60cm (2in) tall and bears bicoloured rose and deep pink flower spikes. Ideal for drying.

'Jewel Box Mixed' has crested blooms in mixed colours: red, pink, salmon, gold and yellow. The plants grow 23cm (9in) high.
'Kimono Mixed' is only 10cm (4in) high and good for containers; the plumes are cream, golden-yellow, orange or scarlet.

Cultivation

Sow the seeds in trays of seed compost in late winter and maintain a temperature of 18°C (64°F). They must be hardened off before planting out in a border or pots in early summer, after all risk of frost has passed.

Set the plants 23-30cm (9-12in) apart in rich well-drained soil in a warm sheltered site.
Pests and diseases Foot and root rot, caused by a fungus, can affect the roots and eventually make the plants wilt or collapse completely. Generally celosias are untroubled by pests.

Celosia 'Jewel Box Mixed'

Centaurea
cornflower

Centaurea cyanus 'Polka Dot'

- ☐ Height 30-90cm (1-3ft)
- ☐ Planting distance 23-30cm (9-12in)
- ☐ Flowers early summer to early autumn
- ☐ Any well-drained soil
- ☐ Sunny position
- ☐ Hardy annual

The cornflower is one of our oldest and best-loved hardy annuals, easy to grow and excellent for cutting. Its wiry stems carry sprays of blue, white, pink, purple, maroon or deep red flowers and long, narrow, silver-grey leaves.

Grow cornflowers on their own in a border, or as part of a cottage garden mixture, perhaps with poppies and marigolds.

Popular varieties
The following varieties have been developed from *Centaurea cyanus*, a cornflower native to Britain.
'Blue Diadem' bears large double, dark blue flowers on 75cm (2½ft) tall plants.
'Dwarf Blue' has large, blue, double flowers and reaches 30cm (1ft) high.
'Frosty' has pink, blue, red and maroon flowers edged white, and white flowers flushed pink. It reaches 60cm (2ft) high.
'Jubilee Gem' has large, double, dark blue flowers and reaches 30cm (12in) high.

'Polka Dot' produces a mixture of blue and red colours, and stands 38-45cm (15-18in) high.
'Tall Double Mixed' comes in shades of pink, red, maroon, blue, mauve and white and reaches 90cm (3ft) high.

The following varieties are developed from sweet sultan (*Centaurea moschata*), an Oriental species with large scented flowers and grey-green, toothed leaves.
'Dairy Maid' has large golden-yellow flowers with fringed petals and prominent centres. It grows to 60cm (2ft) high.
'The Bride', pure white and exceptionally fragrant, reaches a height of 40-60cm (16-24in).

Cultivation
Grow cornflowers in any well-drained garden soil, in a sunny site. Sow the seeds in their flowering site in early autumn – under cloches – or in early to mid spring at fortnightly intervals.

When they are large enough to handle, dwarf varieties should be thinned to 23cm (9in) apart, and tall varieties to 30cm (1ft) apart.

Stake tall varieties in exposed positions with twiggy sticks. Dead-head all cornflowers.
Pests and diseases Petal blight may affect the flowers. Mildew and rust can be a problem.

Cheiranthus
wallflower

Cheiranthus × *allionii* 'Golden Bedder'

- ☐ Height 15-45cm (6-18in)
- ☐ Planting distance 25-38cm (10-15in)
- ☐ Flowers mid spring to early summer
- ☐ Well-drained fertile soil, preferably alkaline or neutral
- ☐ Full sun
- ☐ Hardy biennial

With its dense spikes of richly coloured blooms and its heady fragrance, the wallflower deserves its reputation as the queen of spring and early-summer flowering biennials. Many cultivars are now available, providing the gardener with an enormous range of colours to choose from: shades of yellow, apricot, pink, purple, and strong clear reds, oranges and yellows. All have spikes of freely produced flowers and green lance-shaped leaves.

Most varieties are anything up to 60cm (2ft) high – excellent for growing in borders and formal beds or as cut flowers. But there are dwarf kinds only 23-30cm (9-12in) high which are useful for rockeries and small informal patches in borders near the house so that their scent can waft through the open windows.

Popular varieties
Cheiranthus cheiri has had numerous varieties, tall and dwarf, developed from it. The following are some of the most readily available varieties.
TALL VARIETIES
'Blood Red' has early deep velvety red flowers and reaches 38cm (15in) high.

Cheiranthus cheiri 'Rose Queen'

Cheiranthus cheiri – mixture of tall varieties

'Cloth of Gold' has large, golden, sweet scented flowers and reaches 38cm (15in) high.

'Eastern Queen' has salmon-red flowers and reaches 38cm (15in) high.

'Fire King' has bright scarlet-orange flowers and reaches 38cm (15in) high.

'Ivory White' has cream-white flowers and reaches 38cm (15in) high.

'My Fair Lady Mixed' comes in mixed pastel shades and stands 30-38cm (12-15in) high.

'Persian Carpet' comes in a pastel mixture of cream, orange, apricot, gold, purple and rose. It reaches 38cm (15in) high.

'Primrose Monarch' has primrose-yellow flowers and reaches 38cm (15in) high.

'Rose Queen' has rose-pink flowers and reaches 45cm (18in) high.

'Ruby Gem' has rich ruby-violet flowers and reaches up to 38cm (15in) high.

'White Dame' has cream-white flowers and is 38cm (15in) high.

DWARF VARIETIES

'Dwarf Mixed' includes a good range of colours and reaches 30cm (1ft) high.

'Golden Bedder' has large golden-yellow flowers and reaches 25cm (10in) high.

'Orange Bedder' has rich orange flowers shading to apricot, and reaches 25cm (10in) high.

'Primrose Bedder' has primrose yellow flowers and reaches 25cm (10in) high.

'Scarlet Bedder' has rich scarlet-red flowers and reaches 25cm (10in) high.

'Tom Thumb Mixed' has late-flowering blooms in mixed colours; it is only 15-23cm (6-9in) high.

Cheiranthus × allionii, the Siberian wallflower, has had a handful of varieties developed from it. They form neat compact plants with orange or yellow flowers appearing from late spring till early summer.

'Aurora' grows 25-30cm (10-12in) tall and bears flowers in shades of orange, brown, apricot and mauve.

'Glasnost Mixed' gives 30cm (12in) high plants, with fragrant flowers in a range of pastel colours, including lilac.

'Spring Jester' is a seed mixture producing 30cm (12in) high plants with flowers in shades of apricot, orange, golden-yellow, lemon, lilac and occasionally white.

Cultivation
Sow the seeds thinly in a seed bed in late spring to early summer. When the first true leaves appear, thin out the seedlings to about 15cm (6in) apart.

In mid autumn, plant them out in their flowering site, setting the tall varieties 30-38cm (12-15in) apart and the dwarf varieties 25-30cm (10-12in) apart. Most well-drained garden soils are suitable, though acid soils should be dressed with lime. The planting site must be in full sun.

When the plants reach 12-15cm (5-6in) high, pinch out the tips to encourage bushy growth.

Pests and diseases Cabbage root fly maggots may cause the roots to rot and plants to wilt. Or the plants can become stunted as a result of club root – swellings on the roots.

CHERRY PIE – see *Heliotropium*
CHINA ASTER – see
Callistephus

Chrysanthemum

chrysanthemum

Chrysanthemum frutescens

Chrysanthemum carinatum

☐ Height 15-60cm (6-24in)
☐ Planting distance 15-30cm (6-12in)
☐ Flowers early summer to early autumn
☐ Ordinary garden soil
☐ Sunny site
☐ Hardy annuals

Chrysanthemums form a large genus of plants. Some are grown as hardy and half-hardy annuals and greenhouse plants, while others are true hardy perennials. All annual species are hardy and free-flowering. They form well-branched, bushy plants and produce an abundance of daisy-like flowers from early summer till early autumn. Grow them in informal bedding schemes, as edgings to borders, in tubs, hanging baskets or for cutting.

Popular species
Chrysanthemum carinatum (syn. *C. tricolor*) bears single flowers from early summer to early autumn. These have purple central discs surrounded by ray petals banded in different colours. The plants reach 60cm (2ft) high and should be spaced 30cm (1ft) apart. Popular varieties include 'Court Jesters' (red, pink, orange, yellow, maroon and white banded with red or orange). 'Polar Star' grows up to 90cm (3ft) and bears showy flowers of palest yellow banded with golden-orange on stiff stems, ideal for cutting. 'Rainbow Mixture' has 6cm (2½in) wide flowers brightly banded in various combinations of yellow, scarlet, red, rose-lavender, bronze, orange and white. 'Zebra' is a branching plant with brilliant scarlet flowers.
Chrysanthemum coronarium has double, semi-double or single flowers ranging from white to golden-yellow in mid and late summer. 'Golden Gem' is the most popular variety, reaching 30-45cm (12-18in) high with golden-yellow flowers. Plant 38cm (15in) apart. 'Primrose Gem' is similar, but with pale yellow flowers.
Chrysanthemum frutescens, though really a perennial, is grown as a half-hardy annual and used in containers and for summer bedding schemes. It bears large white or pale yellow flowers from late spring until mid autumn and reaches 30-45cm (12-18in) high. Space the plants 30-45cm (12-18in) apart.
Chrysanthemum multicaule, and its common variety, 'Golden Plate', has small, single golden-yellow flowers. Growing only 15-30cm (6-12in) high, it is useful for window-boxes, tubs and rock gardens. Plant 23cm (9in) apart.
Chrysanthemum palludosum bears an abundance of small white flowers with yellow centres, like mini marguerites, throughout the summer. The 30cm (1ft) high plants can be grown in window-boxes, tubs or as edging. Set them 23cm (9in) apart.
Chrysanthemum parthenium (feverfew) is popular in pots and window-boxes and as edging to summer bedding schemes. It is a compact plant, up to 30cm (12in) high, studded from mid summer to early autumn with masses of small flowers; the light green leaves have a pungent aroma. Popular varieties include 'Golden

Chrysanthemum coronarium

Cladanthus

Palm Springs daisy

Chrysanthemum parthenium 'Golden Ball'

Cladanthus arabicus

Ball', with small rounded golden flowers, and 'Snow Puffs' which has white ball-shaped flowers with an outer ring of petals.

Chrysanthemum segetum bears single yellow flowers with brown central discs from mid summer to early autumn. Plant this 45cm (18in) high species and its varieties 30cm (1ft) apart in a border. 'Eastern Star' (also known as 'Prado') has primrose-yellow flowers.

Cultivation

Annual chrysanthemums will grow and flower freely in any soil, though they give the best results in fertile, well-drained soil in a sunny site. Sow the seeds in their flowering site in early or mid spring, covering them with a sprinkling of soil. When large enough to handle, thin the seedlings to the required spacing. In mild districts and with cloche protection, an autumn sowing gives earlier flowers or pot plants for the greenhouse.

C. frutescens can only be increased from 5-7.5cm (2-3in) long cuttings of non-flowering side-shoots taken in early autumn and rooted under glass.

Pests and diseases Mildew, aphids and caterpillars can cause problems.

☐ Height 75cm (2½ft)
☐ Planting distance 30cm (12in)
☐ Flowers from early summer until autumn
☐ Any well-drained soil
☐ Full sun
☐ Hardy annual

The Palm Springs daisy (*Cladanthus arabicus*) deserves to be better known for it is an easy and accommodating plant, thriving in a wide range of conditions and sites and producing an abundance of flowers from early summer until the first autumn frosts. It grows up to 75cm (2½ft) tall and forms a steadily increasing mound of pale green feathery leaves. These, like the flowers, are pungently aromatic.

The dainty foliage is almost completely hidden by a succession of single daisy-like flowers, golden-yellow and fragrant and about 5cm (2in) wide.

Palm Springs daisies are ideal for growing in groups of five to seven plants in herbaceous and annual borders. They are not suitable for cutting.

Cultivation

Palm Springs daisies will grow in any kind of soil, even poor ones, and in partial shade, but the best results are obtained in light and well-drained soil, in a sunny position.

Sow the seeds thinly in the flowering site, in early to mid spring, covering them lightly with soil. When the seedlings are large enough to handle, thin them out to stand 30cm (12in) apart. When flowering begins, dead-head the blooms regularly to extend the flowering season.

Pests and diseases Generally trouble free.

Clarkia

clarkia

Clarkia amoena

Cleome

spider flower

Cleome spinosa

☐ Height 60cm-1.2m (2-4ft)
☐ Planting distance 60cm (2ft)
☐ Flowers mid summer until autumn
☐ Well-drained fertile soil
☐ Full sun
☐ Half-hardy annual

☐ Height 30-90cm (1-3ft)
☐ Planting distance 30cm (1ft)
☐ Flowers mid summer to early autumn
☐ Light loamy soil
☐ Sunny site
☐ Hardy annual

The tall spikes of clarkias provide a valuable contrast to the rounded blooms of most other annuals. They come in a range of colours – white, pink, salmon, orange, scarlet, purple and lavender – available as single colours or in mixtures. Blooming from mid summer to early autumn, the slender plants are popular for borders, though they can also be grown as pot plants and for cutting.

Popular species and varieties

Clarkia amoena, formerly listed as godetia, bears loose spikes of lilac or pink to red funnel-shaped flowers. The plants reach 60cm (2ft) high.

Clarkia elegans is one of the most popular clarkias, bearing 23-30cm (9-12in) long spikes of double flowers on erect and branching plants, from mid summer till early autumn. The plants reach 60cm (2ft) high. Several varieties have been developed from it, including 'Apple Blossom' (90cm/3ft, double,

soft pink touched with white), 'Love Affair' (red, pink, purple and white double flowers), 'Orange Queen' (double, orange), and 'Royal Bouquet' (double, carnation-like flowers in mixed colours). *Clarkia pulchella* bears spikes of semi-double lavender flowers that form dainty sprays from mid summer to early autumn. It reaches 30-38cm (12-15in) high. Mixed seed selections are available; 'Filigree' has lace-like blooms in white and shades of pink, salmon and purple.

Cultivation

Clarkias like a light, slightly acid loam, slightly moist for *Clarkia amoena.* All need plenty of sun.

Sow the seeds in the flowering site in early spring and then thin to the required spacing when the seedlings are large enough to handle.

Do not feed the plants as this encourages leaf growth at the expense of flowering.

Pests and diseases Grey mould sometimes attacks the base of the stems, and foot and root rot may cause seedlings to collapse.

The spider flower (*Cleome spinosa*) is a handsome plant with globe-shaped flower heads and elegant green, divided leaves. The fragrant flowers open from mid summer until autumn and come in white, delicate pink and purple. In a tub the plants rarely exceed 60cm (2ft), but in well-prepared ground in a border they can grow up to 1.2m (4ft) tall.

Popular varieties

Several varieties have been developed from *Cleome spinosa.*

'**Cherry Queen**' has carmine-pink flowers.

'**Colour Fountain**' has pink, rose, purple, lilac and white flowers.

'**Helen Campbell**' is a white-flowered variety.

Cultivation

Sow the seeds under glass in early spring and keep at a temperature of 18°C (64°F). When the seedlings are large enough to handle prick them out into small pots. Harden off for a few weeks before planting out in late spring. Grow in fertile well-drained soil in full sun.

Pests and diseases Aphids may infest young growth.

CLOUD GRASS – see *Agrostis*

Cobaea

cathedral bell, cup and saucer vine

Cobaea scandens and 'Alba'

- ☐ Height 3-6m (10-20ft)
- ☐ Planting distance 60cm (2ft)
- ☐ Flowers early summer to mid autumn
- ☐ Ordinary well-drained soil
- ☐ Sunny sheltered position
- ☐ Half-hardy annual

Cathedral bell (*Cobaea scandens*) is an annual climber, ideal for providing quick decorative cover for pergolas, trelliswork and other forms of support. The plants may reach 6m (20ft) high, growing vertically at first and then spreading at the top.

From early summer until mid autumn an abundance of purple bell-shaped flowers appear. These are seen against a backdrop of mid to dark green leaves. The variety 'Alba' has greenish-white flowers.

Cultivation
Sow the seeds under glass – one seed in each 7.5cm (3in) pot of potting compost – in early to mid spring. Keep at a temperature of 18°C (64°F).

Harden off the plants before planting them outdoors in early summer. Choose a sunny sheltered position with ordinary well-drained soil. Provide pea sticks, wire mesh or trellis for the plants' tendrils to cling to.
Pests and diseases Watch out for aphids.

COCKSCOMB – see *Celosia*

Coix

Job's tears

Coix lacryma-jobi

- ☐ Height 45-60cm (18-24in)
- ☐ Planting distance 15-23cm (6-9in)
- ☐ Flowers mid summer to early autumn
- ☐ Fertile well-drained garden soil
- ☐ Sunny site
- ☐ Half-hardy annual grass

Job's tears (*Coix lacryma-jobi*), an ornamental grass, is grown for its attractive pearly grey bead-shaped seeds which form in mid summer and last until early autumn. These are borne in small dangling clusters on graceful arching stems which reach up to 45-60cm (18-24in) high and are set with pale green broad leaves. The seeds are unsuitable for drying.

Cultivation
Sow the seeds in late winter or early spring in trays of seed compost at a temperature of 13-16°C (55-61°F). Transplant the seedlings to their flowering site in late spring to early summer, when danger of severe frosts has passed.

The seeds can also be sown outdoors in mid spring.

Grow Job's tears in well-drained soil enriched with humus. The site should be sunny – ideally south-facing.
Pests and diseases Mildew may attack the plants.

Coleus

flame nettle

Coleus blumei 'Wizard Mixed'

- ☐ Height 30-45cm (12-18in)
- ☐ Planting distance 30cm (1ft)
- ☐ Foliage plant
- ☐ Moisture-retentive soil
- ☐ Sunny site or dappled shade
- ☐ Tender perennial grown as annual

Coleus blumei and its varieties are valued for their colourful, ever-green foliage – nettle-like leaves in various shades and patterns of green, yellow, red and maroon. Though most commonly grown as indoor pot plants, they look equally effective in formal beds and containers outdoors, where they provide a splendid setting for summer-flowering plants.

Flowers do appear – tiny blue and white tubular bells – but it is best to remove them as soon as buds form to encourage bushy foliage growth.

Coleus blumei 'Pineapple Beauty'

Coleus blumei mixed

Popular varieties

The following popular varieties have been developed from *Coleus blumei*. Some are in single colours, others are sold as mixtures.

'**Dragon**' is a mixture with large serrated leaves in reds and maroons edged with gold. It reaches 30cm (1ft) high.

'**Fairway**' has delicate foliage on 20-25cm (8-10in) high neatly-growing plants. Distinct colours in various combinations.

'**Fashion Parade**' has elongated, or deeply lobed, serrated or fringed leaves in shades of pink, gold, jade and scarlet. It grows to 30cm (12in) high.

'**Milky Way**' is a dwarf variety, to 15cm (6in) tall, with deeply cut leaves in either vivid or pale colours. Suitable for window-boxes and small pots.

'**Mini Coral**' is tiny, up to 15cm (6in) high and wide and of well-balanced shape; various leaf colour combinations.

'**Molten Lava**' has black and carmine leaves and reaches 23-30cm (9-12in) high.

'**Pineapple Beauty**' has yellow-green leaves with rich maroon markings. It reaches 30-45cm (12-18in) high.

'**Rainbow**' comes in a wide range of bright, rich foliage colours. It is a tall variety, reaching 45cm (18in) high.

'**Rose Wizard**' grows 25-30cm (10-12in) high and has foliage in shades of cream, bright green and pink; good for hanging baskets.

'**Scarlet Poncho**' has maroon leaves with lemon-yellow edging. Its cascading habit makes it an excellent variety for hanging baskets. The plants reach 30cm (1ft) high.

'**Wizard Mixed**' is a mixture of free-branching varieties, up to 30cm (12in) high, coming in a range of bright colours. The shoots do not need to be pinched out.

Cultivation

Sow the seeds in early spring under glass. Pot on as required or plant out in early summer, either singly or in groups, spacing them 30cm (1ft) apart. Coleus grow in any well-drained but moisture retentive soil, in sun or dappled shade.

Pinch out the growing tips and remove flower buds when they appear, to encourage side-branching and healthy growth. Good colour forms can be propagated from tip cuttings taken in late summer and rooted under glass.

Pests and diseases Trouble free.

Collinsia
collinsia

Collinsia heterophylla

☐ Height 60cm (2ft)
☐ Planting distance 15cm (6in)
☐ Flowers early summer to early autumn
☐ Any moist soil
☐ Light shade
☐ Hardy annual

Easily grown and graceful, *Collinsia heterophylla* is popular for its long flowering season. The slender stems, up to 60cm (2ft) high, carry opposite pairs of lance-shaped mid green leaves below loose clusters of showy bicoloured flowers, the upper lips of which are white, the lower ones lilac.

Collinsias are suitable for growing in mixed borders and beds of annuals; they can also be grown as pot plants in the greenhouse.

Cultivation
Sow seeds from early to mid spring where the plants are to flower – successive sowings at fortnightly intervals will extend the flowering season. When the seedlings are large enough to handle, thin them to stand 15cm (6in) apart. Collinsias will grow in most types of soil, though a well-drained but moisture-retentive soil in partial shade gives the best results. Support the plants with twiggy sticks.
Pests and diseases Trouble free.

CONEFLOWER – see *Rudbeckia*

Convolvulus
dwarf morning glory

Convolvulus tricolor 'Dwarf Rainbow Flash'

☐ Height 15-38cm (6-15in)
☐ Planting distance 15-23cm (6-9in)
☐ Flowers mid summer to early autumn
☐ Well-drained soil
☐ Sunny, sheltered site
☐ Hardy annual

Dwarf morning glory, *Convolvulus tricolor,* the only annual in the genus, has all the beauty of its cousin, the white-flowered perennial bindweed (*C. arvensis*), without its strangling habit.

Its funnel-shaped flowers, which are on display from mid summer until early autumn, are a magnificent deep blue with a white or yellow throat. Carried on 30-38cm (12-15in) high bushy and erect plants with oval, dark green

Convolvulus tricolor 'Royal Ensign'

leaves, they look most effective in formal bedding schemes or mixed borders.

Popular varieties
The following favourite varieties have been developed from *Convolvulus tricolor.*
'Blue Ensign' has brilliant blue flowers with yellow and white centres. It is a dwarf variety, 15cm (6in) high.
'Dwarf Rainbow Flash' has large flowers in mixed colours: pink, carmine, rose, deep blue, pale blue, purple and lilac. It is 15cm (6in) high.
'Royal Ensign' has blue flowers with white and yellow centres.

Cultivation
Sow the seeds under glass in pots of seed compost in early spring and keep at a temperature of 15-18°C (59-64°F). When the seedlings are large enough to handle, prick out into boxes. Harden off before planting out in late spring.

Alternatively, sow in the flowering site in mid spring, and thin to 15-23cm (6-9in) apart.

The plants will grow in any well-drained soil, even poor, dry ones, in a sunny sheltered site. Dead-head regularly.
Pests and diseases Trouble free.

Coreopsis

tickseed

Coreopsis tinctoria

□ Height 30-60cm (1-2ft)
□ Planting distance 15-23cm (6-9in)
□ Flowers mid summer to early autumn
□ Fertile, well-drained soil
□ Open sunny site
□ Hardy annual

This genus of free-flowering, bushy plants with deeply cut green leaves and daisy-like blooms has one great asset – it thrives in polluted areas.

Annual tickseeds (perennial tickseeds also exist) have flowers in a range of yellows and chestnuts, appearing between mid summer and early autumn. They look best grown in borders, and can be used for cutting.

Popular species

Coreopsis drummondii, height 60cm (2ft), has bright yellow flowers with deep purple central discs surrounded by red-brown blotches.
Coreopsis tinctoria (syn. *C. bicolor*) carries a profusion of bright yellow flowers on stiff stems about 60cm (2ft) tall. A dwarf variety, reaching 30cm (12in) high, is available.

Cultivation

Sow the seeds in their flowering site from early spring to early summer for a succession of flowers. The best results are achieved in fertile, well-drained soil in an open sunny site. Stake taller plants. Dead-head regularly.
Pests and diseases Trouble free.

CORNCOCKLE – see
Agrostemma
CORNFLOWER – see *Centaurea*

Cosmos

cosmea

Cosmos bipinnatus

□ Height 60-90cm (2-3ft)
□ Planting distance 45-60cm (18-24in)
□ Flowers late summer to early autumn
□ Light soil
□ Full sun
□ Half-hardy annual

An abundance of delicate, richly coloured dahlia-like flowers, borne among pretty light green leaves makes these half-hardy annuals excellent for late summer colour in borders and containers.

The flowers come in pinks, reds and white with yellow centres, or

Cosmos bipinnatus 'Sensation'

Crepis
hawksbeard

Cosmos sulphureus 'Sunny Red'

Crepis rubra 'Alba'

shades of orange, vermilion and yellow. Growing on 60-90cm (2-3ft) high stems, they are also ideal for cutting.

Popular species
Cosmos bipinnatus is the tallest species, reaching 90cm (3ft) high. It has white, crimson, rose or pink flowers with yellow central discs, and finely cut mid green leaves. Popular varieties include 'Candy Stripe' (white flowers with crimson stripes), 'Gloria' (rose-pink, central dark bands; up to 15cm/6in across); 'Psyche' (semi-double and single pink, red or white blooms with frilled petals), 'Purity' (white flowers) and 'Sensation' (white, pink, carmine and crimson flowers).
Cosmos sulphureus reaches just 60cm (2ft) high, and has yellow flowers accompanied by coarsely cut dark green leaves. Popular varieties include 'Bright Lights' (small double yellow, orange or scarlet flowers), 'Diablo' (orange-red flowers), 'Lemon Twist' (acid-yellow flowers) 'Sunny Gold' (semi-double, golden-yellow flowers) and 'Sunny Red' (double vermilion flowers).

Cultivation
Sow the seeds under glass in late winter or early spring and keep at a temperature of 16°C (61°F). Harden off in a cold frame before planting out in late spring.

Cosmeas prefer a poor, light soil in a hot dry corner. Stake the plants and dead-head regularly.
Pests and diseases Aphids sometimes infest young plants.

COTTON THISTLE – see
Onopordum

☐ Height 30cm (12in)
☐ Planting distance 15cm (6in)
☐ Flowers in summer
☐ Any well-drained soil
☐ Full sun
☐ Hardy annual

Most species of the genus *Crepis* are weeds, but a few are suitably handsome for garden decoration, including the annual *Crepis rubra*. This accommodating plant has basal rosettes of pale green, toothed and lance-shaped leaves above which rise 30cm (12in) high flower stems. The stems are topped with a mass of loose clusters of double, dandelion-like flowers throughout the summer months and later. They are rose-pink in the species and white in the variety 'Alba'. Another form 'Snowplume' has white feathery blossoms with a pale apricot centre.

These charming plants are suitable for growing at the front of annual and mixed borders and in rock gardens; they are also long-lasting as cut flowers.

Cultivation
Sow seeds directly in the flowering site in early autumn for early flowering; cover the seedlings with cloches in cold districts. Alternatively, sow in early to mid spring, covering the seeds lightly with soil. Thin all seedlings to stand 15cm (6in) apart when they are large enough to handle.

Crepis grow well in any dry and well-drained soil, particularly poor ones, provided they are given full sun. They are tolerant of exposed sites and thrive in coastal regions. Dead-head regularly to prevent self-seeding; named varieties do not come true to type.
Pests and diseases Generally trouble free.

CUP FLOWER – see
Nierembergia
CUP AND SAUCER VINE – see
Cobaea

Crepis rubra

Cynoglossum

hound's tongue

Cynoglossum amabile

☐ Height 45-60cm (18-24in)
☐ Planting distance 30cm (12in)
☐ Flowers in mid and late summer
☐ Well-drained, fertile soil
☐ Sunny site
☐ Hardy annual/biennial

Sometimes known as Chinese for-get-me-not, the flowers of *Cyno-glossum amabile* are produced in greater profusion than on the ordinary forget-me-not. The leaves are tongue-shaped, grey-green and downy. A true biennial, hound's tongue will flower in the same year from seed, raising its sprays of turquoise-blue flowers on slender stems above the bushy foliage. The variety 'Blue Showers' has sky-blue flowers.

Hound's tongue is suitable for growing in annual and mixed borders, as edging to semi-wild areas and in containers. The flowers last well in water.

Cultivation
Sow seeds in an outdoor nursery bed in early summer; thin out the seedlings and transplant them to their flowering positions in mid autumn. For flowering the same year, sow under glass at a temper-ature of 13-16°C (55-61°F) in late winter; prick off the seedlings into boxes and harden them off in a cold frame before planting out, 30cm (12in) apart, in late spring. The plants self-seed freely and should be dead-headed regularly.

Hound's tongues grow in any good soil that drains freely; they thrive in full sun or partial shade.
Pests and diseases Tobacco mosaic virus may cause mottling of leaves and stunting of plants.

Dahlia

bedding dahlia

Bedding dahlias

☐ Height 30cm-1.2m (1-4ft)
☐ Planting distance 30-60cm (1-2ft)
☐ Flowers mid summer until the first frost
☐ Medium to heavy soil
☐ Open sunny site
☐ Half-hardy annual

A number of dahlia varieties can be grown from seed for flowering the same year. Known as bedding dahlias, they are more modest cousins of the large perennial border dahlias growing from tub-ers. They have similar, though smaller, flowers and vary in height from 30cm (1ft) to 1.2m (4ft). The flowers – in white, yellow, orange, scarlet, crimson and pink – appear in mid summer and continue until the first hard frost.

Use these half-hardy annuals for containers and window-boxes, in bedding schemes and for plant-ing in the foreground of a mixed border.

Popular varieties
The range of varieties available is increasing and changing every year. The following are some of the most popular. The majority come in mixed colours.
'Bambino Mixed' is a miniature variety, growing 30-45cm (12-18in) high and carrying a profu-sion of double flowers. Good for pots and containers.
'Cactus-flowered Hybrids' have semi-double and double flowers with quilled petals. The plants reach 90cm-1.2m (3-4ft) high.
'Collarette Dandy' has single flowers with a small white or yellow collar of inner petals sur-rounding the central disc. The plants reach 45-60cm (18-24in) high.
'Coltness Hybrids', one of the most popular, is a dwarf variety reaching just 50cm (20in) high. The large single flowers are freely produced.
'Diablo' is similar to 'Redskin', but the semi-double flowers and bronze-green foliage are borne on more compact plants, 38-45cm (15-18in) tall.
'Dwarf Amore' bears semi and fully double flowers on bushy plants, 30cm (12in) tall and wide.
'Mignon Silver' has pure white flowers shading to pale yellow-green near the centre. The plants grow 38-50cm (15-20in) high.
'Pompon Mixed' has small ball flowers and reaches 90cm (3ft).
'Redskin' has large semi-double flowers and rich bronze foliage. The plants reach 50cm (20in)

Datura

angel's trumpet

Datura metel 'Flore Pleno'

Bedding dahlia 'Coltness Hybrids'

high. A dwarf mixture produces similar plants, 38cm (15in) tall.

'**Rigoletto**' is an early-flowering, dwarf variety, 30-50cm (12-20in) high, with double and semi-double blooms.

'**Sunburst**' bears single flowers, up to 12.5cm (5in) across, the broad overlapping petals forming circular blooms. Height about 60cm (2ft).

'**Unwin's Dwarf Hybrids**' produce an abundance of double flowers in a particularly wide range of colours. These are long-lasting, and are carried on 45-60cm (18-24in) high plants.

Cultivation

Sow the seeds under glass in late winter and early spring in trays of seed compost, and keep at a temperature of 16°C (61°F). Prick off the seedlings into boxes when large enough to handle, and later into 7.5cm (3in) pots. Harden off from mid spring on and plant out in late spring to early summer, when danger of frost is well over.

Bedding dahlias grow best in a medium to heavy soil in an open sunny position. Enrich poor soils with well-rotted manure several weeks before planting out.

Water regularly in hot weather and dead-head for continuous flowering. Staking is unnecessary.

Pests and diseases Aphids and caterpillars may attack, and earwigs may eat the petals and leaves. Grey mould can be troublesome on flower stalks, buds and older flowers in wet summers.

DAISY – see *Bellis*

☐ Height 60-90cm (2-3ft)
☐ Planting distance 60-75cm (2-2½ft)
☐ Flowers mid summer to early autumn
☐ Rich soil
☐ Sunny, sheltered site
☐ Half-hardy annual

Angel's trumpet could be a misnomer, for these exotic plants are poisonous in all their parts. But in spite of this and their frost tenderness, they produce an impressive show of trumpet-shaped flowers with a strong fragrance that is headiest in the evening.

Daturas are technically shrubby perennials but are usually grown as half-hardy annuals, in mixed borders and bedding schemes. They are ideal as pot and container plants and can be grown in the greenhouse or conservatory in poor summers.

Popular varieties

Datura metel grows 60cm (2ft) or more high. It forms a shrubby plant with red stems set with ovate, dark green leaves. The flowers, 20cm (8in) long, are creamy-white and held erect; pink and purple varieties also exist, and 'Flore Pleno' bears double flowers.

Datura meteloides, a bushy plant, reaches a height of 90cm (3ft) and bears grey and hairy leaves with a pungent aroma. The upright, white or pink-flushed flowers, 15cm (6in) long, are sweetly scented. The variety 'Evening

Datura meteloides

Fragrance' has larger, more strongly scented flowers of pure white, the picotee edges picked out in lavender.

Cultivation

Sow seeds under glass in early spring, at a temperature of 16°C (61°F). When the seedlings are large enough to handle, prick them off into small pots of potting compost and grow on. Harden off the young plants in a cold frame before setting them out when all danger of frost is past.

In the open garden, daturas grow in any fertile garden soil, in a sunny and sheltered position. Grow pot plants in a proprietary compost.

Pests and diseases Trouble free.

Delphinium
larkspur

Delphinium consolida

- ☐ Height 30cm-1.2m (1-4ft)
- ☐ Planting distance 23-30cm (9-12in)
- ☐ Flowers early to late summer
- ☐ Fertile well-drained soil
- ☐ Sunny or lightly shaded site
- ☐ Hardy annual

One of the most enchanting sights in a summer herbaceous border is a mass of blue, white and pink delphinium spires soaring into the sky above attractive fern-like foliage. Two species – *Delphinium ajacis* and *D. consolida* and their varieties – are hardy annuals.

Commonly known as larkspurs, they reach 30cm-1.2m (1-4ft) so should be grown in herbaceous borders where there is plenty of space. Though blue and white are the most common flower colours, shades of pink, lavender and mauve are also available.

Popular species
Delphinium ajacis, or rocket larkspur, reaches 30-90cm (1-3ft) high and has sparsely branching stems bearing spires of loosely arranged flowers. The hyacinth-flowered hybrids are the most commonly

grown – they make excellent cut flowers as well as decoration for borders. They come in blues, purples, pinks and whites. 'Tall Rocket Mixed' reaches 75cm (30in) high and 'Dwarf Rocket Mixed' reaches 38cm (15in) high. *Delphinium consolida*, larkspur, is a taller species reaching 1.2m (4ft) high, with a more branching habit. The flowers are arranged in densely packed spikes and come in blue, red, purple, pink and white. Popular varieties and strains include 'Sublime Mixed' (long spires of double flowers on 90cm/3ft high plants).

Cultivation
Sow the seeds in their flowering site in early to mid spring. Thin to the necessary planting distances when the seedlings are large enough to handle: 23-30cm (9-12in) for rocket larkspur and its varieties, and 30cm (12in) for larkspur and its varieties.

For large, early-flowering plants, seeds may be sown in early autumn.

Annual delphiniums like fer-

tile, well-drained soil in full sun or partial shade. Support tall varieties with twiggy sticks, and cut out faded stems after flowering.
Pests and diseases Slugs and snails and powdery mildew may affect leaves, stems and flowers.

Delphinium ajacis

Dianthus

pinks

Dianthus barbatus

Dianthus chinensis

☐ Height 20-60cm (8-24in)
☐ Planting distance 15-25cm (6-10in)
☐ Flowers early summer until the first frost
☐ Ordinary garden soil
☐ Full sun
☐ Hardy annual and biennial

Dianthus is a large genus of mainly perennials, but it also includes two species which are usually grown as biennials and annuals: *Dianthus barbatus*, commonly known as sweet William, and *Dianthus chinensis*, the Indian pink. Both have fragrant flowers that come in shades of pink, red, cream and white. They appear in summer against a foil of narrow green leaves; they are excellent as cut flowers.

The annual and biennial dianthus are particularly useful for town and coastal gardens as they tolerate pollution and salt spray.

Popular species and varieties

Dianthus barbatus (sweet William) is usually grown as a biennial. In early and mid summer it bears dense heads of sweetly scented single or double flowers in combinations of white, pink and red.

An enormous range of sweet William varieties is available. Most are the standard 30-60cm (1-2ft) high, but a few dwarf varieties, reaching just 20-25cm (8-10in) high, can also be found. Popular varieties include 'Auricula-Eyed' (a mixture of pink, red and crimson flowers with conspicuous white eyes); 'Dunnet's Dark Crimson' (dark crimson flowers); 'Dwarf Double Pinocchio Mixed' (a mixture of dwarf varieties ideal for containers); 'Forerunner Mixed' (compact habit and intense flower colours); 'Harlequin' (pink and white ball-shaped flower heads), 'Indian Carpet' (a dwarf bedding mixture with long-lasting flowers). *Dianthus chinensis* (commonly called Indian pink) has had a range of varieties developed from it, which are grown as hardy annuals. The plants are small and compact with pale to mid green, grass-like foliage and attractive flowers with notched petals in shades of red, pink and white. Often the blooms are patterned or have a darker central zone. They are borne from mid summer until the first frost.

Indian pinks reach 30cm (1ft) high, making excellent edging for borders. They can also be used in formal bedding schemes.

Popular varieties include 'Baby Doll' (a mixture with large single flowers in shades of crimson, rose-pink and white); 'Colour Magician' (an F1 hybrid producing plants whose flower colours on the same plant range from white through pink to deep rose); 'Fire Carpet' (single, bright scarlet flowers); 'Magic Charms' (fringed flowers in shades of pink and red, white or bicoloured); 'Snowfire' (white flowers with scarlet centres), and 'Telstar' (early-flowering, bright crimson, pink, white and bicoloured blooms).

Cultivation

Sow the seeds of sweet William in a seed bed in early summer. Transplant to the flowering site in autumn – to full sun and any well-drained soil. Dress acid soil with lime. Stake only if the site is exposed and the soil rich.

Indian pinks are grown as hardy annuals. Sow the seeds thinly in the flowering position in mid spring, and when the seedlings are large enough to handle, thin to 15cm (6in) apart. Grow them in well-drained alkaline or neutral soil, in full sun.

Pests and diseases Sweet Williams are susceptible to rust.

Dianthus chinensis 'Baby Doll'

Diascia
twinspur

Diascia barberae

☐ Height 30cm (12in)
☐ Planting distance 15cm (6in)
☐ Flowers early summer to early
   autumn
☐ Any well-drained soil
☐ Full sun
☐ Half-hardy annual

The little twinspur (*Diascia barberae*) takes its common name from the shape of its shell-like, two-spurred flowers. They are rosy-pink and borne in loose clusters on top of slender flowering stems from late spring or early summer right through until autumn. Twinspur is a slender plant, clothed with ovate, glossy dark green leaves, and ideal for growing in groups at the front of borders, in bedding schemes and in containers. The variety 'Rose Queen' has exquisite blooms in great profusion.

Cultivation
Sow seeds under glass in late winter or early spring at a temperature of 16°C (61°F), covering them lightly. When the seedlings are large enough to handle, prick them off into boxes of potting compost and harden them off in a cold frame. Transplant the young plants to their flowering sites in late spring.

Any light and well-drained soil in full sun is suitable. Pinch out the growing point to encourage side-branching and dead-head regularly to maintain continuous flowering.

Pests and diseases Generally trouble free.

Digitalis
foxglove

Digitalis purpurea

☐ Height 90cm-1.5m (3-5ft)
☐ Planting distance 60cm (2ft)
☐ Flowers early to mid summer
☐ Any moisture-retentive soil
☐ Partial shade
☐ Hardy biennial

Our native foxglove (*Digitalis purpurea*) is a wonderful combination of strength and delicacy, growing 1.5m (5ft) high in good conditions, yet needing no support for its gracefully arching stems. In early and mid summer these stems, rising from rosettes of green leaves, turn into one-sided spires of spotted red-purple or white bell flowers.

Foxgloves make excellent border plants, even in winter when their rosettes of foliage form good ground cover. They also look most effective growing in a semi-wild corner of the garden.

Popular varieties
Several varieties have been developed from the common foxglove. The following are readily available.

'Alba' has pure white flowers, suitable for cutting.

'Apricot' has flowers in an attractive shade of apricot.

'Excelsior' has tall spikes of white, cream, pink and carmine flowers spotted with maroon.

'Foxy' is a dwarf hybrid strain, growing about 90cm (3ft) tall, with flower spikes in white, cream, pink and carmine all spotted with maroon.

Cultivation
Sow the seeds in late spring to early summer in a nursery bed, by scattering them on the surface and then raking them gently in. Thin to 15cm (6in) apart, when the seedlings are large enough to handle. In early autumn transfer to the flowering position – preferably one in partial shade with ordinary garden soil that will not dry out in summer.

When the central spikes have finished flowering, remove them to encourage side-shoots.

Pests and diseases Trouble free.

Dimorphotheca

star of the veldt, cape marigold

Dimorphotheca aurantiaca

Dimorphotheca 'Glistening White'

- ☐ Height 30-45cm (12-18in)
- ☐ Planting distance 30cm (1ft)
- ☐ Flowers early summer to early autumn
- ☐ Light well-drained soil
- ☐ Sunny position
- ☐ Half-hardy annual

In its native South Africa, star of the veldt grows rapidly and flowers quickly so it can produce its seeds before the dry season sets in. Fortunately, in cooler climates, it lasts longer, producing hundreds of elegant daisy-like flowers from early summer until early autumn. These are brilliant orange, with a dark brown eye and are carried on 30-45cm (12-18in) high stems with narrowly oblong mid-green leaves.

The genus has been reclassified as *Osteospermum*, and seed catalogues may list star of the veldt under either name. Their popularity has risen steadily due to their long flowering season and the brightness of their daisy flowers, sometimes with yellow, sometimes with purple centres. They look magnificent grown in groups in borders and beds, and the dwarf varieties are suitable for sunny rock gardens and for patio containers.

The most popular species, *Dimorphotheca (Osteospermum) aurantiaca*, is a perennial but invariably grown as a half-hardy annual, though it will often survive winters outdoors in mild districts if given cloche protection.

Popular varieties

Several varieties have been developed from *Dimorphotheca aurantiaca*, offering a range of colours and sizes. The following are readily available:

'Giant Mixed' grows 30cm (12in) high and produces plants with a profusion of flowers in all pastel shades – creamy white, orange and salmon.

'Giant Orange' ('Goliath') has exceptionally large, orange-coloured daisy flowers.

'Glistening White' bears silvery and pure white flowers; the plants grow 15-23cm (6-9in) high.

'Hybrids' is a mixed seed selection of plants up to 30cm (12in) high; they bear blush-white, lemon, golden-yellow and salmon-orange flowers.

'Salmon Queen' grows 30cm (12in) tall, with large, 6cm (2½in) wide flowers in pastel shades of salmon and apricot. Set these branching plants 45cm (18in) apart.

'Starshine' bears 5-7.5cm (2-3in) wide, glistening flowers in pink, rose, carmine or white, all with yellow centres. The plants grow to 45cm (18in) high and almost as much across.

'Tetra Pole Star', 38-45cm (15-18in) high, has shiny, 7.5cm (3in) wide silvery flowers with bright violet veins.

Cultivation

Sow the seeds under glass in early spring at a temperature of 18°C (64°F). Harden off in a cold frame before planting out when danger of frost has passed. Space them 30cm (1ft) or more apart.

In mild areas seeds can be sown in the flowering site in early summer. All need a warm sunny situation and light well-drained soil. Thin to 30cm (1ft) apart when the seedlings are large enough to handle.

Dead-head to encourage repeat flowering.

Named varieties can be increased by 7.5cm (3in) tip cuttings taken in late summer and rooted in compost in a cold frame. Over winter the cuttings in a warm greenhouse.

Pests and diseases Grey mould can affect plants in wet weather.

Echium

viper's bugloss

Echium 'Dwarf Hybrids'

Emilia

tassel flower

Emilia javanica

☐ Height 45-60cm (18-24in)
☐ Planting distance 25cm (10in)
☐ Flowers early to late summer
☐ Well-drained garden soil
☐ Sunny site
☐ Half-hardy annual

Tassel flowers are excellent half-hardy annuals for providing a splash of orange, scarlet and gold in sunny dry borders in coastal gardens. Their tassel-like flowers, carried on wiry stems throughout the summer, look most effective in mixed bedding schemes, though they also make excellent subjects for containers, and as cut flowers they are long-lasting in water. Only one species, *Emilia javanica*, is grown in Britain. It reaches 45-60cm (18-24in) high. Mixed seed selections with orange and gold flowers are available.

Cultivation
Sow the seeds in their flowering position – a hot, dry sunny spot with well-drained soil in late spring. Thin to 25cm (10in) apart when the seedlings are large enough to handle. Dead-head to encourage continuous flowering throughout the summer.
Pests and diseases Trouble free.

☐ Height 60-90cm (2-3ft)
☐ Planting distance 23-45cm (9-18in)
☐ Flowers early to late summer
☐ Any well-drained garden soil
☐ Sunny site
☐ Hardy annuals and biennials

Echiums are invaluable in summer beds and borders where their bright upturned bell flowers add colour throughout the summer and are especially attractive to bees. Although of biennial habit, they will flower in their first year from seed and frequently seed themselves.

Popular species and varieties
Echium lycopsis (syn. *E. plantagineum*) is a bushy erect annual growing to a height of 90cm (3ft), its stems set with mid green oblong leaves. From early summer onwards, 25cm (10in) long flower spikes are closely packed with purple or blue tubular blooms. Several seed selections, ideal for containers, are available, including 'Blue Bedder' (30cm/12in high), with deep blue flowers; and 'Dwarf Hybrids' (30cm/12in tall) in a mixture of white, pink, rose and various shades of blue and purple.

Echium vulgare is a biennial usually grown as an annual. It is about 60cm (2ft) high, of bushy but compact habit, with leaves that are lance-shaped and dark green. The tubular flowers are borne in shorter but dense and profuse spikes; they are purple in bud and open violet-blue.

Cultivation
Sow seeds in the flowering site in early spring – or in early autumn, covering the site with cloches during winter. Thin the seedlings when large enough to handle, to stand 45cm (18in) apart for *Echium lycopsis* and 23cm (9in) for dwarf varieties and *E. vulgare*.

Echiums will grow in any kind of soil and site, but flower most profusely in light, well-drained soil and in full sun.
Pests and diseases Trouble free.

Eschscholzia

Californian poppy

Eschscholzia californica 'Monarch Mixed'

Eschscholzia californica

- □ Height 12-38cm (5-15in)
- □ Planting distance 15cm (6in)
- □ Flowers early summer to mid autumn
- □ Any garden soil
- □ Sunny site
- □ Hardy annual

The fragile delicate charm of this group of poppies is apparent from the moment the conical green hats split open around their buds of crumpled silk until the petals fall to reveal long cylindrical seed heads. Produced from early summer until mid autumn, the bright flower display is complemented by the exquisitely cut, blue-green foliage.

Two species and their varieties are popular in gardens, where they can be grown in borders with poor sandy soil, or on sunny banks. They produce self-sown seedlings, so you can rely upon them to appear year after year.

Popular species and varieties

Eschscholzia caespitosa (syn *E. tenuifolia*) has small yellow flowers which appear freely between early summer and early autumn. It is a dwarf species, reaching just 12cm (5in) high, so it looks best grown as edging at the front of a border or in a rockery. Space the plants 15cm (6in) apart. Popular varieties include 'Miniature Primrose' (small lemon-yellow flowers) and 'Sundew' (scented lemon-yellow blooms). *Eschscholzia californica* bears masses of bright orange-yellow flowers from early summer until mid autumn, followed by long cylinder-shaped, blue-green seed pods. The plants reach 30-38cm (12-15in) high. Popular varieties include 'Ballerina' (double red, orange, pink and yellow flowers which are sometimes striped white); 'Dalli' (bicoloured scarlet and yellow flowers on compact plants); 'Monarch Mixed' (single and semi-double blooms in yellow, orange, red and carmine-pink);

'Orange King' (translucent orange flowers) and 'Purple-Violet' (unusual mauve flowers with a hint of red in them).

Cultivation

Sow the seeds in the flowering site in early spring, covering them with just a sprinkling of soil. Thin to 15cm (6in) apart, when the seedlings are large enough to handle.

These poppies will grow in any soil, but thrive in poor sandy soils, and in full sun, which encourages an abundance of flowers with strong colours.

For plants the following year, delay clearing the site until the seeds have scattered.

Pests and diseases Trouble free.

Eschscholzia caespitosa

Euphorbia

euphorbia

Euphorbia marginata

- ☐ Height 60-90cm (2-3ft)
- ☐ Planting distance 30-45cm (12-18in)
- ☐ Foliage plant
- ☐ Ordinary garden soil
- ☐ Sun or partial shade
- ☐ Hardy and half-hardy annual

Annual euphorbias are usually grown in borders for their elegant foliage. They do have flowers – in summer – but these pale into insignificance beside the petal-like bracts in scarlet-red or cream shades, according to species.

The plants form neat bushes 60-90cm (2-3ft) high. They have the advantage of tolerating partial shade as well as sun, and will grow in any ordinary garden soil. Indeed, the foliage colours are more intense when the plants are grown in poor soil.

Popular species

Euphorbia heterophylla, commonly known as fire-on-the-mountain or annual poinsettia, is a neat, bushy, half-hardy annual,

with dark green oval or lance-shaped leaves. At the end of each shoot a 10cm (4in) wide whorl of red bracts appears from mid summer to early autumn, accompanied by small crimson-orange flowers.

Euphorbia lathyris, otherwise known as caper spurge, is an attractive green-leaved species – the long thin leaves being arranged symmetrically on upright stems. In early to mid summer small yellow flowers appear in leafy heads. The plants reach 90cm (3ft) high.

Euphorbia marginata, snow-on-the-mountain, has bright green oval leaves which become edged and veined with white as the plant matures. Insignificant white flowers appear in early autumn. 'Summer Icicle', heavily variegated, is 45cm (18in) tall.

Cultivation

Sow the seeds in a sunny site in early to mid spring. When the seedlings are large enough to

Euphorbia lathyris

handle, thin to 30cm (1ft) apart.

Alternatively give them a head start, and sow under glass at a temperature of 16°C (61°F) in early spring. Harden off before planting out in late spring.

Pests and diseases Trouble free.

EVENING PRIMROSE – see *Oenothera*
EVERLASTING – see *Helichrysum* and *Helipterum*

Felicia

felicia

Felicia bergeriana

☐ Height 15-45cm (6-18in)
☐ Planting distance 15-23cm (6-9in)
☐ Flowers early summer to early autumn
☐ Ordinary well-drained garden soil
☐ Sunny, sheltered position
☐ Half-hardy annual

This little-known South African plant is rather special as it is one of the few daisy look-alikes with blue flowers. These appear in great profusion throughout the summer, their slender blue petals arranged around a yellow central disc. The plants form attractive domes of grey-green foliage, and make excellent window-box fillers or edging for borders.

Popular species
Felicia amelloides, blue marguerite, has sky-blue flowers from early until late summer. They stand 45cm (18in) high, above the domes of mid-green foliage.
Felicia bergeriana, the kingfisher daisy, is a dwarf species (15cm/6in high) with grey-green foliage and steel-blue flowers from early summer until early autumn.

Cultivation
Sow the seeds in pans of John Innes seed compost under glass in late winter to early spring, and keep at a temperature of 16°C (61°F). When the seedlings are large enough to handle, prick out into boxes or pots of potting compost and grow on at 10°C (50°F). Harden off, before planting out in mid to late spring. They will grow in any ordinary well-drained garden soil in a sunny sheltered position.

Dead-head by lightly shearing after the first flush to ensure a second display of flowers.
Pests and diseases Trouble free.

FEVERFEW – see *Chrysanthemum*
FIELD POPPY – see *Papaver*
FIRE-ON-THE-MOUNTAIN – see *Euphorbia*
FLAME NETTLE – see *Coleus*
FLAX – see *Linum*
FLOSS FLOWER – see *Ageratum*
FORGET-ME-NOT – see *Myosotis*
FOUR O'CLOCK PLANT – see *Mirabilis*
FOXGLOVE – see *Digitalis*
FRENCH MARIGOLD – see *Tagetes*

Gaillardia

blanket flower

Gaillardia pulchella

☐ Height 30-60cm (1-2ft)
☐ Planting distance 30cm (1ft)
☐ Flowers mid summer to mid autumn
☐ Any well-drained soil
☐ Sunny site
☐ Hardy annual

This genus of bright daisy-like flowers includes one annual species, *Gaillardia pulchella*. Commonly known as the blanket flower, it has single red flowers edged with yellow from mid summer to mid autumn. They are suitable for decoration in herbaceous borders and also make good cut flowers.

Popular varieties
The following popular varieties have all been developed from *Gaillardia pulchella*.
'Double Mixed' grows 60cm (2ft) high and bears 7.5cm (3in) wide, fully double flowers in cream-white, gold, crimson and bicolours.
'Lorenziana' has double round-headed red, gold or yellow flowers. It grows 30cm (1ft) high.
'Red Plume',30cm (1ft) tall, has a profuse show of striking, deep red double flowers.

Cultivation
Blanket flowers grow reasonably well in most soils in sun or shade, though light well-drained soil in a sunny site gives the best results. Sow the seeds in the flowering site in mid spring and thin to 30cm (1ft) apart. Support with twiggy sticks may be necessary; dead-head to prolong the flowering period.
Pests and diseases Downy mildew sometimes affects the leaves.

Gazania
gazania

Gazania species

Gilia
gilia

Gilia capitata and *Gilia tricolor*

☐ Height 45-60cm (18-24in)
☐ Planting distance 23cm (9in)
☐ Flowers early summer to early autumn
☐ Light well-drained soil
☐ Sunny site
☐ Hardy annual

☐ Height 20-35cm (8-14in)
☐ Planting distance 30cm (1ft)
☐ Flowers mid summer until the first frost
☐ Well-drained soil
☐ Sunny site
☐ Half-hardy annual

Large daisy-like flowers in bright shades of yellow are the principal feature of this mat-forming 23cm (9in) high South African plant. The flowers appear from mid summer until the first frost, but open only in bright sunshine – even then they close again in mid afternoon. The leaves are deep green, with white-felted undersides.

Gazanias are excellent for bedding out, and they also make good cut flowers. They are wind resistant and thrive in seaside gardens.

Popular varieties
Most garden varieties are developed from *Gazania × hybrida*.
'Carnival', an F1 mixture, grows to 35cm (14in) tall, with silver-green foliage and flowers in pink, rose, bronze and red shades, sometimes striped or bicoloured.
'Chansonette', up to 30cm (12in) tall, bears 7.5cm (3in) wide flowers in lemon, orange, gold, apricot and pink-red shades.

'Harlequin Hybrids', 38cm (15in) tall, have brightly coloured flowers in shades of yellow, orange, brown, pink and red, all with a brown zone around the central disc.
'Mini Star Mixed' have bright yellow, red, pink and orange flowers carried on neat, compact plants, 20cm (8in) tall.
'Oranges and Lemons', 20cm (8in) high, bears single, brightly coloured blooms in profusion.
'Talent Mixed' has short stems, to 20cm (8in) high, set with finely cut, silvery leaves and flowers in pastel and strong colours.

Cultivation
Sow the seeds under glass in mid to late winter and keep at a temperature of 16°C (61°F). Prick out into 7.5cm (3in) pots and harden off before planting out in early summer.

Set gazanias 30cm (1ft) apart in well-drained to dry soil in a sunny position.
Pests and diseases Grey mould can affect the plants in wet weather.

GERANIUM – see *Pelargonium*

Gilias are grown for their attractive feathery mid-green foliage and showy flowers which appear from early summer onwards. They are good for massing in beds and borders and as cut flowers.

Popular species
Gilia capitata has pincushion-like heads of lavender-blue flowers from early summer to early autumn on 45cm (18in) high stems.
Gilia tricolor bears clusters of pale violet bell-shaped flowers ringed maroon at the base, in early summer. It grows 60cm (2ft) high.

Cultivation
Sow in the flowering position in early autumn for flowering in early summer of the following year, or in early spring for flowering later in the summer. Ordinary garden soil will suffice, though a light well-drained soil gives the best results. The site should be in full sun. Thin out the seedlings to 23cm (9in) apart when they are strong enough to handle – leave autumn-sown ones until spring.
Pests and diseases Trouble free.

GLOBE AMARANTH – see *Gomphrena*

Godetia
godetia

Godetia grandiflora 'Dwarf Bedding Mixed'

Godetia grandiflora

- ☐ Height 23-75cm (9-30in)
- ☐ Planting distance 15cm (6in)
- ☐ Flowers early to late summer
- ☐ Ordinary well-drained soil
- ☐ Sunny position
- ☐ Hardy annual

Godetias are one of the most popular border plants, thanks to their bushy growth habit, abundance of brightly coloured flowers, and the ease with which they can be grown. The funnel-shaped blooms come in a variety of forms – single, double, semi-double and frilled – and are carried at the top of upright leafy spikes from early to late summer.

They are equally suitable for growing in beds and borders, for pots and containers, and as cut flowers.

Popular varieties
Only one species, *Godetia grandiflora*, is commonly grown and numerous varieties have been developed from it.

'**Azalea-flowered**' has semi-double flowers with wavy-edged petals in shades of pale pink, carmine-pink, salmon-pink and white. The plants stand 38-45cm (15-18in) high.
'**Cherie**' has double, pink, azalea-like blooms on 30cm (12in) high plants.
'**Crimson Glow**' is a dwarf plant, reaching 23cm (9in) high with single red flowers.
'**Double White**' has double white flowers and reaches 38-50cm (15-20in) high.
'**Duchess of Albany**', 30-38cm (12-15in) high, has satin-white, frilled flowers.
'**Dwarf Bedding Mixed**' produces compact plants reaching 23-30cm (9-12in) high, which bear single flowers in mixed colours.
'**Firelight**' is bright crimson, on 30-38cm (12-15in) high plants.
'**Grace Mixed**' is a tall F1 hybrid mixture, up to 75cm (2½ft) high; the flowers are marbled in lavender, salmon, pinks and reds.

'**Salmon Princess**' is a compact plant reaching 25-30cm (10-12in) high, with salmon-pink flowers.
'**Sybil Sherwood**' has lilac-pink flowers edged with white. The plants are 38cm (15in) high.
'**Tall Double Mixed**' has pink, red, rose and mauve double flowers on 75-90cm (2½-3ft) high stems.

Cultivation
Godetias like a well-drained but moisture-retentive soil in a sunny site. If the soil is too rich, excessive foliage will grow at the expense of the flowers.

Sow the seeds in their flowering site in early to mid spring, just covering them with soil. Thin to 15cm (6in) apart.

Stake the taller varieties in exposed positions, and water during dry weather.

Pests and diseases Over-watering can cause yellow, brown, or khaki-coloured patches to appear on the leaves which then fall off prematurely.

Godetia grandiflora 'Azalea-flowered'

Gomphrena
globe amaranth

Gomphrena globosa 'Full Mix'

☐ Height 15-60cm (6-24in)
☐ Planting distance 15-23cm (6-9in)
☐ Flowers mid summer to early autumn
☐ Ordinary well-drained soil
☐ Sunny position
☐ Half-hardy annual

Globe amaranths grow in the wild in India; in Britain they thrive if they are treated as half-hardy annuals and given a sunny position in the garden.

One species and its varieties are generally grown. Botanically known as *Gomphrena globosa*, it bears clover-like flowers in bright orange, yellow, purple, pink and white, accompanied by hairy, light green leaves. The 30cm (1ft) high stems are upright, and the flowers last well, making them excellent for dried flower arrangements. In the garden use them in bedding schemes.

Popular varieties
Single and mixed colour strains are available:

'**Buddy**' is a compact, dwarf form reaching 15cm (6in) high. Its flowers are a vivid deep purple.
'**Full Mix**' is a mixture with orange, purple, pink, red, lavender or white flowers. Also available as single colours. The plants reach 45-60cm (1½-2ft) high.

Cultivation
Sow the seeds in pots or pans of seed compost in early spring under glass and keep at a temperature of 15-18°C (59-64°F). When the seedlings are large enough to handle, prick them out into boxes. Harden off before planting out in late spring when danger of frost has passed.

Plant them in ordinary well-drained garden soil in a sunny position.

For dried flowers, cut the blooms just before they are fully open and hang to dry in bunches upside down in a cool airy place. Gather the blooms in dry weather.
Pests and diseases Trouble free.

Gypsophila
baby's breath

Gypsophila elegans 'Covent Garden'

☐ Height 60cm (2ft)
☐ Planting distance 30cm (1ft)
☐ Flowers late spring to early autumn
☐ Ordinary garden soil
☐ Sunny position
☐ Hardy annual

The soft grey-green foliage and clouds of tiny white or pink flowers that this annual produces from late spring to early autumn serve as a good foil for other border plants and are also good for cutting. Several garden varieties have been developed from *Gypsophila elegans*.

Popular varieties
The following seed strains are readily available:
'**Covent Garden**' has large white flowers excellent for cutting.
'**Giant White**' has exceptionally large white flowers.
'**Improved Mix**' comes in shades of shell-pink, carmine-rose and pure white.
'**Red Cloud**' bears a mass of carmine-pink blooms.

Cultivation
Sow the seeds in their flowering position from mid spring onwards, at fortnightly intervals to ensure a succession of flowers. Thin to 30cm (1ft) apart. Baby's breath will thrive in any well-drained soil in a sunny position; dress acid soils with lime. Support with twiggy sticks.
Pests and diseases Trouble free.

HARE'S TAIL GRASS – see *Lagurus*
HAWKSBEARD – see *Crepis*

Helianthus

sunflower

Helianthus annuus

Helianthus annuus 'Teddy Bear'

'Teddy Bear' is a dwarf variety 60cm (2ft) high, with double golden blooms.

Cultivation

Sow the seeds in a sunny position in well-drained garden soil in early to mid spring. Sunflowers are one of the few annuals that look effective grown as solitary plants. Sow two or three seeds in each flowering site and remove the weakest leaving just the strongest to grow on. Sunflowers growing in a group or row should be thinned to 30-45cm (12-18in) apart.

Support tall sunflowers with strong stakes. Remove dead flowers to prevent self-seeding.

Pests and diseases Grey mould can cause flowers to rot in wet weather late in the season.

☐ Height 60cm-3m (2-10ft)
☐ Planting distance 30-45cm (12-18in)
☐ Flowers late summer to early autumn
☐ Well-drained garden soil
☐ Sunny position
☐ Hardy annual

Sunflowers usually conjure up the image of a solitary yellow flower gazing down to earth from the top of a 3m (10ft) high stem, sparsely clad with huge bristly leaves. Happily for owners of small gardens, not all sunflowers are this tall. A number of lower-growing varieties of *Helianthus annuus*, with more foliage, but equally spectacular blooms, are now available. They offer a large variety of flower forms – double as well as single – and come in varying shades of yellow, orange, red and cream.

Sunflowers look best grown at the back of a border. They also make extremely attractive temporary screens.

Popular varieties

The following is a selection of the most popular annual sunflower varieties.

'Autumn Sunshine' has medium-sized flowers in combinations of yellow, bronze and red. It reaches 1.2m (4ft) high.

'Italian White' has cream flowers with a black central disc and a gold zone. The plants reach 1.2m (4ft) high.

'Lemon Queen' has classic lemon-yellow, brown-centred flowers suitable for cutting. It grows 1.5m (5ft) tall.

'Music Box Mixed' is low-growing, to 70cm (28in) high, with medium-sized flowers that range from yellow and cream to mahogany-red, with black centres.

'Orange Sun', about 1m (3½ft) high, bears fully double, apricot-orange flowers.

'Russian Giant' has large single yellow flowers (reaching 30cm/1ft across) and grows 3m (10ft) high.

'Sunburst' has crimson, gold, bronze and lemon flowers. A well-branching variety, it reaches 1.2m (4ft) high.

'Sunspot', almost a miniature sunflower at 60cm (2ft) high, has 25cm (10in) wide golden-yellow flowers with enormous yellow-green centres.

Helianthus annuus 'Sunburst'

Helichrysum

everlasting, straw flower

Helichrysum 'Bright Bikini'

☐ Height 30cm-1.2m (1-4ft)
☐ Planting distance 30cm (1ft)
☐ Flowers mid summer to early autumn
☐ Light well-drained soil
☐ Open sunny situation
☐ Half-hardy annual

Helichrysum is a large genus which includes shrubs, perennials and annuals. The most common annual grown in Britain is *Helichrysum bracteatum*, and a number of varieties have been developed from it offering the gardener a wide choice of flower colours.

The showy daisy-like flowers of the annual species will be familiar to flower arrangers who often dry them for winter decoration. In the garden they are used to provide colour from mid summer to early autumn in borders and bedding schemes – the dwarf species are also suitable for containers. The plants have mid-green lance-shaped leaves.

Popular varieties
The following varieties are readily available:

'Bright Bikini' is a mixture of dwarf plants, 30-38cm (12-15in) high, bearing a profusion of flowers in bright colours.
'Candy Pink' has particularly large, double candy-pink coloured blooms, 7.5cm (3in) across and grows 90cm-1.2m (3-4ft) tall.
'Frosted Sulphur/Silver Rose' is a mixture of 75-90cm (2½-3ft) tall plants with large double flower of sulphur yellow and clear rose-pink overlaid with silvery white.
'Golden' has golden flowers and reaches 90cm-1.2m (3-4ft) high.
'Hot Bikini' is a dwarf variety reaching 30-38cm (12-15in) high with rich scarlet flowers.
'Monstrosum Double Mixed' has double flowers in white and shades of rose, crimson, yellow and orange. The plants grow 30cm (1ft) high.
'Rose' has rose-pink flowers and reaches 90cm-1.2m (3-4ft) high.
'Salmon Rose' has salmon-pink blooms and reaches 90cm-1.2m (3-4ft) high.
'Snowhite' has double, pure white flowers and reaches 90cm-1.2m (3-4ft) high.

Cultivation
Sow the seeds in pans of seed compost under glass in late winter or early spring and keep at a temperature of 18°C (64°F). Prick out into boxes and harden off before setting out in the flowering site in mid to late spring. An open sunny site with light, well-drained soil is ideal. Rich soil encourages more flowers but reduces the strength of their colours.

Dead-head to encourage flowering on the side shoots.

Cut flowers for drying, before they are fully open and showing the central disc. Tie them in bunches and hang them upside down in a cool room or shed until they are dry. Avoid hanging them in sunlight – the colours fade and stems become brittle.

Pests and diseases Downy mildew, a white fungal growth, can affect the leaves, eventually causing them to drop off.

Heliotropium

heliotrope, cherry pie

Heliotropium 'Marine'

☐ Height 35-60cm (14-24in)
☐ Planting distance 30cm (1ft)
☐ Flowers late spring to mid autumn
☐ Fertile well-drained garden soil
☐ Sunny site
☐ Evergreen shrub treated as half-
   hardy annual

The evergreen hybrid heliotropes received their common name, cherry pie, because the heavy fragrance of their small forget-me-not like flowers resembles that of cherry-pie filling. Great favourites in the formal gardens of Victorian times, they are still much used as dot plants in formal bedding schemes in warm sheltered gardens – heliotropes will not tolerate cold exposed sites.

Dwarf types are suitable for pots and containers and for sunny window-boxes.

The flowers range in colour from dark purple through lilac to white. They appear from late spring until mid autumn and are carried above attractive dark green finely wrinkled leaves.

Popular varieties

These are the most readily available heliotrope varieties:

'Marine' bears large clusters of deep purple flowers, accompanied by dark foliage. It reaches 45cm (18in) high.

'Mini Marine' is a dwarf mixture growing 35-40cm (14-16in) tall. The plants are compact but bushy, branching from the base and have large violet-purple flower clusters and dark green, near bronze foliage.

Cultivation

Sow the seeds in late winter in pots or pans of seed compost. Germinate at a temperature of 16-18°C (61-64°F), and prick out the seedlings when they are large enough to handle into boxes of potting compost. When 7.5cm (3in) high, pinch out the growing tips to encourage bushy growth. Harden off before planting out 30cm (1ft) apart, in late spring, when all danger of frost is past.

Outdoors use heliotrope in bedding schemes and for filling containers. They thrive in fertile well-drained soil, and need full sun, and shelter from winds.

Pests and diseases Trouble free.

Helipterum

Swan River everlasting

Helipterum manglesii

☐ Height 30-60cm (12-24in)
☐ Planting distance 15cm (6in)
☐ Flowers mid summer to early autumn
☐ Any sharply drained soil
☐ Sunny site
☐ Hardy annual

These hardy everlastings, often listed in catalogues under their former names, make enchanting contributions to herbaceous borders, rock gardens and bedding schemes. The daisy-like flowers have a straw-like texture which makes them ideal for drying. They are easily grown plants, revelling in poor soil and full sun and tolerating exposure to winds and sea sprays.

Popular species and varieties

Helipterum humboldtianum (syn. *H. sandfordii*) grows 45cm (18in) tall and has erect flower stems with narrow pointed leaves that are silvery-green and woolly. From mid summer to early autumn the stems are crowned with fragrant clusters of golden-yellow flowers which turn green after drying.

Helipterum manglesii (syn. *Rhodanthe manglesii*), to 38cm (15in), has erect and wiry stems sparsely set with oblong, grey-green leaves and topped with a single red or white, yellow-eyed daisy flower. The flowering season extends from mid summer to early autumn. Varieties include 'Mixed', to 30cm (12in) tall, of compact growth and with a mass of carmine, pink, rose or white flowers. Also available as a separate 'Rose' colour.

Hibiscus
annual hibiscus

Helipterum roseum

Hibiscus 'Southern Belle'

Helipterum roseum (syn. *Acroclinium roseum*) grows 38cm (15in) tall; it resembles *H. manglesii* but bears semi-double, rose-coloured flowers in mid and late summer. The 'Grandiflorum' varieties are 30-45cm (12-18in) high and have double flowers in pink, red, white, with yellow or black centres. The seed strain is available as a mixture or as single colours of red, rose and white. 'Splendidum', up to 60cm (2ft) tall, has large, silky flowers, creamy-white with yellow centres.

Cultivation
Sow the seeds in the flowering site in mid spring. The plants grow best in poor, sharply drained soil in a sunny site. Thin the seedlings to stand 15cm (6in) apart. Avoid transplanting.

Cut the flowers for drying before they are fully open; tie them in bunches and hang them upside down to dry in a cool airy place.

Pests and diseases Aphids may attack young plants.

☐ Height 38-75cm (15-30in)
☐ Planting distance 23cm (9in)
☐ Flowers late summer to early autumn
☐ Rich, moist well-drained soil
☐ Sunny sheltered site
☐ Hardy and half-hardy annuals

There are few more exotic looking plants than the hibiscus hybrids with their wide, funnel-shaped, richly coloured flowers. They are showy but rather short-lived though more blooms follow in quick succession. The plants are suitable as dot plants in mixed borders, for bedding schemes and for growing in tubs on the patio.

Popular species and varieties
Hibiscus moscheutos is a moderately hardy perennial usually treated as a half-hardy annual. The species is rarely grown, having been superseded by F1 hybrids such as 'Disco Belle' (syn. 'Les Belles'). These grow up to 50cm (20in) tall and bear huge, near-circular flowers, 20cm (8in) or more across; they are pure white, sometimes with a rosy centre, or pink or deep cerise red. Also available in the pure white form 'Disco Belle White'.

Hibiscus trionum (flower-of-an-hour) is a hardy bushy annual, up to 75cm (2½ft) tall, with dark green, coarsely toothed leaves. The five-petalled, creamy-white flowers with chocolate-maroon centres are much smaller, about 5cm (2in) wide, and very short-lived, but they are produced continuously during late summer and early autumn. The variety 'Sunnyday' (height 38cm/15in) has cool

Hibiscus moscheutos 'Disco Belle'

lemon-yellow blooms with purple-black centres.

Cultivation
Sow seeds of *Hibiscus trionum* in the flowering site in mid spring and thin the seedlings to 23cm (9in) apart. The species often self-seeds if the soil is left undisturbed.

Sow seeds of the half-hardy hybrids under glass in late winter at a temperature of 16-18°C (61-64°F). When the seedlings are large enough to handle, prick them off singly into 7.5cm (3in) pots of compost and grow on at the same temperature. Harden off in a cold frame before planting out in a sheltered site when all danger of frost has passed.

All annual hibiscus perform best in rich, moist but well-drained soil and in a sunny site.

Pests and diseases Trouble free.

HOLLYHOCK see *Althaea*
HONESTY see *Lunaria*
HOUND'S TONGUE see *Cynoglossum*

Hordeum
squirrel grass

Hordeum jubatum

☐ Height 30-60cm (1-2ft)
☐ Planting distance 15cm (6in)
☐ Flowers early to late summer
☐ Well-drained fertile soil
☐ Sunny site
☐ Hardy annual grass

Hordeum jubatum – commonly referred to as squirrel grass – bears 30cm (1ft) high slender feathery flower heads, similar to ripe barley but without the grain. These appear from early to late summer.

It looks best planted in large drifts, perhaps in beds of annuals to provide welcome relief from bright flower colours. But it is also a popular ornamental grass for flower arrangers.

To dry squirrel grass for winter decoration, cut it in warm dry weather in late summer and hang the grasses upside down to dry in a cool place.

Cultivation
Squirrel grass should be grown in well-drained fertile soil in a sunny site.

Sow the seeds outdoors in mid spring, sprinkling it thinly across the ground and covering it with only a little soil. When the seedlings are large enough to handle, thin them to 10cm (4in) apart.
Pests and diseases Trouble free.

Iberis
candytuft

Iberis umbellata

☐ Height 15-45cm (6-18in) high
☐ Planting distance 15-23cm (6-9in)
☐ Flowers early summer to early autumn
☐ Ordinary well-drained soil
☐ Sunny position
☐ Hardy annual

Easy to grow and generous with their white and pink flowers, candytufts are deservedly popular annuals. As they tolerate smoke and grime, they are a good choice for town gardens, where they can be grown in borders and rockeries, for decoration or for cutting.

To get a continuous display all summer, sow some seeds in autumn and the rest in spring.

Two species and their varieties are found in gardens.

Popular species and varieties
Iberis amara (syn. *I. coronaria*), commonly known as rocket candytuft, is an upright plant, reaching 38cm (15in) high. Its fragrant flowers are excellent for cutting, as well as for border decoration. *Iberis umbellata* is a spreading plant (15-38cm/6-15in high) with compact clusters of white, pink and lavender flowers. Popular varieties include 'Cream Flash' (23-30cm high, creamy-white flowers); 'Dwarf Fairyland Mixed' (25cm/10in high plants with pink, red, maroon, white and lavender flowers); 'Pinnacle' (38-45cm/15-18 in high, pure white, dense and fragrant flowers); and 'Red Flash' (38cm/15in high plants with carmine-red flowers).

Cultivation
Sow the seeds in their flowering site, successively in autumn and in spring to ensure a continuous floral display all summer. Thin the seedlings to 23cm (9in) apart. Candytuft does well in any well-drained garden soil, including poor soil, and in full sun. Deadhead regularly.
Pests and diseases Trouble free.

ICELAND POPPY – see *Papaver*
IMMORTELLE – see
Xeranthemum

Impatiens

busy Lizzie

Impatiens 'Super Elfin Mixed'

Impatiens 'Firelake'

- ☐ Height 15-60cm (6-24in)
- ☐ Planting distance 30cm (12in)
- ☐ Flowers mid spring to mid autumn
- ☐ Fertile well-drained but moisture-retentive soil
- ☐ Sunny or lightly shaded site
- ☐ Half-hardy annual

Busy Lizzies are popular house plants, but introductions of robust F1 hybrids have encouraged gardeners to use them for summer bedding, window-boxes, tubs and hanging baskets.

Here they can be relied upon to produce a mass of flowers in shades of red, pink and white throughout the summer. Combined with the small leaves they form an attractive ground carpet.

Popular varieties
Numerous hybrids have been developed from *Impatiens walleriana*, including the following:
'Accent Formula' is up to 15cm (6in) high, spreading and with large flowers. Seeds are available in single or mixed colours of white, pink, salmon, crimson and violet-purple.
'Blitz Orange' bears large, plentiful flowers in warm orange; the plants grow 23-30cm (9-12in) high.

'Double Confection Mixed' grows 23-30cm (9-12in) high, with semi or fully double flowers in a range of colours.
'Expo Mixed' produces vigorous but compact plants, 20cm (8in) high, in a mixture of colours, often bicoloured.
'Eye-Eye' grows only 15cm (6in) high but is smothered with pastel-coloured flowers, all with a contrasting eye.
'Firelake Mixed', 30-45cm (12-18in) tall, has 5cm (2in) wide flowers in a mixture of colours set among foliage variegated dark red, green, white or cream.
'Futura Mixed' has brightly coloured flowers and a pendulous habit, making it an excellent choice for hanging baskets. The plants reach 20-30cm (8-12in) high. The flowers come in the typical busy Lizzie colours – reds, oranges, pinks and white – either plain or striped.
'King Kong Mixed' has large flowers coming in a mixture of reds, pinks, oranges and whites. The plants are particularly bushy and reach 23-30cm (9-12in) high.
'Mega Orange Star' is 20-25cm (8-10in) high and weather-resistant. The orange-red flowers have prominent white star markings.

'Novette Mixed' carry big bright red, pink and orange flowers early in the summer. The plants reach just 15-20cm (6-8in) high.
'Novette Star Formula' is a bicoloured mixture of bright red, orange, rose-pink and violet.
'Pastel Mixed' is a mixture of dwarf plants (23-30cm/9-12in high), bearing flowers in coral, pink, salmon and white.
'Picotee Swirl' grows to 25cm (10in) tall and is early-flowering; the white to soft-rose flowers have fuchsia edges to the petals.
'Spectra Mixed' is about 30cm (1ft) high, with white, pink, lilac and carmine-red flowers and variegated foliage in cream or bronze.
'Starbright' has spectacularly large bicoloured flowers in shades of orange, pink, rose and violet. Plants grow 15-20cm (6-8in) high.
'Super Elfin' strains grow 20-25cm (8-10in) high and are available as mixtures or single colours.
'Tango' bears large deep orange flowers amid bronze-green foliage. Plants are up to 38cm (15in) high.
'Tempo', up to 25cm (10in) tall, is of branching and pendulous habit; available in seed mixtures and single colours of white, blush-pink, apricot, reds and lavender.
Impatiens balsamina, otherwise known as rose balsam, has pale green lance-shaped leaves and pink flowers from early summer until early autumn. It reaches 75cm (2½ft) high, and looks most effective in bedding schemes. Two popular varieties have been developed from it.

Ipomoea

morning glory

Impatiens 'Novette Star Formula'

'Camellia-flowered' has white, pink, rose and scarlet flowers resembling those of a camellia. The plant has a spreading habit and reaches 40-70cm (16-28in) high.
'Tom Thumb Mixed' has double blooms in shades of red, carmine-pink, salmon-pink, coral and white. The dwarf plants reach just 20-30cm (8-12in) high and are drought-resistant.

Cultivation
Sow seeds in pots or pans of seed compost under glass in early spring, at a temperature of 16-18°C (61-64°F). When the seedlings are large enough to handle, prick out into boxes, and then into 7.5cm (3in) containers of potting compost. Harden off and plant out in late spring to early summer, setting them 30cm (12in) apart.

Give busy Lizzies a site in sun or light shade with fertile, well-drained but moist soil.

Pinch out the growing tips to encourage bushy growth.

Busy Lizzies can also be grown from 7.5-10cm (3-4in) long cuttings of tips on vigorous shoots between summer and early autumn. Root at a temperature of 16°C (61°F). When they have rooted, prick them singly into 7.5cm (3in) pots. Harden off before planting out.
Pests and diseases Aphids may infest leaves and stems, weakening the plants.

INDIAN PINK – see *Dianthus*

Ipomoea violacea

☐ Height 2.4-3m (8-10ft)
☐ Planting distance 30cm (1ft)
☐ Flowers mid summer to early autumn
☐ Rich well-drained soil
☐ Sunny sheltered position
☐ Half-hardy annual

Morning glory is widely regarded as one of the most beautiful climbers. Grown as an annual, its wiry stems twist their way up walls, trellises, pergolas or simple pea-stick supports, decorating them with heart-shaped light green leaves and magnificent trumpet shaped flowers in either a heavenly blue colour fading to white in the centre or red-purple.

Ipomoea purpurea

Popular species
Ipomoea purpurea (syn. *Convolvulus purpureus*) bears purple flowers singly or in small clusters. It is a vigorous climber, to 3m (10ft) high. 'Scarlet Star' is cerise with a white star.
Ipomoea violacea (syn. *I. tricolor*) is a half-hardy perennial usually grown as an annual. A free-flowering species, it carries large red-purple to blue flowers. The plant reaches 2.4m (8ft) high. 'Heavenly Blue' is sky-blue and white-throated.

Cultivation
Sow the seeds under glass in early to mid spring at a temperature of 18°C (64°F). Soak the seeds of *Ipomoea violacea* in water for 24 hours to encourage germination. Move the seedlings to 12cm (5in) pots of potting compost and harden off before planting out in late spring to early summer.

Grow morning glory in rich and well-drained soil in a sheltered sunny position – against a wall or fence or up poles or pea-sticks. Dead-head to prolong the flowering period.
Pests and diseases Aphids may infest young plants.

JOB'S TEARS – see *Coix*
KINGFISHER DAISY – see *Felicia*

Kochia

burning bush, summer cypress

Kochia scoparia 'Trichophylla' — summer

☐ Height 60-90cm (2-3ft)
☐ Planting distance 60cm (2ft)
☐ Foliage plant
☐ Ordinary well-drained soil
☐ Open sunny site
☐ Half-hardy annual

Untidy forms of this intriguing foliage plant grow in the wild from southern Europe to Japan – indeed in mainland Europe it is widely regarded as a weed. But in gardens in Britain summer cypress is grown as a half-hardy annual, its mass of pale green foliage providing welcome relief in bedding schemes of brightly coloured flowering annuals.

The most commonly grown form is *Kochia scoparia* 'Trichophylla'. This forms a neat, symmetrical dome and has the added advantage of gradually turning a rich crimson-purple in autumn, hence its other name, burning bush.

Cultivation

Sow the seeds, where the plants are to grow, in any well-drained soil in an open sunny site in mid

Kochia scoparia 'Trichophylla' — autumn

spring. Thin the seedlings to stand about 60cm (2ft) apart.

If you want to give the plants a head start, sow seeds under glass in early spring and keep at a temperature of 16°C (61°F). Prick out seedlings into large pots and then harden off gradually before planting out in late spring.

Stake plants in exposed sites.
Pests and diseases Trouble free.

Lagurus

hare's tail grass

Lagurus ovatus

☐ Height 30cm (1ft)
☐ Planting distance 15cm (6in)
☐ Flowers early summer to early autumn
☐ Well-drained soil
☐ Sunny position
☐ Hardy annual grass

Hare's tail grass (*Lagurus ovatus*) is a hardy annual often grown in mixed borders for its decorative flowers – delightful 3cm (1½in) long fluffy white heads resembling the tail of a hare or rabbit. These appear from early summer to early autumn carried on slender stems 30cm (1ft) high.

The long, narrow, hairy, grey-green leaves present a pleasant contrast to the soft furry flower heads.

To dry the grass for winter decoration, gather in dry weather in late summer.

Cultivation

Sow the seeds in late summer to early autumn in pots or pans of seed compost and overwinter in a cold frame or cool greenhouse. The following spring (mid spring) set the seedlings in the growing position, spacing them 15cm (6in) apart. A well-drained, fertile soil in a sunny position is suitable.
Pests and diseases Trouble free.

LARKSPUR – see *Delphinium*

Lathyrus

sweet pea

Lathyrus odoratus 'Old-Fashioned Mixed'

Lathyrus odoratus 'Maggie May'

- ☐ Height 30cm-3m (1-10ft)
- ☐ Planting distance 15-25cm (6-10in)
- ☐ Flowers early summer to early autumn
- ☐ Well-drained, medium loam – ideally slightly alkaline
- ☐ Sunny site
- ☐ Hardy annual

The much-loved sweet pea is a versatile plant in the garden. Grown up a wall, fence or another plant, it reaches a height of up to 3m (10ft). It can be grown up pea-sticks in the vegetable patch just for its cut flowers. Or it can be grown without support in a mixed annual border – dwarf varieties look most effective alongside traditional cottage garden plants such as clarkias, candytuft and cornflowers.

The pea-like flowers appear in early summer and, provided all dead blooms are removed immediately, will continue until early autumn. They come in an enormous range of colours – reds, pinks, salmons, purples and white, either one colour or bi-coloured. Most are scented, some more than others.

Popular varieties

All sweet pea varieties grown in

Lathyrus odoratus 'Bouquet Rose'

the garden are developed from *Lathyrus odoratus*. To bring some order to the enormous range available, they are usually organized into groups.

DWARF VARIETIES

Reaching 15-90cm (6-36in) high, these sweet pea varieties can be grown without supports. Use them at the front of borders or to fill window-boxes and containers.

'**Jet Set**' has sweetly scented, frilled flowers in a wide range of colours. It reaches 90cm (3ft) high.

'**Patio**' has fragrant flowers in mixed colours with wavy petals. It grows 30-38cm (12-15in) high.

'**Supersnoop**' has waved flowers in a range of colours, carried on long stems, which make it a suitable dwarf variety for cutting. The plants are without tendrils and have a neat habit, reaching 75-90cm (2½-3ft) high.

GALAXY VARIETIES

These are tall vigorous growing varieties, reaching 1.8-3m (6-10ft) high. Grown for their early, long-lasting display, they produce numerous large flowers in a wide range of colours offered as 'Galaxy Mixed'. Train them up tall supports.

OLD VARIETIES

These have largely been replaced by the more robust bigger-flowered Spencer varieties. Available now only in seed mixtures ('Old-Fashioned Mixed') they have small, dainty flowers with a strong, sweet fragrance. Train up a wall, fence, pergola, or pea-sticks – they grow 1.8-3m (6-10ft) high.

SPENCER VARIETIES

These are the most commonly grown sweet peas. They usually carry four or five particularly large blooms on each stem. Reaching up to 3m (10ft) high, they look most effective grown as climbers. Catalogues list them according to colour. They are suitable for garden decoration, for cutting and for exhibition purposes. Only some have a strong fragrance.

'**Air Warden**' has strong fragrant orange-scarlet flowers.

Lathyrus odoratus 'Xenia Field'

Lathyrus odoratus 'Butterfly Mixed'

'Anniversary' has soft white flowers edged with rose-pink; delicately scented.

'Beaujolais' has rich burgundy maroon blooms.

'Blue Danube' is a blue-flowered variety with frilled petals.

'Bouquet' is a vigorous strain available in single colours (rose, pink, white, lavender, blue) or as mixtures; strongly scented.

'Butterfly Mixed' has cream or white flowers marked, streaked and edged with red, pink, orange, blue or purple.

'Charisma' has wavy carmine-red, long-stemmed flowers.

'Elizabeth Taylor' has clear, rich mauve flowers.

'Giant Waved' has large flowers with wavy petals in a wide range of typical sweet pea colours.

'Herald' has deep rose-pink flowers with a hint of orange in them.

'Hunter's Moon' bears sweetly scented lemon-cream flowers.

'Leamington' has deep lavender-blue flowers with a sweet scent.

'Love Match' comes in mixed colours. The flowers are bicoloured and have frilled petals.

'Maggie May' bears wavy-edged, strongly fragrant blooms of sky-blue flushed with white.

'Maroon Magic' is a scented variety, with wavy, maroon-purple flowers on long stems.

'Mrs. R. Bolton' has pale pink flowers resembling the colour of almond blossom.

'Noel Sutton' is rich blue-mauve with a strong fragrance.

'Pennine Floss' is a strongly-scented variety, with red-purple wavy flowers.

'Princess Elizabeth' has cream to salmon-pink flowers.

'Red Ensign' is strong-growing, with scented, deep scarlet flowers.

'Romance' is a bicoloured seed mixture, producing frilled and scented flowers in a range of colours.

'Rosy Frills' has white flowers with frilled petals edged deep rose-pink.

'White Supreme' has strongly scented, pure white flowers.

'Winston Churchill' has rich crimson-red flowers with frilled petals.

'World's Children' is free-flowering, with long-stemmed flowers bicoloured in fiery red and orange.

'Xenia Field' is delicately blush-pink on cream ground, shading to apple-blossom pink.

Cultivation
Many sweet pea varieties have seeds with thick coats, so it pays to nick them with a sharp knife or soak them in water for 12 hours to speed up germination.

Sow the seeds in boxes or pans of seed compost in early autumn or early spring at a temperature of 16°C (61°F). Pot the seedlings into 7.5cm (3in) pots of potting compost. When they reach 10cm (4in) high, pinch out the growing tips to encourage strong side-shoots. Harden off in a cold frame before planting out – autumn-sown ones in mid-spring, early spring-sown ones in late spring.

The seeds can be sown directly in the flowering site in early to mid autumn or early spring, and then thinned to 15cm (6in) in mid spring. An autumn sowing gives the best results, but young plants have to be protected with cloches in cold areas. Remove the cloches in mid spring.

Sweet peas will grow in any ordinary garden soil in a sunny site. But for the best results plant them in deeply dug, well-manured and well-drained, slightly alkaline loam.

Dead-head and remove any seed pods so flowering continues until early autumn.

Pests and diseases Mildew may occur on the leaves and stems and wilt may cause the leaves to turn yellow and the plants to wilt. Virus diseases can be a problem.

Lathyrus 'Madrid Jet Set Scarlet'

Lavatera
mallow

Lavatera trimestris 'Silver Cup'

☐ Height 50-90cm (20-36in)
☐ Planting distance 45cm (18in)
☐ Flowers mid summer to early autumn
☐ Ordinary well-drained soil
☐ Sunny site
☐ Hardy annual

One species of mallow (*Lavatera trimestris*) and its varieties are grown as annuals. This is a bushy plant some 60-90cm (2-3ft) high with attractive trumpet-shaped hibiscus-like flowers coming in shades of pink and white. These appear during the summer months, and are shown off to best effect in herbaceous borders.

Popular varieties
Several varieties have been developed from *Lavatera trimestris*, including the following:
'**Loveliness**' is an old variety producing rose-pink flowers in late summer and early autumn. The plants are 90cm (3ft) high.
'**Mont Blanc**' has glistening large white flowers in mid summer on dwarf compact plants, 50-60cm (20-24in) high.

'**Ruby Regis**' grows 60cm (2ft) high and bears a profusion of large, deep cerise-red flowers.
'**Silver Cup**' has bright pink flowers shaded silvery pink. It stands 60cm (2ft) high.
'**Tanagra**' has large glistening cerise-pink blooms. It is a tall variety reaching 90cm (3ft).

Cultivation
Sow mallow directly in its flowering site in early autumn or mid spring, just covering the seeds with soil. It will flourish in most well-drained garden soils though rich soils should be avoided as they encourage leafy growth at the expense of flowers. Thin out the seedlings to 45cm (18in) apart in mid spring.

Mallow seeds itself freely and produces plants the following season if the soil around is left undisturbed.
Pests and diseases Leaf spot (yellow-brown spots) may affect leaves and stems.

Layia
tidy-tips

Layia elegans

☐ Height 45cm (18in)
☐ Planting distance 25cm (10in)
☐ Flowers early summer to mid autumn
☐ Any well-drained soil
☐ Sunny site
☐ Hardy annual

The charm of tidy-tips (*Layia elegans*) lies in the neat white tips of the pale yellow petals giving each flower an attractive fringe. The petals themselves surround a bright yellow central disc.

Tidy-tips is a bushy well-branched plant, some 45cm (18in) high with pleasantly scented grey-green leaves. It is suitable for growing in herbaceous borders and summer beds of annuals. It provides a long succession of daisy flowers from early summer until mid autumn; they are useful for cutting as well as garden decoration.

Cultivation
Sow the seeds in the flowering site in early to mid spring, just covering them with soil. Well-drained sandy soil gives the best results, though the plants will grow in any soil provided they receive plenty of sunlight.

Thin the seedlings, when large enough to handle, to stand 25cm (10in) apart.
Pests and diseases Trouble free.

Leptosiphon

leptosiphon

Leptosiphon 'Rainbow Mixture'

☐ Height 10-15cm (4-6in)
☐ Planting distance 7.5-10cm (3-4in)
☐ Flowers early summer to early autumn
☐ Ordinary well-drained soil
☐ Sunny open site
☐ Hardy annual

Almost everyone who comes across the hybrid mixtures of this unjustly neglected annual is enchanted by it. The tiny flowers are scattered in profusion over the plant and come in a random collection of pink, red, orange, yellow, cream and white. They appear from early summer to early autumn on straight slender stems above finely divided deep green foliage, which forms mounds 10-15cm (4-6in) high.

Use leptosiphon hybrids to edge borders, to cheer up earth-filled cracks in paving or small pockets of soil between rocks or stones. They are also suitable for growing in window boxes and other shallow containers.

'Rainbow Mixture' and 'Stardust Hybrids Mixed' are the mixtures most commonly sold in garden centres, or found in mail order catalogues.

Cultivation

Sow the seeds in ordinary well-drained soil in an open sunny site in mid spring, covering them with just a little soil. Thin the seedlings to 7.5cm-10cm (3-4in) apart.
Pests and diseases Trouble free.

Limnanthes

poached egg flower

Limnanthes douglasii

☐ Height 15cm (6in)
☐ Planting distance 15cm (6in)
☐ Flowers late spring to late summer
☐ Ordinary garden soil
☐ Open sunny site
☐ Hardy annual

The common name of *Limnanthes douglasii* – poached egg flower – aptly describes the colour scheme of its blooms: a large yolk-yellow centre surrounded by white. Bowl-shaped, softly waved and with a delicate fragrance, these blooms are set off to perfection by glossy, pale yellow-green, deeply cut foliage. Bees and other nectar-loving insects find them irresistible.

Poached egg flower reaches 15cm (6in) high and spreads quickly. It looks best grown in clumps in rockeries, at the front of borders or along the edges of paths – where the seedlings will swiftly colonize the cracks between paving stones.

Cultivation

Poached egg flowers thrive in ordinary garden soil in open sunny positions though they need a cool root run. Such conditions are usually found along paths or between rocks and paving.

Sow the seeds in the flowering site in early autumn for a late spring floral display, or in early spring for a mid to late summer display. Cover them with just a little soil. Thin to 15cm (6in) apart. Seedlings from an autumn sowing should be protected with cloches during the cold winter months.

The plants usually seed themselves prolifically, so be ready for more poached egg flowers in successive years. These are unlikely to be as strong and robust as those grown from fresh packets of seeds.
Pests and diseases Trouble free.

Limonium

sea lavender, statice

Limonium suworowii

□ Height 45cm (18in)
□ Planting distance 30cm (1ft)
□ Flowers mid summer to early autumn
□ Ordinary well-drained soil
□ Open sunny site
□ Half-hardy annual

Statice or sea lavender is perhaps more often seen in dried flower arrangements than gardens, its tiny bright yellow, purple, pink, blue and white blooms providing an invaluable splash of colour indoors in winter. The individual funnel-shaped flowers are tiny, but they are clustered together in spikes at the top of 45cm (18in) high stems. Flower spikes are accompanied by small mid-green lance-shaped and stem-clasping leaves. For drying, cut the flower stems before the flowers have opened fully, tie them in bundles and hang them upside down to dry in a cool, airy and shady place.

Statice is suitable for growing in large clumps in herbaceous borders. Two species and their varieties are generally available.

Popular species

Limonium sinuatum is a tender perennial species usually grown as a half-hardy annual. The 45cm (18in) long stems carry 7.5-10cm (3-4in) long clusters of white or blue flowers surrounded by green bracts from mid summer to early autumn. This is the most commonly grown statice, and the one used for drying. Popular varieties developed from it include 'Beidermeier Mixed' (height 30-38cm/12-15in, white, rose, blue, apricot, yellow and purple); 'Formula Mixture' (pastel shades of rose, cream-yellow, light blue and white); 'Sunburst' (available in a mixture or as single colours of white, yellow, rose and pale and dark blue).

Limonium suworowii is a half-hardy annual grown for its cut flowers – it is not suitable for drying. The 45cm (18in) high plants carry tall thin spikes of tiny rose-pink flowers.

Cultivation

Sow the seeds thinly in pots or pans of seed compost under glass in late winter to early spring and keep at a temperature of 13-16°C (55-61°F). When the seedlings are large enough to handle, prick out into boxes. Harden off before planting out in late spring.

Plant statice in ordinary well-drained soil in a sunny site.

You can sow directly in the flowering site in mid spring and thin out to the appropriate spacings; the blooms will appear later and may be damaged by autumn frosts.

Pests and diseases Grey mould and mildew can affect the plants.

Limonium sinuatum 'Beidermeier Mixed'

Linaria

Moroccan toadflax

Linaria maroccana 'Fairy Bouquet'

☐ Height 23-60cm (9-24in)
☐ Planting distance 15cm (6in)
☐ Flowers early to mid summer
☐ Ordinary well-drained soil
☐ Sunny site
☐ Hardy annual

Moroccan toadflax (*Linaria maroccana*) is a narrow upright plant some 23-60cm (9-24in) high with slender light green leaves. It bears spikes of narrow tubular flowers, resembling miniature snapdragons, which can be bright yellow, red, pink or mauve often blotched with white.

Flowering throughout the summer, toadflax is an extremely versatile plant. It is suitable for annual and mixed borders, for rock gardens, and also for edging a path. For best effect grow in groups of five or seven plants.

Popular varieties
The following varieties have been developed from *Linaria maroccana*.
'Fairy Bouquet' is a seed mixture producing compact plants reaching just 23cm (9in) high. The flowers come in shades of red, pink, purple, yellow and cream, all with white throats. This is a particularly easy toadflax to grow. **'Northern Lights'** reaches 60cm (2ft) high and has flowers in shades of bronze, red, purple, pink, yellow and cream. Some of the flowers are bicoloured.

Cultivation
Sow the seeds in the flowering site in early autumn (for large early flowers) or in early to mid spring. Make successive sowings to extend the flowering season.

Thin the seedlings to 15cm (6in) apart.

Toadflax seeds itself freely so plants will appear the following year if the surrounding soil is left undisturbed.

Moroccan toadflax grows in any ordinary well-drained garden soil; on particularly heavy clay soil it's advisable to add some grit to aid drainage. A sunny position is essential.
Pests and diseases Trouble free.

Linum

flax

Linum grandiflorum 'Rubrum'

☐ Height 30-45cm (12-18in)
☐ Planting distance 12cm (5in)
☐ Flowers early to late summer
☐ Well-drained garden soil
☐ Open sunny position
☐ Hardy annual

With their elegant five-petalled flowers in bright clear colours, and the slender fresh green leaves, flaxes of any kind are welcome in the garden. *Linum grandiflorum* is the most widely grown of the annual species. It produces a long succession of rose-red, cup-shaped flowers from early to late summer.

Popular varieties
Named varieties are more popular than the species.
'Bright Eyes' has ivory-white flowers with crimson centres. It is up to 45cm (18in) high.
'Rubrum', scarlet flax, grows about 30cm (1ft) high, with brilliant crimson satiny flowers.

Cultivation
Sow the seeds in the flowering site in early autumn or early to mid spring. Make successive sowings at monthly intervals in the spring for a continuous display all summer. Thin to 15cm (6in) apart.

If flax flowers are to achieve their full brilliance, they must have plenty of sun. Flax grows in any ordinary well-drained soil, flourishing in limy soil and also tolerating acid conditions.
Pests and diseases Trouble free.

LIVINGSTONE DAISY – see *Mesembryanthemum*

Lobelia

lobelia

Lobelia erinus 'Cascade Mixed'

□ Height 10-23cm (4-9in)
□ Planting distance 10cm (4in)
□ Flowers late spring to autumn
□ Fertile moisture-retentive soil
□ Sunny or partially shaded site
□ Half-hardy perennial grown as an
  annual

Though grown as an annual, *Lobelia erinus* is correctly a half-hardy perennial. It is a small plant, only 10-23cm (4-9in) high, with light green leaves, and it produces a mass of small blue flowers from late spring until autumn frost.

More popular than the species are the many varieties which may be either compact, making neat 10-15cm (4-6in) high domes, or trailing in a spread of 30cm (1ft) across. The colour range of the varieties embraces white, pale blue, deep purplish-blue and wine-red.

The varieties with a compact habit are normally used to edge beds while those with a trailing habit look effective in hanging baskets, window-boxes and other containers.

Popular varieties
The following varieties are readily available.

Lobelia erinus 'Rosamund'

'**Blue Moon**' is a compact, early-flowering variety. The large flowers are clear blue.
'**Cambridge Blue**' is neat and compact with light blue flowers.
'**Cascade Mixed**' is a mixture of cascading varieties coming in blue, mauve, red and white, usually with white eyes.
'**Crystal Palace**' is a compact variety bearing rich deep blue flowers. The foliage is bronze-coloured.

Lobelia erinus 'Mrs Clibran'

'**Lilac Fountain**' is a trailing variety, with pale lilac-pink flowers. Other strains in this series include white and blue-coloured varieties.
'**Mrs Clibran**' is a compact plant bearing rich violet-blue flowers with white eyes.
'**Red Cascade**' is a trailing variety with wine-red, white-eyed flowers.
'**Rosamund**' is a compact variety bearing crimson flowers with white eyes.
'**Sapphire**' is a trailing variety with white-eyed, glossy deep blue flowers.
'**Snowball**' is a compact variety with white flowers, though some are slightly tinged with blue.

Cultivation
Sow the seeds in late winter in pans of seed compost and keep at a temperature of 16-18°C (61-64°F). Prick out the seedlings in groups of three or four – they're too small to prick out individually – and grow on at a temperature of 13-16°C (55-61°F). Harden off and plant out in late spring.

Plant lobelia in rich moist soil in a sheltered, sunny or partially shady position.
Pests and diseases Damping off and root rot can cause the plants to wilt and stem rot may show as pale spots on the leaves of seedlings.

LOVE-IN-A-MIST – see *Nigella*
LOVE-LIES-BLEEDING – see
Amaranthus

Lunaria

honesty, moneywort

Lunaria annua

☐ Height 75cm (2½ft)
☐ Planting distance 30cm (1ft)
☐ Flowers mid spring to early summer
☐ Any well-drained soil
☐ Partially shaded site
☐ Hardy biennial

Although *Lunaria annua* (also known as *Lunaria biennis*) can be grown as an annual, it is naturally a biennial and, treated as such, produces finer flowers. These are borne in loose fragrant clusters from mid spring to early summer. The true species has pale lavender flowers while the varieties range from white to rich purple and red.

The flowers of both species and varieties are followed in summer by silvery-white seed pods that can be used for indoor decoration.

Popular varieties

'Mixed' has rich purple or purple-red – some with white markings – and white flowers.

'Variegata Stella' bears pure white flowers and foliage strongly variegated with creamy white.

Cultivation

Sow the seeds outdoors in a nursery bed (or in their flowering position) in late spring to early summer. Thin out to 15cm (6in) apart, and then transplant to the flowering site in early autumn spacing them 30cm (1ft) apart. Honesty grows best in well-drained soil in partial shade.

Pests and diseases Trouble free.

Lupinus

lupin

Lupinus nanus 'Pixie Delight'

☐ Height 45cm (18in)
☐ Planting distance 20-25cm (8-10in)
☐ Flowers mid summer to mid autumn
☐ Acid to neutral well-drained soil
☐ Sun or partial shade
☐ Hardy annual

To most people, lupins are the perennial Russell lupins, but a few annual types are also grown. *Lupinus nanus*, the best known of these, is generally available only in its 45cm (18in) high dwarf form 'Pixie Delight'. This is a mixed strain whose flowers may be white, pink, red, lavender, purple, blue or bicoloured.

'Pixie Delight' has colourful spikes which appear from mid summer to mid autumn, persisting long after perennial lupins have faded. Carried on bushy plants with leaves divided into softy hairy green leaflets, they are excellent for producing a band of medium height colour in a mixed border. But they also look effective grown in a mass on their own or in containers on the patio.

Cultivation

Soak the hard seeds in water for 12 hours, before sowing them outdoors in their flowering site in early autumn (in mild parts of the country), or in early spring. Thin the seedlings to stand 20-25cm (8-10in) apart.

Lupins grow in sun or partial shade, doing best in light, neutral to acid soils and thriving on poor soils.

'Pixie Delight' should not require support. Dead-head regularly – the poisonous seed pods appeal to children and, if eaten, cause upset stomachs.

Pests and diseases Trouble free.

Malcolmia

Virginia stock

Malcolmia maritima

☐ Height 20cm (8in)
☐ Mid spring to autumn
☐ Ordinary well-drained soil
☐ Sunny site
☐ Hardy annual

The flowers of *Malcolmia maritima*, an easily grown 20cm (8in) high hardy annual, have a delightfully old-fashioned look. Little cross-shaped blooms, they come in white, pink, red, lavender and purple (usually sold as a mixture) and have a sweet scent. If sown in succession from early spring to mid summer they will produce flowers from mid spring through to autumn – expect flowering to begin four weeks after sowing, and to continue for six to eight weeks.

Cultivation
Sow the seeds thinly between early spring and mid summer in ordinary well-drained soil, preferably in a sunny site. Rake the seed into the soil so it is only just covered. It's important to scatter the seed thinly as seedlings are best left to grow into one another to form a drift. Virginia stock self-seeds freely.
Pests and diseases Trouble free.

MALLOW – see *Lavatera*

Malope

mallow-wort

Malope trifida

☐ Height 90cm (3ft)
☐ Planting distance 23cm (9in)
☐ Flowers early summer until early
   autumn
☐ Ordinary garden soil
☐ Sunny site
☐ Hardy annual

Mallow-wort is one of the easiest – and showiest – of hardy annuals. Its striking trumpet-shaped flowers add bright colours to annual and mixed borders all summer, and they are also good for cutting. The species, *Malope trifida*, grows to 90cm (3ft) high, bearing its blooms in large clusters. The form usually offered is 'Grandiflora', with large flowers borne in great profusion.

Seed mixtures, producing white, rose-pink, crimson or rich purple flowers, are readily available as well as single-coloured strains, such as 'Pink Queen' and 'White Queen'.

Cultivation
Sow seeds outdoors in the flowering site, just covering them with soil. When the seedlings are large enough to handle, thin them out to 23cm (9in) apart.

Malopes will grow in any kind of soil, preferably light and well-drained; they do best in a sunny position. Self-sown seedlings occur if the surrounding soil is left undisturbed.
Pests and diseases Trouble free.

MARGUERITE, BLUE – see *Felicia*
MARIGOLD – see *Calendula* and *Tagetes*
MARVEL OF PERU – see *Mirabilis*
MASK FLOWER – see *Alonsoa*

Matthiola

stock

Matthiola incana 'Ten Week Stock'

☐ Height 30-75cm (12-30in)
☐ Planting distance 23-30cm (9-12in)
☐ Flowers early to late summer
☐ Fertile garden soil
☐ Sunny or lightly shaded site
☐ Hardy annual and biennial

Their heavenly scent and dense spikes of pastel and rich-coloured flowers have made stocks age old favourites for cottage gardens, formal bedding schemes, mixed borders and as cut flowers. The spikes are borne on erect stems clothed with narrow, grey-green and felted leaves.

Popular varieties
Most garden varieties have been developed from *Matthiola incana*, commonly known as stock.
'Brompton Stocks' are upright bushy plants reaching 45cm (18in) high. These late spring-flowering stocks have single or double blooms and come in shades of red, pink, purple, yellow and white. Usually sold as a mixture, they should be treated as biennials.
'East Lothian Stock', sometimes known as the Intermediate group, produces bushy plants reaching 38cm (15in) high. They bear flowers in mixed colours throughout the summer and can be grown as annuals or biennials.
'Night-scented Stock', the common name for *Matthiola bicornis*, is a 38cm (15in) high annual plant with a bushy habit. The lilac-grey or purple flowers, which are borne from mid to late summer, remain

Mentzelia
mentzelia

Matthiola incana 'Brompton Stock'

Mentzelia lindleyi

☐ Height 45cm (18in)
☐ Planting distance 23cm (9in)
☐ Flowers early to late summer
☐ Well-drained garden soil
☐ Sunny site
☐ Hardy annual

closed during the day, but at night they open to release the sweet fragrance for which they are renowned.

'Ten Week Stocks' are exceptionally fragrant, early-flowering varieties in mixed colours which, as their name implies, flower 10-12 weeks after being sown. Varieties include **'Dwarf'** which has compact plants 30cm (1ft) high, carrying large flowers in mixed pastel and rich colours. They make ideal bedding plants.

'Trysomic Seven Week' produces dwarf bushy plants 30cm (1ft) high. The double blooms – in mixed colours – come out seven weeks after sowing, making them the earliest flowering stocks. Treat them as annuals.

Cultivation
Sow annual stocks – 'Ten Week', 'East Lothian' and 'Night Scented' – directly in the flowering site in mid spring, just covering the seeds with soil. They grow in any fertile garden soil in either sun or partial shade. Thin the seedlings to stand 30cm (1ft) apart.

For early flowering, sow under glass in late winter to early spring and keep at a temperature of 13-15°C (55-59°F). Prick out into boxes and harden off in a cold

frame before planting out in mid to late spring.

The 'Trysomic Seven Week' and 'Selectable Doubles' – strains with double flowers – should be sown under glass, as already described, the temperature lowered to 10°C (50°F) for a couple of days before pricking out. This drop in temperature will exaggerate the difference in seedling leaf colour between the pale yellow-green double plants and green singles. Discard the singles if double-flowered plants only are wanted.

The 'Brompton Stocks' are treated as biennials. Sow the seeds in a seed bed in early summer. Thin when the seedlings are large enough to handle and then transfer to the flowering site in autumn, setting the plants 30cm (1ft) apart.

All stock varieties thrive in fertile soil in sun or light shade.

Pests and diseases Flea beetles may attack seedlings, eating small holes in the leaves; caterpillars feed on the leaves of older plants and aphids can be a problem. Troublesome diseases include club root and mildew.

Mentzelia lindleyi, sometimes called *Bartonia aurea*, is a robust, freely branching, slightly sprawling annual some 45cm (18in) high. From mid to late summer it produces a long succession of fragrant, brilliant yellow flowers. These open from gracefully pointed buds into flowers composed of five broad petals arranged around a mass of slender golden stamens. The small narrow leaves are a rich green and set on succulent stems.

This annual is a native of California so it should be grown in full sun. If the weather is cool and cloudy the flowers may fail to open properly. However it does have a reputation for standing up well to wind.

Cultivation
Sow the seeds during early and mid spring in a sunny site where they are to flower. They grow best in light fertile soil, though any well-drained soil gives good results. Cover the seeds with just a little soil. Thin to 23cm (9in) apart.

Pests and diseases Trouble free.

Mesembryanthemum

Livingstone daisy

Mesembryanthemum criniflorum 'Magic Carpet'

☐ Height 10-15cm (4-6in)
☐ Planting distance 10-15cm (4-6in)
☐ Flowers early to late summer
☐ Any well-drained soil
☐ Sunny site
☐ Half-hardy annual

Originating in South Africa, the Livingstone daisy has astonishingly brilliant pink, lavender, red, orange and yellow flowers and thick pale green leaves which have a glistening, sugary appearance. The flowers are daisy-like, with slender petals, and put on their dazzling display from early to late summer, provided they are grown in a dry, sunny position.

As the plants are less than 15cm (6in) high and have a trailing habit, they look most effective on banks, in rock gardens and along the edges of borders. Grow them in large drifts.

Popular varieties

Garden varieties rather than the true species are usually available. They have been developed from *Mesembryanthemum criniflorum.*
'Lunette' has flowers with clear yellow petals arranged around a deep rust-red central disc.
'Magic Carpet Mixed' is a mixture of red, orange, pink, lavender and yellow flowers, some with a white band around the dark central discs.

Cultivation

Sow the seeds under glass in early spring and keep at a temperature of 15°C (59°F). Prick out the seedlings into boxes when they are large enough to handle and harden off before planting out in late spring. Set the plants 15cm (6in) apart. Choose a position in full sun and in well-drained soil. The plants thrive in sandy soils.

Seeds can be sown directly in the flowering site in mid spring, but they won't flower as early as plants started off under glass. Thin to 15cm (6in) apart.

Mesembryanthemum 'Magic Carpet Mixed'

Pests and diseases Plants may collapse due to the fungus foot rot.

MIGNONETTE – see *Reseda*

Mimulus

monkey flower

Mimulus cupreus 'Queen's Prize Strain'

☐ Height 15-30cm (6-12in)
☐ Planting distance 23cm (9in)
☐ Flowers early summer to mid autumn
☐ Moisture-retentive soil
☐ Sunny or lightly shaded site
☐ Half-hardy annual

Mimulus is a large genus of mainly perennial garden plants but one species and its varieties is grown as a half-hardy annual – *Mimulus cupreus*. This produces flowers (said to resemble the face of a grinning monkey) in great profusion from early summer until mid autumn – bright red, orange and yellow blooms.

The annual monkey flower is one of the few bedding plants to tolerate light shade and flourish in damp soil. It is useful for filling window-boxes and hanging baskets out of the sun or edging lightly shaded borders.

Popular varieties

Several varieties are available:
'Calypso Mixed' has robust plants, to 30cm (1ft), bearing a mass of orange, yellow, burgundy and pink flowers singly or in bicolours.
'Magic' is early-flowering, in a mixture of bright red, orange, yellow and crimson, as well as

Mimulus cupreus 'Red Emperor'

pink, pale yellow and several bicolours. Height 15cm (6in).
'Queen's Prize Strain' has flowers in mixed colours with some mottled or spotted. The plants reach 30cm (1ft) high.
'Red Emperor' has dazzling scarlet-red flowers and reaches 15cm (6in) high.

Cultivation

Sow the seeds under glass in early spring and keep at a temperature of 13-16°C (55-61°F). When the seedlings are large enough to handle, prick them out into boxes. Harden off in a cold frame before planting out in late spring to early summer.

Monkey flowers grow in any moisture-retentive soil, in sun or light shade.
Pests and diseases Trouble free.

Mirabilis

marvel of Peru, four o'clock plant

Mirabilis jalapa

☐ Height 60cm (2ft)
☐ Planting distance 30cm (1ft)
☐ Flowers mid summer to early autumn
☐ Light, moderately rich soil
☐ Sheltered sunny sight
☐ Tender perennial grown as a half-hardy annual

Marvel of Peru or four o'clock plant, botanically known as *Mirabilis jalapa*, has fragrant, trumpet-shaped flowers in yellow, red, crimson, rose-pink or white, often striped, veined or mottled with contrasting colours. These usually open from mid to late afternoon and fade the following morning, though in cool dull weather they open earlier and stay fresh for longer the following day. Appearing from mid summer to early autumn, they are carried on erect 60cm (2ft) high plants, and are set against a foil of heart-shaped mid-green leaves.

The plants are suitable for growing in clumps in sunny borders.

Cultivation

Sow the seeds under glass in late winter to early spring and germinate at a temperature of 18°C (64°F). Prick out the seedlings into boxes when large enough to handle, and harden off before planting out in late spring to early summer. Set the plants 30cm (1ft) apart in groups of five or seven.
Pests and diseases Aphids may infest young growths.

Molucella
bells of Ireland, shellflower

Myosotis
forget-me-not

Myosotis alpestris

Molucella laevis

☐ Height 60cm (2ft)
☐ Planting distance 23cm (9in)
☐ Flowers late summer to early autumn
☐ Light rich soil
☐ Open sunny site
☐ Half-hardy annual

Bells of Ireland – a misleading name, as the species *Molucella laevis* comes from Syria – is a favourite among flower arrangers, not because of its flowers, which are small and insignificant, but because of large pale green bell-like calyces which surround them. These are arranged in tall graceful spikes 23cm (9in) long and borne on erect stems clothed with light green rounded leaves.

Bells of Ireland make unusual border decorations as well as cut flowers that last for months in water. They can also be dried for winter arrangements. Pick in warm dry weather towards the end of summer.

Cultivation
Sow the seeds under glass in early spring at a temperature of 15°C (59°F), just covering them with compost. Prick out the seedlings into boxes and harden off in a cold frame before planting out in late spring, 23cm (9in) apart. Bells of Ireland will grow in any ordinary garden soil, though well-drained rich soil in an open sunny site provides the perfect conditions.

As the plants are moderately hardy, seeds can also be sown in the flowering site in mid spring and the seedlings thinned to 23cm (9in) apart.

Pests and diseases Trouble free.

MONARCH OF THE VELDT – see *Venidium*
MONEYWORT – see *Lunaria*
MONKEY FLOWER – see *Mimulus*
MORNING GLORY – see *Convolvulus* and *Ipomoea*
MOROCCAN TOADFLAX – see *Linaria*
MULLEIN – see *Verbascum*

☐ Height 15-38cm (6-15in)
☐ Planting distance 15cm (6in)
☐ Flowers mid spring to early summer
☐ Fertile well-drained but moisture-retentive soil
☐ Partial shade
☐ Hardy biennial

Forget-me-nots provide a delightful succession of tiny pure blue – or pink – flowers, each with a white or yellow eye, from mid spring to early summer. They are used mainly for bedding with spring-flowering bulbs, though they also make attractive long-lasting cut flowers – only when the sprigs are taken indoors is the neatness and delicate colouring of the tiny flowers fully appreciated. They are also useful plants for the front of mixed borders, wild gardens and shrubberies.

Popular varieties
The varieties available all stem from *Myosotis alpestris* and *M. sylvatica* and include the following:
'Blue Ball' forms compact ball-shaped plants just 15-20cm (6-8in) high, bearing indigo-blue flowers. It is an excellent edging variety.
'Blue Bouquet' is a tall variety, 38cm (15in) high, with sprays of large deep blue flowers. Useful for cutting and in bedding schemes.
'Carmine King' has rich pink flowers on compact plants and reaches 20cm (8in) high.
'Compindi', of compact habit and 15-20cm (6-8in) high, has deep blue flowers.
'Rose Pink' is a mid-pink variety.

Myosotis alpestris 'Rose Pink'

Nemesia
nemesia

Nemesia strumosa 'Carnival Mixed'

The compact plants are just 15cm (6in) tall.

'Royal Blue' reaches 30cm (1ft) high and has loose sprays of indigo-blue flowers. It is one of the first varieties to bloom.

'Spring Symphony Mixed' is an early-flowering strain, with plants up to 20cm (8in) high and with white, rose-pink and ultra-marine-blue flowers. Compact and good for edging.

Cultivation
For the best results, forget-me-nots should be raised as biennials. Sow the seeds in trays in early summer, then transplant to the flowering site in autumn, setting them 15cm (6in) apart. For the best results grow them in fertile well-drained but moisture-retentive soil in partial shade, though ordinary garden soil in sun or shade is quite adequate.

Forget-me-nots self-seed and hybridize easily.

Pests and diseases Grey mould and mildew can cause problems.

NASTURTIUM – see
Tropaeolum
NATAL GRASS – see
Tricholaena

☐ Height 20-25cm (8-10in)
☐ Planting distance 10-15cm (4-6in)
☐ Flowers early to late summer
☐ Moist rich soil
☐ Sunny position
☐ Half-hardy annual

This bushy annual, with its solid mass of funnel-shaped blooms in many vivid colours, puts on a splendid show all summer long if grown in fertile moist soil in a sunny position. It is useful in bedding schemes and containers and long-lasting as a cut flower.

Popular varieties
Numerous varieties have been developed from *Nemesia strumosa*.

'Carnival Mixed' produces compact plants 23cm (9in) high which become smothered with a mixture of brightly coloured flowers.

'Snow Princess' grows 20cm (8in) high and has glistening white, yellow-throated flowers.

'Suttons Sparklers' is a mixture of bicoloured and tricoloured flowers. The plants reach 20cm (8in) high.

'Triumph Red', up to 25cm (10in) tall, is compact and early-flowering, with bright red flowers.

Cultivation
Sow the seeds under glass in early spring, at a temperature of 15°C (59°F), just covering them with compost. Prick out the seedlings into boxes and harden off before planting out in late spring. Ideally grow nemesia in a fertile moist soil in full sun.

Pests and diseases Foot and root rot may be a problem, causing the plants to collapse.

Nemesia strumosa 'Suttons Sparklers'

Nemophila
nemophila

Nemophila menziesii

☐ Height 15-23cm (6-9in)
☐ Planting distance 15cm (6in)
☐ Flowers early to late summer
☐ Moist good garden soil
☐ Sun or partial shade
☐ Hardy annual

The two species grown in gardens – *Nemophila maculata* and *Nemophila menziesii* – are bushy, compact plants suitable for growing at the front of borders or for edging paths. They bear a profusion of small cup-shaped flowers in blue and white or purple and white, and have light green leaves.

Popular species
Nemophila maculata has white flowers with purple veins and purple blotches on the petal tips. The spreading stems carry lobed leaves and reach 15cm (6in) high. *Nemophila menziesii*, commonly called baby-blue-eyes, has white-centred sky-blue flowers. Reaching 23cm (9in) high, the plants bear feathery leaves. 'Pennie Black' has deep purple, near black flowers edged with silvery-white.

Cultivation
Sow the seeds shallowly in their flowering site in early autumn or early spring. In mid spring thin to 15cm (6in) apart. Nemophila grows well in sun or partial shade in any ordinary soil, but for the best results, sow in moist rich soil.
Pests and diseases Aphids may infest young shoots.

Nemophila maculata

Nicandra
shoo-fly, apple of Peru

Nicandra physalodes

☐ Height 90cm (3ft)
☐ Planting distance 30cm (1ft)
☐ Flowers mid summer to early autumn
☐ Deep moist rich soil
☐ Sunny position
☐ Hardy annual

If you're looking for an unusual plant to fill a gap in a border, *Nicandra physalodes* is worth considering. It is a vigorous plant, easily grown and robust, its branching growth reaching 90cm (3ft), with lush mid-green toothed leaves, small but pretty lilac-blue bell-shaped flowers and fruits enclosed in attractive green lantern-like calyces. Another benefit is its supposed ability to repel flies, hence one of its common names, shoo-fly.

The flowers appear from early to late summer, though they open only for a few hours at midday. Expect the fruits to form between late summer and mid autumn; dried they are suitable for winter decoration.

Cultivation
Sow the seeds under glass in early spring at a temperature of 15°C (59°F). Prick out the seedlings into 7.5cm (3in) pots. Harden off before planting out in late spring, setting the plants 30cm (1ft) apart. Alternatively sow the seeds in the flowering position in mid spring.

Shoo-fly thrives in deep moist and rich soil in a sunny position.
Pests and diseases Trouble free.

Nicotiana
tobacco plant

Nicotiana 'Nicki'

☐ Height 25-90cm (10in-3ft)
☐ Planting distance 23-30cm (9-12in)
☐ Flowers early summer to early
   autumn
☐ Rich well-drained soil
☐ Sunny site
☐ Half-hardy annual

Tobacco plants have long been valued for the heady evening fragrance of their flowers. Species and varieties grown in the past mainly flowered in the evening, but modern breeding programmes have resulted in hybrids and varieties whose flowers open during daylight hours.

The plants have rosettes of pale green leaves at the base, from which rise elegant branching stems. The star-shaped flowers are carried in clusters throughout the summer and come in a mixture of white, soft pink, lavender-pink, deep red and lime-green.

With their long flowering period, tobacco plants are ideal for group planting in borders and summer beds; the dwarf types do well in pots and containers.

Popular varieties

Most hybrids and varieties are developed from *Nicotiana alata*.

'Domino Mixed' are compact plants just 30cm (1ft) high, carrying flowers in red, pink, mauve, lilac, lime and white.

'Evening Fragrance' has flowers with a particularly heady scent. They come in pink, red, lilac, mauve and white on 90cm (3ft) high plants.

'Lime Green' has greenish-yellow flowers and reaches 75cm (30in) high.

'Merlin' is a dwarf mixture, up to 23cm (9in) high, with blooms in crimson, white, lime-green and bicoloured purple.

'Nicki' has strongly fragrant flowers in a mixture of colours – pink, white, red, mauve, maroon and lime-green. It reaches 30cm (1ft).

'Roulette' seed strain comes in a mixture of colours, often white-eyed, and bright green foliage. Plants grow to 30cm (1ft).

'Sensation Mixed' has flowers in a wide range of colours – white, pink, red and mauve – and reaches 75cm (30in) high.

Cultivation

Sow the seeds under glass in late winter to early spring at a temperature of 18°C (64°F). Prick out the seedlings into boxes. Harden off before planting out in late spring. Set the plants 23-30cm (9-12in) apart in rich well-drained soil in a sunny site. Dead-head.

Pests and diseases Aphids can attack young plants.

Nicotiana 'Lime Green'

Nierembergia
cup flower

Nierembergia caerulea 'Purple Robe'

☐ Height 15-20cm (6-8in)
☐ Planting distance 20cm (8in)
☐ Flowers early summer to early autumn
☐ Moist, but well-drained soil
☐ Sunny sheltered site
☐ Tender perennial grown as half-hardy annual

Though perennial, the species most commonly grown in Britain, *Nierembergia caerulea*, is tender and usually treated as an annual. Its fine green foliage forms neat hummocks which become covered with small pale lavender flowers with yellow throats from early summer to early autumn. 'Mont Blanc' is smothered with glistening white flowers; 'Purple Robe' has deep violet flowers. Cup flower looks most effective as edging to beds and borders and is ideal for container growing.

Cultivation
Sow the seeds in pots or pans under glass in late winter or early spring at a temperature of 15°C (59°F). Prick out the seedlings into boxes and harden off before planting out in late spring.

The plants will grow in ordinary soil, although a moist but well-drained soil gives the best results. Choose a sunny sheltered site.
Pests and diseases Trouble free.

Nigella
nigella

Nigella hispanica

☐ Height 60cm (2ft)
☐ Planting distance 23cm (9in)
☐ Flowers early summer to early autumn
☐ Any good soil
☐ Sunny position
☐ Hardy annual

The blue, white and pink flowers of this enchanting annual bloom all summer long in a haze of feathery, soft green foliage. As the flowers fade, each seed pod swells and ripens into a pale brown, red-barred spiky globe, suitable for drying for winter decoration.

Invaluable for the border, nigella also provides superb cut flowers. Two species and their varieties are widely grown in gardens.

Popular species
Nigella damascena (love-in-a-mist) has showy blue or white flowers surrounded by a leafy green crown of thread-like bracts from early to late summer. Popular varieties include 'Miss Jekyll' (large bright blue flowers) and 'Persian Jewels' (light and dark blue, rose-pink and white flowers). *Nigella hispanica* has larger blue flowers than the more commonly grown love-in-a-mist. Appearing from mid summer to early autumn, these have a slight scent and a cluster of red stamens. The seed pods are less inflated than those of love-in-a-mist.

Cultivation
Sow the seeds in any well-cultivated soil in a sunny position in early spring, just covering them with soil. Thin to 23cm (9in) apart. Dead-head for larger, later flowers, unless you want the seed pods.
Pests and diseases Trouble free.

Nigella damascena 'Persian Jewels'

Ocimum
basil

Ocimum basilicum 'Purpureum'

☐ Height 30-45cm (12-18in)
☐ Planting distance 30cm (1ft)
☐ Flowers late summer
☐ Any well-drained soil
☐ Sunny and sheltered site
☐ Half-hardy annual foliage plant

Better known for its culinary uses, sweet basil (*Ocimum basilicum*) has given rise to several ornamental varieties which are popular in summer bedding schemes and as container and pot plants. The purple foliage provides strong colour contrasts and can also be used in cooking like its green-leaved relation.

The small pinkish-white or purple flower spikes borne on bushy plants are of little significance compared with the shiny purple leaves, almost black in the variety 'Purpureum' and wavy-edged in 'Purple Ruffles'.

Cultivation
Sow seeds in pots or pans in the greenhouse in mid spring, at a temperature of 13°C (55°F). Prick the seedlings out into trays when large enough to handle and grow on at the same temperature. Harden the young plants off in a cold frame before planting them out in late spring when all danger of frost is past.

Basil thrives in light and well-drained garden soil and needs a sheltered site in full sun. Pinch out the flowers to encourage leaf growth.

Pests and diseases Trouble free.

Oenothera
evening primrose

Oenothera biennis

☐ Height 90cm (3ft)
☐ Planting distance 30cm (1ft)
☐ Flowers early summer to mid autumn
☐ Ordinary well-drained soil
☐ Sunny site
☐ Hardy biennial

Most evening primroses are perennials, but one species, *Oenothera biennis*, is a hardy biennial. Ideal for the back of a border or a wild garden, its pale yellow funnel-shaped flowers open out in the evening from early summer to mid autumn. The lance-shaped mid-green leaves, arranged in a large rosette on 90cm (3ft) high erect stems, make a perfect foil for the slightly fragrant and short-lived flowers.

If allowed to self-seed, evening primrose spreads like a weed.

Cultivation
Sow the seeds in pots or pans of seed compost in a cold frame in mid spring. Prick out the seedlings and grow them on in a nursery bed until mid autumn, when they can be planted out in the flowering position – preferably in ordinary well-drained soil in an open sunny site. Water the plants well in dry weather.

Pests and diseases Mildew can cause a white powdery coating on the leaves.

Onopordum
Scotch thistle, cotton thistle

Onopordum acanthium

☐ Height 1.8m (6ft)
☐ Planting distance 75cm (30in)
☐ Flowers mid to late summer
☐ Rich or ordinary garden soil
☐ Sunny or partially shaded site
☐ Hardy biennial

Scotch thistle (*Onopordum acanthium*) makes an excellent specimen plant in a border, large shrubbery or wild garden. It is grown for its dramatic foliage – broad silver-grey spiny leaves covered with white cobweb-like hairs – though purple thistle-like flowers do appear from mid to late summer.

Cultivation
Sow the seeds directly in the flowering site and thin to 75cm (30in) apart. If the plants are to reach their maximum size (1.8m/6ft tall), they should be grown in rich soil. However, ordinary garden soil in full sun or partial shade still gives good results. Remove dead flowers to prevent self-seeding.

Pests and diseases Trouble free.

OUR LADY'S MILK THISTLE – see *Silybum*
PAINTED TONGUE – see *Salpiglossis*
PALM SPRINGS DAISY – see *Cladanthus*
PANSY – see *Viola*

Papaver
poppy

Papaver nudicaule

Papaver somniferum 'Danebrog'

☐ Height 30-75cm (12-30in)
☐ Planting distance 30-45cm (12-18in)
☐ Flowers early to late summer
☐ Ordinary well-drained soil
☐ Sunny site
☐ Hardy annual and biennial

The simple delicate petals of poppies come in such bright colours that few gardeners can resist them. Several species and their varieties are grown in gardens. Some have single flowers with four broad overlapping petals arranged in a characteristic bowl-shape, while others have double flowers – ball-like blooms formed from many petals.

Poppies are suitable for a variety of situations in the garden, though sun is essential.

Popular species
Papaver nudicaule, the Iceland poppy, comes from the sub-Arctic, and is one of the most elegant poppies. The slender leafless stems carry white or yellow fragrant flowers in early summer. Only at the base of the 45-75cm (18-30in) high stems is there a rosette of smooth, soft green leaves. This is one of the few poppies suitable for cutting for indoor flower arrange-

ments. When you cut it, select buds just starting to show colour, and scald the stems in hot water after cutting, to seal the ends.

Numerous garden varieties have been developed from the species, offering a wide range of flower colours: 'Champagne Bubbles' has large pink, salmon, apricot, orange, golden-yellow and scarlet flowers, single or bicoloured, and reaches 60cm (2ft) high; 'Garden Gnome Mixed' is a compact strain, growing only 30cm (12in) high, with flowers in scarlet, salmon, orange, yellow or white.

Papaver rhoeas, the field poppy, has scarlet-red flowers with black centres from early to late summer, on erect 60cm (2ft) high stems. These are accompanied by pale green deeply lobed leaves. Field poppies look their best grown in large drifts on grassy banks or in a semi-wild grassed area.

Several garden varieties have been developed, the most popular being the 'Shirley' strains, with single flowers in white, rose, pink, salmon, orange and red in 'Shirley Single Mixed' and similar, but double flowers in 'Shirley Double Mixed'; both grow to 60cm (2ft) tall. *Papaver rhoeas commutatum* is

a subspecies, with single flowers of crimson with large black blotches. *Papaver somniferum*, the opium poppy, has large white, red, pink or mauve flowers from early to late summer, followed by bulbous, flat-capped and poisonous seed pods in autumn. The plants reach 75cm (30in) high and carry deeply lobed smooth, pale green leaves.

Several varieties with double flowers are available. 'Peony Flowered Mixed' has flowers resembling peonies in a mixture of white, pink or purple; 'White Cloud', on 90cm (3ft) tall stems, has extra large white flowers; 'Danebrog' has single blood-red flowers prominently marked with white in the centre, and with fringed petals.

Cultivation
Poppies grow in ordinary well-drained soil in a sunny position. Sow biennials (*Papaver nudicaule*) in the flowering site in early summer. Protect the seedlings with cloches during the winter months and then thin to 30-45cm (12-18in) apart the following spring.

Sow annuals in the flowering site in mid spring, just covering them with soil. Thin to 30cm (1ft) apart. Staking should not be necessary. Dead-head regularly to prevent self-seeding. Try to avoid transplanting.

Pests and diseases Downy mildew can cause yellow blotches on the leaves. Otherwise trouble free.

PEARL GRASS – see *Briza*

Papaver somniferum

Papaver somniferum 'Peony Flowered'

Papaver rhoeas commutatum

Pelargonium
pelargonium, geranium

Zonal pelargonium 'Ringo Scarlet'

Zonal pelargonium 'Michelle'

□ Height 15-60cm (6-24in)
□ Planting distance 20-30cm (8-12in)
□ Flowers late spring to mid autumn
□ Ordinary well-drained garden soil
□ Full sun
□ Tender perennials, grown as half-hardy annuals

Formal beds, hanging baskets, window-boxes and pots on balconies all abound with brightly coloured pelargoniums in summer. These tender perennials, grown outdoors as half-hardy bedding plants, come in an enormous range of forms. The flowers, which can be white, red, pink, rose-pink, salmon and mauve, are borne on either upright or pendulous plants, with variously shaped and coloured leaves.

Popular varieties
Pelargoniums are divided into several groups, according to their hybrid provenance, flower type or general growth habit.
REGAL PELARGONIUMS, also known as *Pelargonium* x *domesticum*, are a hybrid race of erect, shrubby plants up to 60cm (2ft) tall, with light green lobed leaves that are lightly toothed.

The exotic flowers are borne in dense clusters, often veined or marked with contrasting colours and often with frilled petals. Suitable for pot cultivation, outdoors and under glass.
'Applause' has pink flowers with frilled petals.
'Aztec' has pink flowers with dark maroon veining and a white base.
'Grand Slam' has crimson-red flowers.
'Velvet Duet' has purple-pink flowers fading to white.
ZONAL PELARGONIUMS are the most commonly grown varieties, sometimes listed as *Pelargonium* x *hortorum*. Distinguished by their rounded, pale to mid green leaves, usually though not always with a conspicuous brown or maroon zone, the upright plants reach 30-60cm (1-2ft) in height. They are suitable for bedding schemes and containers and are available in numerous seed selections, mainly F1 hybrids:
'Eyes Right' has huge flower clusters in shades of pink and rose-red with scarlet eyes.
'Hollywood Star' bears tightly packed flower heads, rosy-pink and white-centred.

'L'Amour' is a seed mixture producing compact plants, branching from the base and bearing clusters of semi or fully double flowers in shades of pink, red and white.
'Masquerade' is a bicoloured mixture bearing scarlet, pink, cerise or salmon flowers, all with white eyes.
'Orange Appeal' has large, pure orange flower heads.
'Orbit Series' is available as a mixture or in single colours of apple-blossom pink, deep pink, scarlet, violet or white.
'Ringo Scarlet' has glossy, rich scarlet flowers above dark green, zoned foliage; 'Ringo White' has pure white flowers and light green leaves.
'Sensation Mixed', so-called floribunda geraniums, come as mixed seeds or in single colours of rose, scarlet, cherry, blush-pink and coral.
'Startel' has dense flower heads in white, shades of pink and red, and heavily zoned leaves.

Fancy-leaved pelargoniums have leaves so heavily marked that they outshine the flowers:
'A Happy Thought' has green leaves with yellow markings, and red flowers.
'Mrs Henry Cox' has yellow, green, red and copper leaves, with salmon-pink flowers.

Miniature zonal pelargoniums, suitable for window boxes and edging include:
'Michelle' has delicate salmon-pink flowers and zoned leaves.
'Playboy Speckles', 23cm (9in) high, compact and bushy, with bicoloured pink and white blooms.

Ivy-leaved pelargonium 'Cornel'

Ivy-leaved pelargonium 'Snow Queen'

Regal pelargonium 'Velvet Duet'

Zonal pelargonium 'Mrs Henry Cox'

'Red Black Vesuvius' is 15cm (6in) tall, with cerise-pink flowers and heavily zoned, almost black leaves.

'Video Mixed', to 25cm (10in) high, in a range of clear colours and with deep green, zoned leaves.

Cascading zonal pelargoniums do not trail but branch naturally from the base to cascade over hanging baskets, window-boxes and tubs:

'Breakaway Red' and **'Breakaway Salmon'** are both 25cm (10in) tall, with deep red or salmon flowers and lightly zoned leaves.

'Continental Cascade' is a mixture of lilac-pink, rose-pink and orange-red, single flowers on short stems.

'Palais' bears large trusses of semi-double, coral-pink flowers.

Zonal pelargonium 'Red Black Vesuvius'

Zonal pelargonium 'Hollywood Star'

'Red Fountain', single flowers of vermilion-red above strongly zoned leaves.

IVY-LEAVED PELARGONIUMS are trailing plants with stems up to 90cm (3ft) long and mid green fleshy leaves like those of ivy. They are ideal for hanging baskets and deep window-boxes. Varieties and hybrids bred from the species *Pelargonium peltatum* include:

'Butterfly', compact, with double lilac flowers.

'Cezanne' has large shiny, velvety red flowers and rich green leaves.

'Cornel' has pink flowers with a hint of lavender in them.

'Ingress' bears compact clusters of clear rose-pink flowers.

'Lulu' trails to 45cm (1½ft), and has deep violet flowers.

'Mexican Beauty' has single crimson flowers.

'Salmon Queen' has deep pink, semi or fully double flowers.

'Snow Queen' has double white flowers tinged with lilac.

'Summer Showers' has a mixture of pink, red, mauve and white flowers.

SCENTED PELARGONIUMS are grown for the strong scent of their leaves; they bear typical five-petalled flowers but these are small and insignificant. Suitable for pot and tub cultivation.

'Chocolate Peppermint' has peppermint scented leaves and blush-pink flowers.

'Citronella' has white flowers and leaves with a strong lemon scent.

'Grey Lady Plymouth' has foliage smelling of eucalyptus, and blush-pink flowers.

Cultivation

Pelargoniums are usually grown from cuttings though many zonal and ivy-leaved varieties are easily grown from seed. For cuttings, buy stock plants from a nursery or garden centre in late spring.

Take 7.5cm (3in) long tip cuttings in mid to late summer and insert them in 6cm (2½in) pots of potting compost, placed on an open

Penstemon
penstemon

Perilla
perilla

Penstemon hartwegii 'Skyline'

Perilla frutescens 'Nankinensis'

□ Height 60cm (2ft)
□ Planting distance 30cm (1ft)
□ Foliage plant
□ Fertile, well-drained soil
□ Sunny site
□ Half-hardy annual

Zonal pelargonium 'White Orbit'

greenhouse bench. When the cuttings have rooted, pot them on as necessary.

Alternatively, overwinter mature plants in a frost-free greenhouse and take tip cuttings from these in early spring.

When young plants are about 15cm (6in) high, pinch out the growing tips to encourage bushy side-growth.

Sow seeds of zonal pelargoniums in late winter in pots or pans of seed compost at a temperature of 16-18°C (61-64°F). Prick out the seedlings into boxes and pot on as necessary.

Plant out pelargoniums between late spring and early summer, when all danger of frost has passed. Set them in ordinary well-drained soil in full sun.

In mid autumn, transfer the plants to pots of potting compost and keep them at a temperature of 10°C (50°F).
Pests and diseases Whitefly sometimes gather on leaves.

□ Height 30-60cm (1-2ft)
□ Planting distance 30cm (1ft)
□ Flowers mid to late summer
□ Ordinary well-drained soil
□ Full sun
□ Half-hardy annual

Most of the species in this genus are hardy perennials grown in rock gardens and borders, but some outstanding hybrids, developed from *Penstemon hartwegii*, are half-hardy and best treated as bedding plants. With their long spikes of tubular red, pink, purple and white flowers, penstemons are an attractive halfway house between foxgloves and snapdragons.

Popular varieties
The following are readily available from seed.
'Early Bird Mixed' has spikes of white, pink, mauve, lavender and scarlet flowers on 45-50cm (18-20in) high plants.
'Skyline' has bell-shaped pink, red and white flowers. The plants stand 45-60cm (18-24in) high.

Cultivation
Sow the seeds under glass in late winter and early spring and keep at a temperature of 13-18°C (55-64°F). Harden off before planting out in late spring, 30cm (1ft) apart in well-drained soil in sun.
Pests and diseases Trouble free.

The attractive purple-red leaves of *Perilla frutescens* make it a popular specimen plant for formal beds, its dark foliage contrasting well with bright summer flowers.

It is a coarse-looking plant, which will reach 60cm (2ft) high, given the right growing conditions. If you bruise the pointed oval, toothed leaves, they give off a spicy smell, reminiscent of their oriental (Chinese) origins.

The most popular variety is 'Foliis Atropurpurea Laciniata' which has crumpled, deeply cut foliage. 'Nankinensis' ('Crispa') has bronze leaves with wrinkled edges.

Cultivation
Sow the seeds in late winter to early spring in pots or pans of seed compost at a temperature of 18°C (64°F). Prick out the seedlings, when they are large enough to handle, into boxes. Harden off before planting out in late spring, setting the plants 30cm (1ft) apart. Grow in any good soil in an open sunny site.
Pests and diseases Generally trouble free.

Petunia

petunia

Petunia 'Brass Band'

Petunia 'Dwarf Resisto'

☐ Height 20-45cm (8-18in)
☐ Planting distance 15-30cm (6-12in)
☐ Flowers early summer to first autumn frost
☐ Any well-drained soil
☐ Sunny site
☐ Half-hardy annual

Petunia 'Daddy Mixed'

Since the first plants were introduced to Europe about 1830, the petunia has grown in favour until it is now one of the most popular summer annuals.

Flowering from early summer until the first severe frost, petunias are ideal for edging beds or filling window-boxes, tubs and hanging baskets. The trumpet-shaped flowers come in white, pink, red, lavender, blue and yellow, sometimes bicoloured or veined and sometimes with ruffled edges.

Popular varieties
Petunias are usually divided into two groups.
GRANDIFLORA VARIETIES have a slightly trailing habit and large showy flowers, some of which are double. As they are not weather-resistant they do best in a sheltered position.
'Blue Picotee' has deep violet-blue flowers with wavy petals edged with pure white.
'Daddy Mixed' has large burgundy, mauve and pink flowers, with distinct dark veining.

'Picotee Mixed' has flowers in plum-purple, deep-blue, scarlet or rose, all with a broad white edge and waved petals.
'Razzle Dazzle' has red, rose, and deep blue flowers striped white.
'Strawberry Tart', up to 45cm (18in), has double flowers of ruffled petals in cerise-red with bold white markings.
MULTIFLORA VARIETIES grow into bushy plants bearing large numbers of small flowers. They are more weather-resistant than the grandiflora varieties.
'Brass Band' has deep primrose-yellow flowers.
'Carpet Mixed' produces low, spreading plants, only 20cm (8in) high, with pink, rose, red, plum, blue and white flowers.

'Dwarf Resisto' is a short variety, just 30cm (1ft) high, with a mixture of flowers in the typical petunia colours.
'Mirage Series' comes between grandiflora and multiflora petunias. They are large-flowered and weather-resistant; seeds are available as mixtures or in single colours.

Cultivation
Sow the seeds under glass in early spring at a temperature of 15°C (59°F). Prick out the seedlings into seed boxes. Harden off before planting out in late spring to early summer in light well-drained soil in a sheltered sunny site. Dead-head the plants regularly.
Pests and diseases Aphids may infest young plants, and virus diseases may distort the leaves, stunt the plants and reduce flowering.

Petunia 'Picotee Mixed'

Phacelia

phacelia

Phacelia campanularia

□ Height 23cm (9in)
□ Planting distance 15cm (6in)
□ Flowers early summer to early autumn
□ Well-drained garden soil
□ Sunny situation
□ Hardy annual

The intense blue bell-shaped flowers of *Phacelia campanularia* make this hardy annual an attractive addition to a rockery or unusual edging · for a border. Appearing from early summer to early autumn, the flowers are carried on 23cm (9in) high plants with lush green irregularly toothed leaves. When these are crushed they give off a strong but pleasant fragrance.

Bees find the blue flowers particularly attractive.

Cultivation

Sow the seeds in the flowering site in early to mid spring, just covering them with soil. Thin the seedlings to 15cm (6in) apart.

In a warm sheltered garden the seeds can be sown in early autumn for earlier flowering plants. Protect them with cloches during the winter.

Phacelia will grow in any well-drained and light soil and thrive especially in sandy soils. The situation must be sunny.

Pests and diseases Slugs may eat the seedlings.

PHEASANT'S EYE – see *Adonis*

Phlox

phlox

Phlox drummondii 'Beauty Mixed'

□ Height 10-30cm (4-12in)
□ Planting distance 23cm (9in)
□ Flowers mid summer to early autumn
□ Fertile well-drained soil
□ Open sunny site
□ Half-hardy annual

Annual phlox (*Phlox drummondii*) is one of the traditional bedding plants, its compact bushy plants and brightly coloured flowers making attractive edgings to formal bedding schemes and borders. The red, mauve, pink and white flowers are borne in tightly clustered round heads, each individual flower with a zone around its eye in a contrasting colour. The leaves are light green and lance-shaped, but the flowers are so profuse that you hardly notice them.

Phlox flowers from mid summer until early autumn. Dead-heading, though time-consuming, will extend the season.

Popular varieties

The following seed selections are readily available.

'**Beauty Mixed**' is a dwarf variety just 15cm (6in) high with large flowers in clear red, pink, mauve and white.

'**Carnival Mixed**' bears large flowers in mixed colours, each with a clearly defined eye. The plants reach 25-30cm (10-12in) high.

'**Large Flowered Mixed**' is a tall variety 30cm (1ft) high with large blooms in mixed colours.

'**Petticoat**' grows only 10cm (4in) high, but is smothered with a mass of small flowers in shades of white, pink, red, violet and lavender, often bicoloured.

'**Twinkles Dwarf Star Mixed**' has star-like flowers in mixed colours. As its name implies, the plants reach just 15cm (6in) high.

Cultivation

Sow the seeds in pots or boxes of John Innes seed compost during early spring and germinate at a temperature of 15°C (59°F). Prick out the seedlings into boxes of potting compost. Harden off before planting out in late spring.

Grow phlox in any fertile, well-drained garden soil in an open sunny site. Dead-head regularly.

Pests and diseases Slugs feed on young stems and leaves, and mildew may appear on the leaves.

Phlox drummondii 'Twinkles Dwarf Star Mixed'

Portulaca

sun plant

Portulaca grandiflora

- ☐ Height 15-23cm (6-9in)
- ☐ Planting distance 15cm (6in)
- ☐ Flowers early summer to autumn
- ☐ Well-drained garden soil
- ☐ Sunny site
- ☐ Half-hardy annual

A swathe of sun plants (*Portulaca grandiflora*) makes a gloriously bright display, especially when the flowers are allowed to tumble down a bank. The elegant cylindrical succulent leaves form dense mats 15-23cm (6-9in) high and are smothered in summer by single or double flowers in a range of colours.

Popular varieties
Several varieties are available.
'**Double Mixed**' has double flowers in rich shades.
'**Sundance**' is semi-trailing, with double, brightly coloured flowers.

Cultivation
Sow the seeds under glass in early spring at a temperature of 18°C (64°F). Prick out the seedlings into boxes of potting compost and harden off before planting out in late spring, in a sunny site and well-drained soil.
Pests and diseases Aphids may make the plants sticky.

POT MARIGOLD – see
Calendula
PRICKLY POPPY – see
Argemone

Primula

polyanthus

Primula Polyanthus hybrids

- ☐ Height 15-30cm (6-12in)
- ☐ Planting distance 30cm (1ft)
- ☐ Flowers early to late spring
- ☐ Moist fertile soil
- ☐ Partially shaded site
- ☐ Short-lived perennial treated as biennial

Primula is an enormous genus of hardy and half-hardy perennials, but one group within the genus, the polyanthuses, are usually grown as biennials for bedding.

The polyanthus has been popular since its introduction in the 19th century. It is developed in part from the common primrose (*Primula vulgaris*) and has retained the characteristic bright green, corrugated leaves of that species. But only with the development of the large-flowered hybrids has the polyanthus become widely used in bedding. These large-flowered hybrids produce blooms in compact long-lasting clusters on tall sturdy stems 23-30cm (9-12in) high. The flowers appear from early to late spring in a wide spectrum of colours.

Popular varieties
Several seed selections are available, usually mixed strains.
'**Crescendo**' has giant flowers in shades of primrose, yellow, red, pink, blue and white, and reaches 30cm (1ft) high.
'**Fancy Shades Mixed**' is about 18cm (7in) tall, with flower heads in shades of bronze, peach,

Primula Polyanthus 'Pacific Giant Blue'

amber, rose-pink, cream and white.
'**Giant Superb Mixed**' has large flowers on sturdy 20cm (8in) tall plants; colours include white, yellow, crimson-red and blue.
'**Jackpot Mixed**' has short flower stems topped with yellow-eyed blooms in full colour range.
'**Pacific Giant**' has enormous blooms coming in a wide range of colours. The plants reach 30cm (1ft) high.
'**Spring Rainbow**' grows 20cm (8in) high and has several stems to each plant, bearing dense clusters of flowers from scarlet, rose, pink and orange to yellow, white and blue.

Hybrids bred from *Primula vulgaris* are smaller than polyanthus primroses, up to 15cm (6in) tall, with clusters of often stemless

Primula vulgaris

flowers. They include:
'Husky', with an abundance of lavender, pink, rose, blue, yellow and white flowers.
'Rosebud Mixed' has clusters of rose-shaped, frilled flowers, in pink, red, apricot and orange edged with gold or silver.
'Wanda Hybrids' bloom prolifically and are exceptionally cold-resistant. Strong bright colours and often bronze foliage. Available as mixtures or in single colours.

Cultivation
Sow the seeds under glass between spring and mid summer. Germination is often erratic and slow. Prick out in a cold frame or into boxes of potting compost when the seedlings are large enough to handle. Plant out in autumn, setting the plants 30cm (1ft) apart. Polyanthuses grow best in a partially shaded site in moist fertile soil.
Pests and diseases Slugs and snails sometimes eat the flowers.

PRINCE OF WALES'
FEATHERS – see *Celosia*
PRINCE'S FEATHER – see
Amaranthus
PURPLE ORACH – see *Atriplex*

Reseda
mignonette

Reseda odorata

☐ Height 30cm (1ft)
☐ Planting distance 25cm (10in)
☐ Flowers early summer to mid autumn
☐ Fertile well-drained soil
☐ Site in sun or dappled shade
☐ Hardy annual

Mignonette has always been a favourite in the garden for its unforgettable fragrance, which fills the air between early summer and mid autumn, when the flowers are out. To look at, the plants have only modest charm – the leaves resemble those of spinach, and the flower spikes consist of minute yellow-green blooms with tufted brown stamens.

Popular varieties
Several varieties have been developed from *Reseda odorata*.
'Fragrant Beauty' has particularly strongly scented lime-green and red tinged flowers on plants 30cm (1ft) high.
'Machet' has red-tinged flowers. The plants reach 30cm (1ft) high.

Cultivation
Sow the seeds in fertile well-drained soil – ideally alkaline – in full sun or dappled shade. Just cover them with soil and firm thoroughly. Thin the seedlings to 25cm (10in) apart.
For early-flowering plants, sow the seeds under glass in late winter to early spring at a temperature of 13°C (55°F). Prick out into boxes and harden off, before planting out in late spring in the flowering position.
Pests and diseases Trouble free.

Ricinus
castor oil plant

Ricinus communis

☐ Height 1.5m (5ft)
☐ Planting distance 90cm (3ft)
☐ Foliage plant
☐ Rich soil
☐ Sunny site
☐ Tender shrub grown as half-hardy annual

This tropical plant, whose seeds are used to make castor oil, is a particularly striking half-hardy annual. Robust and shrubby, it will grow 1.5m (5ft) high, and nearly as wide, in the course of a year. The leaves, up to 30cm (1ft) across, are hand-shaped. In the species, *Ricinus communis*, these are green, but varieties exist with brown, maroon or bronze-green foliage.
Castor oil plants make eye-catching specimen plants.

Cultivation
Soak the seeds in water for 24 hours to speed up germination, then sow them in individual pots under glass in late winter to early spring. Keep at a temperature of 21°C (70°F). Harden off before planting out in late spring.
Space the plants 90cm (3ft) apart in rich soil and in a sunny site. Stake in exposed sites.
Pests and diseases Trouble free.

ROCKET LARKSPUR – see
Delphinium
RUBY GRASS – see *Tricholaena*

Rudbeckia

coneflower

Rudbeckia hirta

☐ Height 45-90cm (1½-3ft)
☐ Planting distance 30-60cm (1-2ft)
☐ Flowers mid summer to late autumn
☐ Any well-drained soil
☐ Open sunny site
☐ Short-lived perennial grown as hardy annual

Rudbeckia hirta and its varieties are excellent annuals for producing colour in herbaceous borders towards the end of summer. Displaying a mass of large yellow or orange daisy-like flowers with conspicuous cone-like central discs, the plants stand 45-90cm (1½-3ft) high with oblong mid green leaves and bristly, branching stems. Some varieties will continue to flower for a few years. Excellent for cutting.

Popular varieties

'Gloriosa' has huge single flowers in shades of yellow, orange, bronze and mahogany. The plants reach 90cm (3ft) high.

'Goldilocks' bears large double and semi-double golden-yellow blooms. The plants reach 45-60cm (18-24in) high, and have a particularly long flowering season.

'Green Eyes' (75cm/2½ft) is a well-branched variety bearing golden-yellow pointed flowers, with olive-green centres.

'Marmalade' has single golden-orange flowers with black centres, and reaches 60cm (2ft) high.

'Nutmeg' grows 60-75cm (2-2½ft) tall and has double flowers ranging from clear and golden-yellow to orange-brown, often with contrasting zones of red.

'Rustic Dwarf Mixed' bears a

Rudbeckia hirta 'Rustic Dwarf Mixed'

mixture of large single flowers in shades of golden-yellow, mahogany-red and bronze.

'Sonora' is a low-growing, spreading variety, up to 38cm (15in) tall, with a profusion of large, golden-yellow flowers. These have a bronzy-brown zone around the dark centres and appear until well into autumn.

'Sputnik' ('Kelvedon Star') has large 10cm (4in) wide flowers of bright yellow petals surrounding a prominent dark brown centre. The plants grow up to 90cm (3ft) tall, and the flowers are especially long-lasting when cut.

Cultivation

Sow the seeds in pots or pans of seed compost during autumn or early to mid spring and place in a cold frame. Prick the seedlings out into boxes when they are large enough to handle. Plant out in late spring in the flowering site – an open sunny position with well-cultivated and well-drained soil. Set them 30-60cm (1-2ft) apart; tall varieties need staking in windy sites.

After the first main flowering, give the plants a liquid foliar feed to encourage more blooms. The

'Gloriosa' varieties are often perennial in habit and will flower for a couple of years if the crowns are protected with a deep winter mulch.

Pests and diseases Slugs and snails may eat the leaves and stems.

Rudbeckia hirta 'Goldilocks'

Salpiglossis

painted tongue, velvet flower

Salpiglossis sinuata 'Splash'

☐ Height 30-60cm (12-24in)
☐ Planting distance 23cm (9in)
☐ Flowers mid summer to early autumn
☐ Rich soil
☐ Open sunny site
☐ Half-hardy annual

The velvety funnel-shaped blooms of this Chilean half-hardy annual create a dramatic effect in the mixed border with their kaleidoscope of purples, reds, pinks, oranges and yellows. The flowers, many of which are veined in deeper or contrasting colours, are produced from mid summer to early autumn.

Salpiglossis sinuata, the species usually grown, and its hybrid varieties make good pot plants in the greenhouse and on the patio; they add a wealth of colour to summer borders and last well in water.

Popular varieties
Several seed selections are available, including the following:
'Bolero' is a vigorous variety bearing a mixture of richly coloured flowers.
'Casino Mixed' has strongly veined flowers in shades of red, rose, yellow, orange and purple; good for bedding.
'Festival Mixed' are bushy and compact plants, only 30cm (12in) high and bear large flowers in scarlet, crimson, pink, rose, lavender and gold.
'Splash' is a bushy strain bearing a profusion of brightly coloured flowers. It will grow in poor soil.

Cultivation
Sow the seeds under glass in late winter to early spring at a temperature of 18°C (64°F). When the seedlings are large enough to handle, prick out into boxes. Harden off before planting out in late spring 23cm (9in) apart, in rich soil and a sunny site.

The seeds can be sown directly into the flowering site in mid to late spring in mild areas.

Support the plants with twiggy sticks, and remove dead flower spikes to increase the size of blooms on the side-shoots.

Pests and diseases Aphids may infest the stems. Foot rot and root rot can cause plants to collapse.

Salvia

salvia

Salvia splendens 'Blaze of Fire'

☐ Height 38-90cm (15-36in)
☐ Planting distance 30-45cm (12-18in)
☐ Flowers mid summer to autumn
☐ Ordinary well-drained soil
☐ Sunny position
☐ Half-hardy annual

When considering salvias, many gardeners never look beyond *Salvia splendens*, the bedding plant with spikes of red flowers seen in almost every park in the country. But salvias form a large genus incorporating shrubs and perennials as well as annuals. Here, annual and tender perennial species used in bedding schemes are described. All have spikes of tubular flowers, but they come in a range of colours.

Popular species
Salvia argentea is a short-lived perennial grown as a biennial foliage plant. Reaching 60cm (2ft) high, the plant forms attractive rosettes of oval leaves covered with silky, silvery white hairs. If the white flowers flushed with purple do appear remove them to encourage healthy foliage. Plant 38-45cm (15-18in) apart in a rockery, on a wall, or as a dot plant.
Salvia farinacea, commonly known as mealy-cup sage, is a 75-90cm (30-36in) tall tender perennial, usually grown as a half-hardy annual. It bears spikes of blue flowers flushed with purple from mid summer to autumn. A waxy dusting which gives a grey-green appearance covers the stems and foliage. The variety

Salvia argentea

'Victoria' (height 45cm/18in) is widely grown, its dense spikes of violet-blue flowers looking at home in formal bedding schemes. The flowers are excellent for cutting.

Salvia horminum, an annual, has an upright branching habit and reaches 45cm (18in) high. The pale pink or purple flowers appear from mid summer to early autumn, but it is the deep purple bracts around the flowers that give this species its decorative appeal. 'Colour Blend', offering a mixture of pink, violet-blue and white coloured bracts, and 'Claryssa Pink' – a pink-flowered variety – are also available. The flower spikes can be dried as everlastings.

Salvia patens, another perennial species grown as an annual, is distinguished by its striking clear gentian-blue flowers which appear from late summer to early autumn. These are widely spaced on 60cm (2ft) high slender stems. The upright well-branched plants bear mid-green oval leaves.

Salvia splendens, otherwise called scarlet sage, has spikes of brilliant red flowers between mid summer and autumn, accompanied by rich green foliage. Reaching just 38cm (15in) high, this species and its varieties are some of the most popular annuals for formal bedding schemes. Though the red-flowered varieties are most commonly seen, cultivars with blooms in shades of pink and purple are also available. 'Blaze of Fire' is an early-flowering variety with vivid scarlet flowers; 'Laser Purple'

Salvia horminum

Salvia horminum 'Claryssa Pink'

Salvia patens

has rich deep purple flowers; 'Phoenix Mixed', up to 25cm (10in) tall, has scarlet, purple, white, deep or pale pink and lilac flowers; 'Rambo' is especially vigorous, growing to 60cm (2ft) high, with vivid scarlet flower spikes and deep green foliage; 'Tom Thumb' is a dwarf variety, just 15-20cm (6-8in) high, with shining scarlet flowers.

Cultivation

Sow the seeds in pots or pans of seed compost in late winter and early spring at a temperature of 18°C (64°F). Prick out the seedlings into boxes when they are large enough to handle and harden off before planting out in late spring. Set the plants about 30cm (1ft) apart.

Salvia argentea may be difficult to grow from seed. Buy the plants from a garden centre and set out in late spring.

Grow all salvias in ordinary well-drained garden soil in a sunny position.

When the plants are 5-7.5cm (2-3in) high, pinch out the growing tips to encourage branching and bushy growth.

Pests and diseases Trouble free.

Scabiosa

sweet scabious

Scabiosa atropurpurea

□ Height 45-90cm (18-36in)
□ Planting distance 23cm (9in)
□ Flowers mid summer to early autumn
□ Fertile well-drained soil
□ Open sunny site
□ Hardy annual

The sweet scabious (*Scabiosa atropurpurea*) is an airy graceful plant. Its closely packed fragrant flowers (in shades of blue, mauve, purple, red, pink and white) are carried on slender stems 90cm (3ft) tall. Its foliage is elegantly divided. The plant is ideal both for cutting and for a border.

Popular varieties

Several popular varieties have been developed from *Scabiosa atropurpurea*.

'Blue Moon' has lavender-blue flowers, excellent for cutting. Left, the flowers fade to attractive papery blue-eyed seed heads.

'Dwarf Double Mixed' is a short variety reaching just 45cm (18in) high, but it carries large fragrant flowers in mixed colours.

'Stellata' is a 75cm (30in) high plant with silvery blue flowers which develop into attractive large round seed heads with a greenish, spiny, star-like centre. These are excellent for dried flower arrangements.

Cultivation

Sow the seeds in the flowering site in early autumn or early to mid spring. They grow in any fertile well-drained soil in an open sunny site. Protect autumn-sown seedlings with cloches over winter. Thin out all the seedlings in spring to 23cm (9in) apart.

Stake tall varieties in windy situations. To encourage further flowering, cut the stems at the first joint as blooms fade.

Pests and diseases Slugs and snails often damage young plants. Root rot may cause the plants to collapse and powdery mildew may appear on the leaves.

SCARLET PIMPERNEL – see *Anagallis*
SCARLET SAGE – see *Salvia*

Schizanthus

poor man's orchid, butterfly flower

Schizanthus pinnatus 'Dwarf Bouquet Mixed'

☐ Height 30-45cm (12-18in)
☐ Planting distance 30cm (1ft)
☐ Flowers early summer to early autumn
☐ Fertile moisture-retentive soil
☐ Sheltered sunny site
☐ Half-hardy annual

This Chilean annual has orchid-like blooms in shades of pink, red and purple blotched with yellow. Each has a pale throat veined with a darker colour. The flowers appear between early summer and early autumn and are given a perfect setting by the exquisite pale green, almost fern-like foliage. They are good for cutting.

Schizanthus pinnatus and its varieties are usually grown as indoor pot plants, but several dwarf varieties have been developed for growing outdoors as bedding plants in a warm sheltered spot.

Popular varieties

The following seed selections are readily available.

'Butterfly Mixture' grows to 45cm (18in) high and bears dainty flowers in pink, carmine, purple, crimson and white.

'Disco' has neat compact plants 30cm (1ft) high covered with a profusion of flowers in mixed colours.

'Dwarf Bouquet Mixed' has 30-38cm (12-15in) high plants smothered in red, pink, amber and salmon blooms.

Cultivation

Sow the seeds under glass in early spring, just covering them with compost. Keep at a temperature of 16°C (61°F) until they germinate. Prick out into boxes and harden off before planting out in late spring 30cm (1ft) apart.

Poor man's orchid grows best in fertile moisture-retentive soil in a sunny sheltered site.

Pests and diseases Aphids may infest young plants.

SCOTCH THISTLE – see *Onopordum*
SEA LAVENDER – see *Limonium*

Senecio

silver-leaved cineraria

Senecio maritimus 'Silver Dust'

☐ Height 23-45cm (9-18in)
☐ Planting distance 30cm (1ft)
☐ Foliage plant
☐ Dry to well-drained soil
☐ Sunny site
☐ Half-hardy shrub grown as annual

Arching sprays of intricately dissected, white felted leaves make *Senecio maritimus* (syn. *S. bicolor*) an excellent foliage plant for summer bedding schemes.

Silver-leaved cineraria is evergreen, near-hardy in many regions and will survive most winters, but it is usually treated as an annual bedding plant since the lustrous foliage becomes coarse in subsequent years. Clusters of groundsel-like yellow flowers appear during summer but are best removed as they are less attractive than the silvery leaves.

Popular varieties

Varieties developed from the species offer different leaf forms.

'Cirrhus' has bright silver, rounded leaves.

'Dwarf Silver' is only 23cm (9in) tall and suitable for window-boxes; the bright silver foliage is deeply cut and fringed.

'Silver Dust' forms a mound of silvery fern-like foliage.

Cultivation

Sow the seeds in pans or boxes in late winter to early spring, at a temperature of 16°C (61°F). Prick out the seedlings into pots or boxes and harden off before planting out in late spring. Set the plants 30cm (1ft) apart in good soil in sun.

Pests and diseases Birds may attack the leaves and powdery mildew can be a problem.

SHELLFLOWER – see *Molucella*
SHOO-FLY – see *Nicandra*

Silene

campion, catchfly

Silene coeli-rosa 'Red Angel'

Silene pendula

□ Height 15-45cm (6-18in)
□ Planting distance 15cm (6in)
□ Flowers late spring to early autumn
□ Any well-drained soil
□ Sunny or lightly shaded site
□ Hardy annual

Campion and its many varieties are easily grown, hardy annuals valued for their prolific flowering through summer. The slender stems carry delicate, five-petalled, cup-shaped flowers in attractive shades of blue, lilac, pink and white, with contrasting centres. They are suitable as cut flowers.

Their fragile appearance belies their robust growth habit, and they are seen to best advantage in large swathes in cottage-garden beds and borders; the dwarf species and varieties are ideal for rock gardens and as edging.

Popular species

Silene coeli-rosa (syn. *Viscaria elegans*) grows 45cm (18in) tall, its slender stems set with oblong, grey-green leaves and topped with white-eyed rose-purple flowers in succession from early to late summer. Several varieties are popular, including the 'Angel' series (height 25cm/10in), available in blue, rose-cerise or as a mixture. 'Brilliant Mixture' (38cm/25in) produces flowers in bright shades of pink, red, blue and white, all with a dark centre. 'Fire King' (25-38cm/10-15in) is vivid red; 'Royal Collection' (38cm/15in) bears large flowers in a range of bold colours; and 'Treasure Island Mixed' (30-45cm/12-18in) comes in soft shades of blue, purple, pink, crimson, and white.

Silene pendula is rather different, growing only 15-23cm (6-9in) high. It is the most widely grown of the annual species, forming compact plants ideal for edging. The erect stems bear loose clusters of pale pink flowers above mounds of pointed, mid green and hairy leaves. Popular varieties include 'Dwarf Mixed' (23cm/9in) with flowers in white or shades of pink. 'Peach Blossom' (15cm/6in) is of branching and cascading habit and suitable for hanging baskets, its stems are covered with a profusion of double flowers that open from deep pink buds to become salmon pink and when mature turn near white.

Cultivation

Sow the seeds in the flowering site in early to mid spring and thin the seedlings to their required spacings. Seeds of *Silene pendula* and its varieties can also be sown outdoors in early autumn, for flowering in late spring, and given cloche protection during winter.

All campions will grow in ordinary garden soil provided it is well-drained; they tolerate light shade but perform best in an open and sunny position.

Pests and diseases Trouble free.

Silybum

blessed thistle, Our Lady's milk thistle

Silybum marianum

☐ Height 1.2m (4ft)
☐ Planting distance 60cm (2ft)
☐ Flowers mid summer to early autumn
☐ Any garden soil
☐ Open sunny site
☐ Hardy annual

The fast-growing *Silybum marianum* is chiefly cultivated for its striking foliage of ovate, glossy dark green and spiny leaves heavily marbled with white veins. They are carried in flat, wide-spreading rosettes topped from mid summer onwards with tall stems carrying deep violet-red thistle-like flowers.

Cultivation

Sow seeds in the flowering site in early spring or early autumn, just covering them with soil. Thin the seedlings to 60cm (2ft) apart. Any soil is suitable, at the back of a border or in a semi-wild garden in full sun.

Pests and diseases Trouble free.

SLIPPER FLOWER – see
Calceolaria
SNAPDRAGON – see
Antirrhinum
SNOW-ON-THE-MOUNTAIN –
see *Euphorbia*
SPIDER FLOWER – see *Cleome*
STATICE – see *Limonium*
STRAW FLOWER – see
Helichrysum
SUNFLOWER – see *Helianthus*
SWEET PEA – see *Lathyrus*
SWEET SULTAN – see
Centaurea
SWEET WILLIAM – see
Dianthus

Tagetes

marigold

Tagetes patula 'Tiger Eyes'

☐ Height 15-75cm (6-30in)
☐ Planting distance 30-45cm (12-18in)
☐ Flowers mid summer to autumn
☐ Ordinary garden soil
☐ Open sunny site
☐ Half-hardy annual

French and African marigolds are without doubt two of the most popular sources of orange and yellow colour in summer bedding schemes. And they are also among the easiest to cultivate.

The flowers are single, semi-double or double and come in every shade of orange, yellow and mahogany-red. They are excellent for cutting as well as for garden decoration. When crushed, the deeply cut green leaves give off a pungent smell.

Popular varieties

Three species and their varieties are generally available.

Tagetes erecta, African marigold, has given rise to numerous varieties, many of which are F1 hybrids of uniform vigour and flower size. Popular tall types (60-75cm/2-2½ft) with double flowers up to 15cm (6in) across, include 'Crackerjack Mixed' (orange, gold and lemon); 'Doubloon' (primrose-yellow); and the 'Jubilee' series (a

Tagetes patula 'Honeycomb'

Tagetes patula 'Mischief Gold'

Tagetes erecta 'Inca Gold'

mixture of yellow, orange and gold). Dwarf, double-flowered varieties (25-45cm/10-18in) include the 'Inca' series (mixed or single colours of gold, bright yellow and deep orange); and 'Sunspot Mixed' (yellow, gold and orange, frilled petals).

Afro-French varieties are hybrids between African and French marigolds. They grow 30cm (12in) high and bear a profusion of frilled, double blooms. Popular types include 'Caribbean Parade' (lemon-yellow to deep orange, often bicoloured); and 'Seven Star Red' (mahogany-red).

Tagetes patula, the French marigold, is a dwarf plant and excellent for edging and window-boxes. The numerous varieties range in height from 15cm (6in) to 25-30cm (10-12in). The majority bear double or crested flowers, and dainty, single-flowered types are also available. Double-flowered varieties include the 'Boy O'Boy' series (mixtures or single colours of yellow, gold, orange and mahogany-red); 'Goldfinch' (golden-yellow, crested); 'Goldie' (golden-yellow, red-blotched); 'Honeycomb' (red and yellow, crested); 'Queen Bee' (interlaced red and yellow); 'Royal Crested' (mixed colours, crested); and 'Tiger Eyes' (red and deep orange, crested).

Single-flowered French marigolds include 'Naughty Marietta'

(golden-yellow, maroon blotches); 'Fantasia' (clear lemon, orange and combinations of red and yellow); and the 'Mischief' series (available as a mixture or in yellow, gold, mahogany and red and gold).

Tagetes tenuifolia pumila, the signet marigold, is a more delicate plant with slender growth and finely divided, light green, sweet-smelling leaves. Its yellow flowers are much smaller than those of the other marigolds. Varieties include 'Lemon Gem' (pale yellow) and 'Golden Gem' (golden-yellow).

Cultivation

Sow the seeds under glass in early to mid spring, just covering them with compost and keep at a temperature of 18°C (64°F). When the seedlings are large enough to handle, prick out into boxes and harden off before planting out in late spring to early summer. Most varieties should be set 30cm (1ft) apart, the taller African marigolds 45cm (18in) apart.

Marigolds grow in any garden soil – even poor dry conditions – though a moderately rich soil is ideal. Give them an open sunny site, and dead-head regularly.

Pests and diseases Foot rot may make the plants collapse and grey mould can rot the flower heads. Slugs and snails eat the plants.

TIDY TIPS – see *Layia*

Tagetes tenuifolia pumila 'Golden Gem'

Torenia

wishbone flower

Torenia fournieri

- ☐ Height 10-30cm (4-12in)
- ☐ Planting distance 15-23cm (6-9in)
- ☐ Flowers mid summer to early autumn
- ☐ Moist garden soil
- ☐ Partial shade
- ☐ Half-hardy annual

The wishbone flower (*Torenia fournieri*) takes its common name from the shape of the stamens in the throat of the trumpet-shaped flowers. These are borne in such profusion throughout summer as to almost hide the pointed and finely toothed, pale green leaves. The flowers are bicoloured, with violet-purple lips and throats of lilac-purple with yellow splashes.

The wishbone flower is valued by gardeners for its exotic blooms and for its preference for shade. It is suitable for bedding schemes and also makes a fine pot plant.

A few seed varieties are available, including the small 'Pink Panda' which grows 10-20cm (4-8in) high; the flowers are a blend of white and cerise-pink.

Cultivation

Sow the seeds in early spring in pans of compost at a temperature of 18°C (64°F), just covering them. When the seedlings are large enough to handle, prick them off singly into small pots; harden them off in a cold frame before planting out in early summer.

Wishbone flowers thrive in any good, moist soil and need a sheltered and shaded site. Pinch out the growing tips on the young plants to encourage bushy growth.

Pests and diseases Trouble free.

Trachymene

blue lace flower

Trachymene caerulea

- ☐ Height 45cm (18in)
- ☐ Planting distance 23cm (9in)
- ☐ Flowers mid to late summer
- ☐ Any good garden soil
- ☐ Sheltered sunny site
- ☐ Half-hardy annual

The modest lavender-blue flowers of *Trachymene caerulea* (syn. *Didiscus caeruleus*), the blue lace flower, make a welcome change from the strong, startling colours characteristic of so many annuals and biennials. Composed of dainty florets arranged in small round umbels, they resemble the cushions of the annual scabious. They have a slight scent and appear from mid to late summer.

The flowers are carried on 45cm (18in) high bushy plants with light green deeply divided leaves sticky to the touch.

Blue lace flowers look best grown in groups among other annuals in a sunny border. Their long, stiff stems make them good for cutting.

Cultivation

Sow the seeds under glass in early spring and keep at a temperature of 15°C (59°F). As soon as the seedlings are large enough to handle, prick them out into 7.5cm (3in) pots or seed boxes. Harden off in a cold frame, before planting out in late spring.

Blue lace flowers grow in any good garden soil in a sheltered sunny position. The plants may need the support of twiggy sticks.

Pests and diseases Trouble free.

Tricholaena

Natal grass, ruby grass

Tricholaena rosea

- ☐ Height 75cm (2½ft)
- ☐ Planting distance 30cm (1ft)
- ☐ Flowers early to late summer
- ☐ Well-drained fertile soil
- ☐ Open sunny position
- ☐ Tender perennial grown as half-hardy annual

Tricholaena rosea is an ornamental grass grown for its attractive flower heads which appear from early to late summer. Slender and graceful, these 25cm (10in) long reddish-maroon fluffy spikelets fade to a silvery-pink colour with age.

This is a clump-forming species reaching 75cm (2½ft) high, excellent for growing at the front of a border or in an isolated patch on its own. A sunny open position is essential for it to thrive.

Cultivation

Sow the seeds in late winter or early spring in trays of seed compost. Keep at a temperature of 13-16°C (55-61°F). Harden off before transplanting the seedlings to the flowering site in late spring or early summer, when the danger of frost has passed.

Alternatively, sow the seeds in the flowering site in late spring; thin the seedlings to stand 30cm (1ft) apart.

Natal grass should be grown in fertile well-drained soil in an open sunny position.

Pests and diseases Trouble free.

Tropaeolum

nasturtium

Tropaeolum majus 'Alaska Mixed'

Tropaeolum majus 'Climbing Mixed'

☐ Height 23cm-3.6m (9in-12ft)
☐ Planting distance 38cm (15in)
☐ Flowers early summer to early autumn
☐ Poor soil
☐ Sunny site
☐ Hardy annual

The spurred, lightly perfumed orange and yellow flowers, trailing stems and round, smooth, green leaves of this hardy annual are one of the most familiar summer sights in gardens. The blooms appear from early summer until early autumn and grow on compact, trailing or climbing plants according to variety.

Nasturtiums can be grown in containers and hanging baskets, in bedding schemes or the fronts of borders, and they can be trained up a wall or trellis. However, blackflies find the smooth green leaves irresistible, and will destroy the plants if they are not controlled.

Popular varieties

Most garden varieties have been developed from *Tropaeolum majus* and include the following.

COMPACT VARIETIES

These have a compact bushy habit and reach 23cm (9in) high.

'Alaska Mixed' has single red and orange flowers. The pale green leaves are marbled with cream.

'Empress of India' has deep crimson-scarlet flowers and dark green leaves.

'Tom Thumb Mixed' has single flowers in shades of red, orange and yellow.

'Whirlybird Mixed' has a mass of semi-double blooms in mixed colours. These are held well above the foliage and face upwards. Single colours – scarlet, mahogany, cherry, tangerine, orange, gold and cream – are also available.

SEMI-TRAILING VARIETIES

These have a trailing habit and reach 30-38cm (12-15in) high.

'Double Gleam Mixed' has fragrant double and semi-double flowers in golden-yellow, orange and scarlet.

'Jewel Mixed' is an early-flowering mixture with semi-double blooms in mixed colours.

CLIMBING VARIETIES reach 1.8m (6ft) or more high and are suitable for training up trellis and walls.

'Climbing Mixed' is a free-flowering variety with single flowers in crimson, orange, yellow, cream and bicolours.

Tropaeolum peregrinum is a short-lived perennial species usually grown as an annual. Rapidly reaching 3.6m (12ft) high in one season, it bears irregularly shaped yellow flowers with green spurs from mid summer to mid autumn among blue-green leaves. It will tolerate shade.

Cultivation

Sow the seeds 2cm (¾in) deep in poor soil in a sunny site. Thin to 38cm (15in) apart. With *Tropaeolum peregrinum* sow two seeds where one plant is required and if both germinate remove one. This species requires ordinary garden soil.

To cultivate plants for hanging baskets, sow the seeds in late winter to early spring in pots or pans of seed compost at a temperature of 13-16°C (55-61°F). When the seedlings are large enough to handle, pot them singly in 7.5cm (3in) pots of compost and pot on as required. Harden off and plant out in early summer.

Pests and diseases Blackfly may infest leaves and stems and virus diseases may affect leaves.

TWINSPUR – see *Diascia*

Tropaeolum majus 'Whirlybird'

Tropaeolum peregrinum

Tropaeolum majus 'Empress of India'

Ursinia

ursinia

Ursinia anethoides

☐ Height 45cm (18in)
☐ Planting distance 25-30cm (10-12in)
☐ Flowers early summer to early autumn
☐ Light, poor soil
☐ Open sunny site
☐ Tender perennial treated as half-hardy annual

This South African daisy-like annual is a particularly bright and graceful plant. The pale green finely dissected foliage forms a misty green mass, above which brilliant orange-yellow, purple-centred flowers are borne. The floral display extends from early summer to early autumn. When each flower fades, the protective sepals around it become white.

Ursinias look best grown in mixed borders, in bedding schemes or in containers. They thrive in coastal gardens. The variety 'Solar Fire' (height 30cm/12in) has bright orange flowers.

Cultivation

Sow the seeds under glass in early spring at a temperature of 15°C (59°F), just covering them with compost. Prick out the seedlings into boxes. Harden off before planting out in late spring 25-30cm (10-12in) apart.

For the best results, grow in light, even poor soil in an open sunny site. The plants may need support with twiggy sticks.

Pests and diseases Trouble free.

VELVET FLOWER – see *Salpiglossis*

Venidium

monarch of the veldt

Venidium fastuosum

☐ Height 60cm (2ft)
☐ Planting distance 30cm (1ft)
☐ Flowers early summer to early autumn
☐ Well-drained fertile soil
☐ Sunny site
☐ Half-hardy annual

Monarch of the veldt (*Venidium fastuosum*), a half-hardy annual from South Africa, deserves more attention from gardeners. Its large sunflower-like blooms are particularly striking – rich orange with a black central disc – and are attractively set off by silver-white, deeply lobed woolly leaves. The variety 'Zulu Prince' has creamy-white flowers with a black central zone.

Appearing between early summer and mid autumn, they look best planted in bold drifts in borders and beds. They are long-lasting as cut flowers.

Cultivation

In early to mid spring, sow the seeds under glass at a temperature of 16°C (61°F), just covering them with compost. Prick out the seedlings into boxes or pots and harden off before planting outdoors in late spring, 30cm (1ft) apart.

For late-flowering plants, sow the seeds directly in the flowering site in late spring, later thinning the seedlings.

Monarch of the veldt grows reasonably well in most soils, though well-drained soil enriched with organic matter is ideal. The site must be sunny. Usually the plants need staking.

Pests and diseases Trouble free.

Verbascum

mullein

Verbascum phlomoides

Verbascum bombyciferum

☐ Height 90cm-1.8m (3-6ft)
☐ Planting distance 30-60cm (1-2ft)
☐ Flowers late spring to early autumn
☐ Ordinary well-drained soil
☐ Sunny site
☐ Hardy biennial

Mulleins are stately plants, excellent for growing at the backs of borders, in groups in island beds or in wild gardens. The spikes of yellow flowers are carried 90cm-1.8m (3-6ft) high above rosettes of white-felted leaves, and appear between late spring and early autumn.

Popular species

Verbascum bombyciferum has silvery branching stems covered with sulphur-yellow flowers between early to mid summer. It reaches 1.2-1.8m (4-6ft) high and the plants should be grown 45-60cm (18-24in) apart. 'Silver Lining' has pale yellow flowers.

Verbascum phlomoides has spikes of clustered creamy-white flowers between late spring and early autumn and oblong, grey woolly leaves. This 1.8m (6ft) high species is most suitable for wild gardens where, left alone, it self-seeds easily. Plant 45cm (18in) apart.

Verbascum phoeniceum bears spikes of flowers in shades of white, pink and purple from late spring to early autumn. Its dark green leaves are arranged in a rosette around the base of the plant. Reaching 1.05-1.35m (3½-4½ft) high, this species is usually grown as an annual and planted 38-45cm (15-18in) apart. A hybrid strain, 'Choice Mixed' grows only 60cm (2ft) high and bears white, pink, salmon, mauve and blue flowers.

Verbascum thapsus, a native of Britain, has spikes of yellow flowers from early to late summer and toothed leaves covered with white woolly hairs. It reaches 90cm (3ft) high and should be planted 30cm (1ft) apart, ideally in a wild garden.

Cultivation

Sow the seeds of biennial species in mid spring in pans of seed compost and place in a cold frame. Prick out the seedlings and plant them 15cm (6in) apart in nursery rows outdoors, finally moving the plants to their flowering site in early autumn.

Verbascum phoeniceum can be grown as an annual. Sow the seeds under glass in late winter to early spring at a temperature of 13°C (55°F). Prick out the seedlings into boxes and harden off before planting out in mid spring 38-45cm (15-18in) apart.

Grow mulleins in ordinary well-drained soil in full sun. Stake in exposed positions.

Pests and diseases Trouble free.

Verbena

verbena

Verbena × hybrida 'Dwarf Jewels'

☐ Height 15-30cm (6-12in)
☐ Planting distance 25-38cm (10-15in)
☐ Flowers early summer to first autumn frost
☐ Fertile well-drained soil
☐ Open sunny site
☐ Hardy annual

The many varieties of *Verbena × hybrida* are beautiful plants that, throughout the summer, produce tight clusters of small pale-eyed primrose-like flowers in scarlet, crimson, purple, lavender-pink and white. Providing a foil for these gay colours are attractively toothed, dark green leaves.

The bushy plants are popular for summer bedding and borders, and the dwarf varieties are ideal for containers, edging and for window-boxes.

Popular varieties
The following are readily available as seed strains.
'Amethyst' has cobalt-blue flowers with a white eye and reaches 23-30cm (9-12in) high.
'Blaze' is a compact variety reaching 23cm (9in) high with scarlet flowers.
'Blue Lagoon' has true blue flowers without an eye; it grows 23cm (9in) high.
'Delight' has coral-pink flowers flushed with salmon. It is a small variety, just 15cm (6in) high.
'Dwarf Jewels' is a mixture of dwarf varieties 25-30cm (10-12in) high bearing red, purple, lavender-pink and white flowers.
'Imagination' bears deep violet-blue flowers and grows 30cm (12in) tall.
'Peaches and Cream' is only 20cm (8in) high but smothered with a mass of blooms in pastel shades of coral, salmon and cream.
'Showtime' comes in a range of brilliant colours, some with bold central eyes. They grow to 25cm (10in) high.
'Sissinghurst' is 25-30cm (10-12in) high with pretty rose-pink flowers.

Cultivation
Sow the seeds under glass in late winter, just covering them with compost and keep at 18-21°C (64-70°F). Prick out the seedlings into boxes and harden off before planting out in late spring.

Grow verbenas in any light, fertile soil in a sunny open border. Pinch out the tips of young plants to encourage bushy growth. Deadhead to prolong the flowering season.

Pests and diseases Trouble free.

Verbena × hybrida 'Sissinghurst'

Viola

pansy

Viola × *wittrockiana* 'Arkwright Ruby'

☐ Height 15-23cm (6-9in)
☐ Planting distance 25cm (10in)
☐ Flowers throughout the year
☐ Fertile moist soil
☐ Sunny or partially shaded site
☐ Hardy biennial

Annual pansies (*Viola* × *wittrock-iana*) are among the best loved garden plants with their enchanting flowers and diverse colours. Given a lightly shaded position and moist soil, each plant will quickly form a well-spread tuft of colour.

It is quite possible to have pansies in the garden for most of the year. From late spring to early autumn there are the summer-flowering varieties, while winter-flowering ones start to bloom in autumn and, in mild winters, will continue until the spring.

Pansies make enchanting ground cover plants or informal edgings for roses and other shrubs. They can also be used to provide splashes of colour in spaces among border perennials or to fill containers and window-boxes. The small-flowered varieties look most effective in rock gardens.

Popular varieties
Numerous varieties and seed selections are available, in mixtures or as separate colours. Unless stated, they are spring/summer flowering.

'**Arkwright Ruby**' has rich red-brown flowers.

'**Azure Blue**' has flowers in shades of cool blue.

'**Bambini**' has small flowers in pale pink, apricot, yellow, blue, copper, bronze and red, all with whiskered faces.

'**Chalon Giants**' come in deep shades of blue, mahogany-red and yellow with dark blotches. Their petals are waved and frilled.

'**Clear Crystal Mixed**' is a mixture of gold, red, orange, violet and white flowers without any patterns on them.

'**Crimson Queen**' has velvety red flowers with dark blotches.

'**Early Flowering Mixed**' is a winter-flowering selection. The flowers come in shades of red, bronze, yellow and violet-blue; some are plain, others have blotches or whiskered markings.

'**Majestic Giants**' has large red,

Viola × *wittrockiana* 'Rippling Waters'

yellow and blue flowers with dark central blotches.

'**Paper White**' has white flowers with a yellow eye.

'**Queen of Planets**' has very large flowers in rich, bright yellow, violet, red and maroon.

'**Rippling Waters**' has deep purple-blue flowers with a broad cream-white edging.

'**Roggli Giants**' has large velvety flowers in mixed colours: blues, reds, violets, and yellows.

'**Ullswater Blue**' has gentian

Viola × wittrockiana 'Early Flowering'

Viola tricolor

blue flowers with darker blotches. **'Universal Mixed'** is a winter and summer-flowering selection in a range of clear and blotched colours (single colours available). *Viola tricolor* (heartsease or wild pansy) has very small bicoloured flowers in cream, yellow, purple-red or blue-black.

Cultivation
Pansies give of their best when grown as biennials. Sow the seeds in an outdoor nursery bed in mid to late summer and thin to 12cm (4in) apart. Transplant to the flowering site in autumn. The soil should be fertile and moist but well-drained, and the site should be in sun or partial shade. Dead-head regularly.
Pests and diseases Pansy sickness causes plants to collapse.

VIPER'S BUGLOSS – see *Echium*
VIRGINIA STOCK – see
Malcolmia
WALLFLOWER – see
Cheiranthus
WISHBONE FLOWER – see
Torenia
WOODRUFF – see *Asperula*

Viola × wittrockiana 'Crimson Queen'

Viola × *wittrockiana* 'Paper White'

Viola tricolor

Viola 'Bambini'

Xeranthemum

common immortelle

Xeranthemum annuum

☐ Height 60cm (2ft)
☐ Planting distance 45cm (18in)
☐ Flowers mid summer to early autumn
☐ Light well-drained garden soil
☐ Sunny site
☐ Hardy annual

Common immortelle (*Xeranthemum annuum*) is an attractive daisy-like annual, grown for its everlasting flowers – the petals keep their colour for a long time after drying, making the flowers excellent for winter decoration. Coming in a range of pinks, lilacs, purples and white, the dainty single or double blooms appear between mid summer and early autumn, 60cm (2ft) above ground on wiry stems. They are accompanied by small narrow silver leaves.

'Double Mixed', the variety usually sold, has white, purple, lilac and rose flowers.

Cultivation

Sow the seeds in the flowering position in early spring – any well-drained, even poor soil is ideal. The site must be sunny. Thin to 45cm (18in) apart.

For indoor decoration, cut the flowers before they are fully open. Tie them in bunches and hang upside down in a cool dry place.

Pests and diseases Trouble free.

Zea

ornamental sweetcorn

Zea mays 'Gracillima Variegata'

☐ Height 90cm-1.5m (3-5ft)
☐ Planting distance 45cm (18in)
☐ Flowers early to mid summer
☐ Rich soil
☐ Open sunny site
☐ Half-hardy annual

Several varieties of sweetcorn (*Zea mays*) have variegated foliage or coloured cobs, which make them suitable for garden decoration. Grow them as dot plants in summer bedding schemes or use them to fill gaps in mixed and herbaceous borders.

They are tall plants, reaching up to 1.5m (5ft) high, so they will have considerable impact wherever you plant them – ideally in an open sunny site, but protected from strong winds.

The cobs appear between early and mid summer, but before and after the leaves make an attractive display.

Popular varieties

The following varieties are grown for garden decoration.

'**Gigantea Quadricolor**' is a robust 1.5m (5ft) high variety with leaves variegated with white, pale yellow and pink.

'**Gracillima Variegata**' is a dwarf variety 90cm (3ft) high with slender white-striped leaves.

'**Japonica**' reaches 1.2-1.5m (4-5ft) high and has green leaves with white stripes.

'**Rainbow**', 1.5m (5ft) high, has green leaves and coloured cobs composed of yellow, red, orange and purple-blue seeds. When ripe, and dried, the cobs can be used for winter decoration.

'**Strawberry Corn**' is a green-leaved variety reaching 1.5m (5ft) high with strawberry-shaped maroon cobs.

Cultivation

Sow the seeds under glass in mid spring, setting them singly 1cm (½in) deep in 7.5cm (3in) pots of seed compost. Keep at a temperature of 16-18°C (61-64°F). When the seedlings are 12-15cm (5-6in) high, harden off and plant out 45cm (18in) apart. This should be done in late spring.

Alternatively, sow the seeds in the open in late spring. Sow the seeds in groups of three, 1cm (½in) deep and 45cm (18in) apart, later removing two plants from each group to leave the strongest.

An open sunny site, protected from strong winds, is essential for ornamental sweetcorn. Ideally the soil should have been enriched with well-rotted manure.

Pests and diseases Birds may damage the cobs.

Zinnia

youth and old age

Zinnia elegans 'Early Wonder Mixed'

☐ Height 15-75cm (6-30in)
☐ Planting distance 15-30cm (6-12in)
☐ Flowers mid summer to early autumn
☐ Fertile well-drained soil
☐ Sunny site
☐ Half-hardy annual

The species name, *elegans*, has become increasingly inappropriate for this Mexican half-hardy annual as breeders produce ever-larger flowers on ever-smaller plants. However, in compensation, there is now a wide range of flower colours: white, cream, yellow, orange, scarlet, crimson, purple and even green.

The flowers of almost all the varieties are fully double and resemble solid, drier-petalled ball dahlias. They appear from mid summer to early autumn and last well as cut flowers.

Popular varieties

Varieties developed from *Zinnia elegans* offer tall or dwarf plants.
TALL VARIETIES reach 60-75cm (2-2½ft) high and are suitable for bedding or cutting.
'Early Wonder Mixed' is an early-flowering variety offering all the typical zinnia colours.
'Envy' has chartreuse green blooms, which make it popular among flower arrangers.
'Peppermint Sticks' is a dahlia-flowered strain with flowers striped or streaked with contrasting colours.

'State Fair' is a vigorous variety with salmon, orange, lavender, purple, rose, scarlet and yellow flowers.
DWARF VARIETIES are 30-45cm (12-18in) high and are good as edging plants or for bedding and pots.
'Fairyland' is a compact variety bearing a profusion of small flowers in red, orange, yellow, pink, purple, cream and gold.
'Persian Carpet' has miniature double flowers in yellow, orange, mahogany-red, maroon, chocolate and cream.
'Thumbelina' grows as small, 15cm (6in) high plants with double and semi-double flowers in mixed colours.

Cultivation

Sow the seeds under glass at a temperature of 21°C (70°F), setting the seeds singly in 7.5cm (3in) whalehide pots, as zinnias dislike root disturbance. Harden off and plant out when danger of frost has passed in late spring, setting tall-flowered varieties 30cm (1ft) apart and dwarf varieties 15cm (6in) apart. Grow them in fertile well-drained soil in full sun.

You can sow seeds directly in the flowering site in late spring.
Pests and diseases Viruses may cause mottling of the leaves.

Zinnia elegans 'State Fair'

Early bulbs Dainty snowdrops and brilliant early crocuses announce the end of winter.

A-Z of bulbs and corms

Bulbs, corms, tubers and rhizomes are perennial plants in which the lower part of the stem has evolved into an underground food store. Compared to other perennials, bulbs are cheap to buy, easy to grow and, apart from such notable exceptions as dahlias, demand little attention after planting.

There are bulbs for every garden, whatever its size and soil type, and for every situation. Bulbs can be grown in formal beds or naturalized in grass, in pockets in the rock garden or gaps in herbaceous borders; they can be grown in raised beds, in pots, tubs and window-boxes, as well as providing blooms for cut flowers.

Bulbs bloom throughout the year – snowdrops, aconites and tiny irises in winter, followed by swathes of cheerful crocuses, golden daffodils and narcissi, muscaris, hyacinths and tulips in almost every colour. Late spring welcomes fritillaries and bluebells, lily-of-the-valley, irises and alliums, and with summer come the glorious lilies, crocosmias and gladioli. Finally it is the turn of dahlias, colchicums and other autumn crocuses, sternbergias and the exotic nerines.

Many bulbs die down and disappear underground after flowering; others leave a mess of untidy leaves. Don't be tempted to remove the foliage until it has withered – it needs exposure to sun and air to replenish the bulbs for the following year. Half-hardy types, such as gladioli, dahlias and begonias, must be lifted before the first frost, dried off and kept in frost-free storage for next year's colourful display.

SEASONAL BULBS

Coming in all colours, sizes and shapes, the flowers of bulbs provide year-round impact in the garden.

Bulbous plants deserve to be popular. Their flowers have some of the most beautiful and striking colours to be found in the garden, and they offer an enormous variety of shapes. They range in height from miniatures, such as crocuses, for the rockery to lilies up to 3m (10ft) tall which should be planted at the back of a border. There are bulbs, corms or tubers in flower at any time of the year, and forms suitable for almost any garden situation.

Such diversity provides plenty of scope for associations of bulbs on their own or partnered with trees, shrubs and other plants.

Spring is the time for crocuses, anemones, narcissi, and scillas which are often planted in informal groupings, while tulips and hyacinths can be bedded out in more formal displays, or grown in containers and window-boxes.

In summer use bulbous plants in mixed borders. The tall summer hyacinth (*Galtonia candicans*) with dangling bell-like flowers on 1.2m (4ft) stems in mid and late summer would look pretty against a background of the pink and grey-green leaves of *Fuchsia magellanica* 'Versicolor'. Complete the grouping with the silver-grey foliage and magenta blooms of rose campion (*Lychnis coronaria*) set in front.

In autumn the elegant pink blooms of *Nerine bowdenii* look even more beautiful when fronted by the pale blue of *Lobelia erinus* 'Cambridge Blue'. This partnership can be extended with clumps of lily turf (*Liriope muscari*) which has grassy leaves and spikes of violet blooms reminiscent of grape hyacinths. At the same time of year, the white goblets of *Colchicum autumnale* 'Album' make a fine contrast for the autumn-tinted leaves of deciduous shrubs.

In semi-woodland, enliven the dull days of mid and late winter with snowdrops, *Cyclamen coum* and winter aconite (*Eranthis hyemalis*). Their white, pink and yellow flowers bring a foretaste of spring beneath the bare branches and yellow flowers of the wintersweet (*Chimonanthus praecox*); add *Iris histrioides* 'Major' for a touch of blue. The green flowers and evergreen, fingered foliage of *Helleborus foetidus* would add height and leafy interest.

▲ **Winter cheer** Undeterred by the weather, glistening white snowdrops and golden aconites (*Eranthis*) are the first to announce the coming of longer and warmer days. They are soon joined by the silver-blue flowers of diminutive *Scilla tubergeniana*.

► **Early-summer bulbs** The ornamental onion (*Allium albopilosum*) mingles its heads of metallic-pink flowers with the velvety blue of flag irises. They brighten up borders before perennials come into their own.

▲ **Golden trumpets** True harbingers of spring, trumpet daffodils are ideal for naturalizing, beneath deciduous trees and in rough grass where they can be left to colonize over the years. 'Golden Harvest' is one of the first to flower, bringing life to a gaunt silhouette of bare-stemmed honey locust (*Gleditsia triacanthos*).

► **Trouble-free bulbs** One of the joys of bulb-growing is the ease with which many appear year after year, making few demands but producing a steadily increasing show of flowers. Here, cyclamineus narcissi, with their long golden trumpets and backswept petals, jostle against hyacinth-like sprays of the pure white form of striped squill (*Puschkinia scilloides*).

◄ **Exotic lilies** The magnificent blooms of lilies bring a touch of class and sophistication to the garden. The Asiatic hybrids come in a range of colours and are particularly easy to grow in mixed borders where they reach a manageable height of about 90cm (3ft). The sturdy stems grow unsupported and bear a succession of upward-facing blooms in early summer.

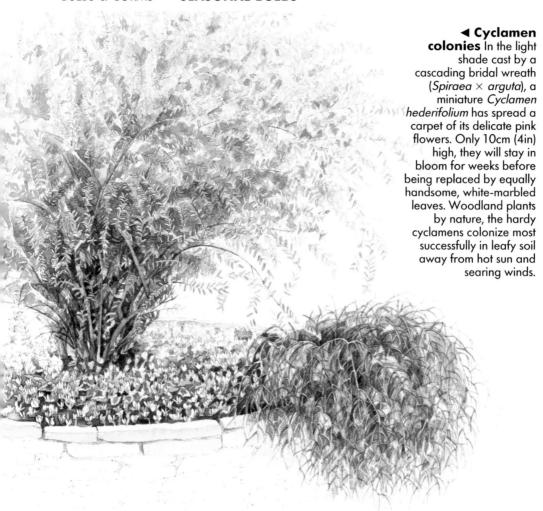

◄ **Cyclamen colonies** In the light shade cast by a cascading bridal wreath (*Spiraea* × *arguta*), a miniature *Cyclamen hederifolium* has spread a carpet of its delicate pink flowers. Only 10cm (4in) high, they will stay in bloom for weeks before being replaced by equally handsome, white-marbled leaves. Woodland plants by nature, the hardy cyclamens colonize most successfully in leafy soil away from hot sun and searing winds.

◄ **Bedding hyacinths** The deliciously scented hyacinths, in shades of blue, pink, white and yellow, are popular winter-flowering indoor bulbs, but they are perfectly hardy. Ideal for spring beds, containers and window-boxes, the elegant flower spikes blend happily with other spring flowers, such as short-growing tulips, winter pansies, primulas and polyanthus primroses.

▲ Formal bedding Tulips are traditional in late-spring bedding schemes, lifting their goblets most often above classic combinations of forget-me-nots and wallflowers. Here, a bed of mixed tulips, including the stunning near-black 'Queen of the Night', is underplanted with pansies.

▼ Late-winter scene Miniature bulbs hold the stage against a backdrop of winter-flowering jasmine (*Jasminum nudiflorum*). Its yellow starry flowers reflect the blue of tiny *Iris histrioides*, deep pink *Cyclamen coum*, white snowdrops (*Galanthus nivalis*) and the golden goblets of *Crocus aureus*.

▲ Stately crown imperials
Resentful of disturbance, the tall spring-flowering crown imperial (*Fritillaria imperialis*) adorns its tall stems with crowns of nodding bells, yellow in the variety 'Lutea'. They are partnered by clumps of American trout lily (*Erythronium revolutum* 'White Beauty') whose creamy, reflexed flowers are held above brown-mottled leaves.

Allium
ornamental onion

Allium giganteum

☐ Height 30-150cm (1-5ft)
☐ Planting distance 8-30cm (3-12in)
☐ Flowers in summer
☐ Any well-drained soil
☐ Sunny open position
☐ Bulbs available in autumn

Ornamental onions are becoming increasingly popular because of their easy-going nature, tough constitution and long-lasting flowers. The flowers appear in summer and, according to variety, range in colour from white, yellow and blue to deep lilac and rose. Some alliums are ideal for mixed or herbaceous borders, others for rock gardens, sink gardens and even indoor displays. Their onion-like smell is only a problem when leaves and stems are bruised.

Popular species
Allium albopilosum (syn. *christophii*) is best grown among herbaceous plants that hide its untidy grey-blue leaves without giving too much shade. Plant the bulbs 10-12cm (4-5in) apart. In early summer the large heads of striking star-shaped lilac-pink flowers appear on stems 60cm (2ft) tall. The seed heads that follow in autumn and winter are excellent for indoor flower arrangements.
Allium caeruleum (syn. *azureum*) has densely packed balls of star-like flax-blue flowers among long thin mid-green leaves in early and mid summer. Set the bulbs 15cm (6in) apart. As the flowers are carried on 60cm (2ft) high stems, they are suitable as cut flowers.
Allium giganteum stands well above most other herbaceous plants, often reaching an impressive height of 1.5m (5ft). It is

Allium moly

grown for its large decorative flower heads: balls of mauve star-shaped florets that appear in early summer. Like many of the ornamental onions, it has long thin grey-blue leaves. Plant 23-30cm (9-12in) apart.
Allium moly forms a vivid display in early and mid summer with its bright yellow star-shaped flowers among grey lance-shaped leaves. It reaches only 30cm (12in) high, but is particularly invasive, so avoid planting it among small delicate plants. Space the bulbs 10cm (4in) apart.
Allium oreophilum var. *ostrowskianum*, a popular member of the family, reaches only 30cm (12in) high. Planted 8cm (3in) apart it can spread rapidly. The small rose-coloured flowers and drooping grey-blue leaves are excellent for livening up rockeries in early summer.
Allium roseum has elegant rosy-pink star-shaped flowers that come out in early summer. It reaches 30cm (1ft) high and has long, broad, mid-green leaves. Plant the bulbs 10cm (4in) apart, in a sunny and sheltered site.

Cultivation
Alliums grow best in ordinary, well-drained soil in open sunny sites. Plant the bulbs in early to mid autumn, setting them in clumps of six or more so the flowers have impact. Cover each bulb with soil to twice its depth – if the dormant bulb is 4cm (1½in) high plant it 8cm (3in) deep.

Every spring apply a dressing of general fertilizer or bone-meal. When the flowers are over, cut off the heads (some make good dried arrangements). In autumn, remove the dead leaves and stems. Tall alliums growing in a windy position may need support with canes.
Propagation Detach bulblets from the base of mature bulbs in autumn or in spring and replant immediately in moist soil. Or increase from ripe, home-saved seed.
Pests and diseases Young shoots, leaves and stems are often eaten by slugs. White rot can cause the leaves to turn yellow and die back – the roots also rot and the bulbs become covered with a fluffy white fungus growth.

Allium oreophilum var. *ostrowskianum*

Alstroemeria

Peruvian lily

Alstroemeria aurantiaca

- ☐ Height 60-90cm (2-3ft)
- ☐ Planting distance 30cm (1ft)
- ☐ Flowers early to late summer
- ☐ Well-drained fertile soil
- ☐ Sheltered sunny position
- ☐ Tubers available in late winter and early spring

The beautiful Peruvian lilies provide glorious colour both outdoors in the herbaceous border and as long-lasting cut flowers in the home. Their lily-like flowers, ranging in colour from light pink to yellow, flame or orange, appear in the summer and are carried on slender stems adorned with silvery twisted leaves. Being delicate plants, they make greatest impact when grown in clumps.

Popular species

Alstroemeria aurantiaca is one of the hardiest and most flamboyant of the garden Peruvian lilies. Its fiery orange, trumpet-shaped flowers, splashed with maroon on the upper petals, create a magnificent blaze of colour in summer. Popular varieties include 'Orange King' with orange blooms, and 'Lutea' which has bright yellow flowers with carmine markings. All stand 90cm (3ft) high.

'Ligtu Hybrids' are near hardy and come in a wide range of pastel colours: white, cream, pink, rose, flame orange and yellow. They stand 60-90cm (2-3ft) high and flower in summer.

Cultivation

Plant the tubers in early spring in any well-drained soil; Peruvian lilies dislike root disturbance so give them a sheltered site where they can be left undisturbed for several years. Arrange the tubers in groups, setting each one at a depth of 15cm (6in). Place them 30cm (1ft) apart. Peruvian lilies usually take two years to become established, so don't expect top growth in the first year. The plants may need sticks for support.

Apply liquid manure during and after flowering. Dead-head the flowers regularly and cut the stems back to the ground in autumn when the leaves have died down. Protect from winter frosts with a deep mulch of composted forest bark.

Propagation Every three or four years divide established plants into 10-15cm (4-6in) clusters in early or mid spring, and replant them immediately.

Pests and diseases Slugs may eat the young shoots, leaves and stems, checking any early growth. The plants can also be stunted by a virus disease, made apparent by yellow mottling on the leaves.

Alstroemeria 'Ligtu Hybrids'

Amaryllis

amaryllis

Amaryllis belladonna 'Parkeri'

- ☐ Height 60-75cm (2-2½ft)
- ☐ Planting distance 30cm (1ft)
- ☐ Flowers early to mid autumn
- ☐ Well-drained fertile soil
- ☐ Sheltered sunny site
- ☐ Bulbs available in summer

Only one species of true amaryllis grows outdoors, *Amaryllis belladonna* (the showy *Hippeastrum*, often sold as amaryllis, only grows indoors). *A. belladonna* saves its magnificent display of satiny pink, fragrant flowers until autumn. The long purple stems are leafless at flowering time so surround them with other plant foliage, but don't create too much shade. Popular varieties of *A. belladonna* include 'Hathor' – pure white flowers with a yellow throat, and 'Parkeri' – deep pink with a yellow throat.

Cultivation

The ideal situation for *A. belladonna* is the foot of a south-facing wall where it can get maximum benefit from the summer sunshine, and protection for the young leaves when they appear in late winter and early spring. Plant in early or mid summer setting the bulbs 15-20cm (6-8in) deep in good, well-drained soil. Remove faded flowers and the stems and leaves when they die down.

Propagation Lift mature plants when the leaves turn yellow in summer, detach the offsets and replant immediately.

Pests and diseases Narcissus fly maggots may tunnel in the bulbs.

AMERICAN TROUT LILY – see *Erythronium*

Anemone
anemone

Anemone blanda

- ☐ Height 15-30cm (6-12in)
- ☐ Planting distance 10-15cm (4-6in)
- ☐ Flowers late winter to mid spring
- ☐ Good well-drained soil
- ☐ Sunny or partially shaded site
- ☐ Tubers available in autumn and winter

Spring-flowering anemones have tuberous roots or corms. They are ideal for naturalizing in a semi-wild, shady or wooded corner of the garden, for introducing spring colour to a rockery, and for cutting.

Popular species
Anemone blanda stands only 15cm (6in) high and looks enchanting in a semi-natural setting. If left undisturbed, it will form an extensive carpet of white, pink or blue flowers from late winter to early spring. It tolerates dappled shade so a good site for it is under a deciduous tree. Here the flowers provide ground interest before the tree leaves are fully out. For blue flowers select such varieties as 'Blue Pearl', 'Violet Pearl' or 'Atrocaerulea'. For white flowers there's 'White Splendour', and for pink flowers 'Pink Star'. Mixtures are also available.

Anemone coronaria, sometimes called the poppy anemone, is the red, blue, cream or purple species often seen in florists'. Two strains are widely available: 'De Caen' which produces up to 20 single saucer-shaped flowers in a season, and 'St Brigid', a double or semi-double strain. Mixtures and named varieties of single colours are easily obtained. All grow about 30cm (1ft) high and are suitable for the front of a border.

Anemone × *fulgens*, a hybrid, has striking scarlet flowers and stands

Anemone coronaria 'De Caen'

30cm (1ft) high; it forms an eye-catching sight throughout spring. *Anemone nemorosa*, the wood anemone, is native to English woodland so it looks best in a semi-natural setting where its clusters of feathery leaves, 15cm (6in) high, are superb for ground cover in early and mid spring. The flowers are naturally white tinged pink, but lavender ones such as 'Robinsoniana' and blue forms such as 'Royal Blue' are sometimes available.

Cultivation
Plant the tubers 5cm (2in) deep and 10-15cm (4-6in) apart in any rich, well-drained soil from early to mid autumn. *A. coronaria* and *A.* × *fulgens* do best in sunny sites while *A. blanda* and *A. nemorosa* prefer partial shade. With succession planting every three months, *A. coronaria* can be in flower for most of the year, protected with cloches during the winter. *A. coronaria* and *A.* × *fulgens* deteriorate quickly and should be replaced after a couple of years.

Anemone nemorosa

Propagation When the top growth dies down in late summer lift the corms and separate and replant the offsets.

Pests and diseases Watch out for and remove caterpillars and cutworms eating the leaves, flower buds and stems of established plants. Few pests and diseases attack species anemones, but 'De Caen' and 'St Brigid' can be susceptible to a rust disease.

ANGEL'S FISHING ROD – see *Dierama*

Anthericum liliago

Anthericum

St Bernard's lily

Anthericum liliago

☐ Height 45-60cm (1½-2ft)
☐ Planting distance 30cm (1ft)
☐ Flowers late spring to early summer
☐ Well-drained, moisture-retentive soil
☐ Partial shade or sun
☐ Tuberous roots available in autumn

The starry white flowers of *Anthericum liliago*, one of two hardy species in this genus, appear in late spring and early summer. With its grass-like leaves and delicate flowers, *A. liliago* is best grown in herbaceous borders in groups of five or more plants.

Cultivation

Choose a lightly shaded or sunny spot with soil that is humus-rich and well-drained but unlikely to dry out in summer. Plant the tuberous roots 10cm (4in) deep in autumn. In early spring mulch with garden compost or well-rotted manure. Cut the stems back to ground level after flowering.
Propagation Divide overcrowded plants between mid autumn and early spring; or raise new plants from seed, sown in spring in a cold frame.
Pests and diseases Generally trouble free.

AUNT ELIZA – see *Curtonus*
AUTUMN CROCUS – see
Colchicum

Begonia

begonia

Begonia × *tuberhybrida* (fimbriata)

☐ Height 15-60cm (6-24in)
☐ Planting distance 38cm (15in)
☐ Flowers early summer to early autumn
☐ Rich, moist well-drained soil
☐ Sun or partial shade
☐ Tubers available late winter/spring

The tuberous begonia, with its vibrant scarlet, orange, yellow, white or pink blooms borne through the summer, is often regarded as the queen of bedding plants. It is ideal for adding summer colour to pots, window-boxes, hanging baskets and borders, in sun or shade. The half-hardy *Begonia* × *tuberhybrida* will grow happily outdoors during the summer, provided it is planted in a rich, moist but well-drained soil. The varieties developed from this hybrid are divided into four groups.

Popular varieties

Multiflora non-stop varieties have clusters of small bright flowers carried well above the foliage. The plants grow 15cm (6in) high and have a compact, neat bushy habit that makes them excellent as bedding for flower beds and containers. The varieties come in a wide range of colours – some with unusual foliage colours as well. 'Switzerland' has deep

Begonia × *tuberhybrida* (pendula)

orange-scarlet flowers and bronze leaves; 'Mme Helene Harms' has semi-double copper-yellow flowers, and 'Bouton Rose' is bicoloured pink and white.
Pendula varieties have a slender, trailing habit that makes them suitable for hanging baskets and window-boxes. From early summer till early autumn they bear an abundance of semi-double white, yellow, orange, scarlet, salmon or rose flowers, according to variety.
Large camellia-flowered (double) varieties have blooms 7.5-15cm (3-6in) across. The plants reach up to 30-60cm (1-2ft) high and grow well in containers. An enormous number of varieties is on sale, offering almost every shade of orange, yellow, red and pink imaginable.

Brodiaea
brodiaea

Brodiaea laxa

☐ Height 45-60cm (1½-2ft)
☐ Planting distance 5-7.5cm (2-3in)
☐ Flowers late spring to early summer
☐ Well-drained soil
☐ Sheltered sunny site
☐ Corms available in autumn

Summer-flowering brodiaeas are reasonably hardy when planted in their favourite position – a sheltered bed at the foot of a south-facing wall. The plants have only a few long, narrow, green leaves at the bottom of the stem and look best when grown in groups. The flowers are star-shaped or trumpet-shaped, according to species, and range from blue to mauve in colour. Carried on 45-60cm (1½-2ft) high upright stems, they make excellent cut flowers.

Popular species
Brodiaea coronaria (syn. *grandiflora*) reaches 45cm (1½ft) high and has starry, blue-mauve flowers in late spring/early summer.
Brodiaea laxa has loose clusters of dark blue trumpet-shaped flowers that resemble a tiny *Agapanthus*. The flowers appear in early to mid summer on 60cm (2ft) stems.
Brodiaea × tubergenii is similar to *B. laxa* but with paler coloured flowers that come out in late spring and early summer. The plants are 45cm (1½ft) high.

Cultivation
Plant the corms in early autumn in small or large groups and space them 5-7.5cm (2-3in) apart. For the best results choose a sheltered sunny site and well-drained soil.
Propagation Remove and replant offsets every four years.
Pests and diseases Trouble free.

Begonia × *tuberhybrida* (large camellia-flowered)

Fimbriata varieties are vigorous, weather-resistant in spite of their fragile appearance. They bear fully double flowers with frilled petals and come in white and shades of pink, orange and yellow.

Cultivation
Start the tubers in late winter or early spring – hollow-side facing up – in 7.5cm (3in) deep boxes of moist peat substitute. Keep them at a temperature of 18°C (64°F). When leafy shoots appear, transfer them to individual pots of potting compost. Plant out in early summer in flower beds or containers, once the risk of frost is over. Fill the containers with a proprietary potting compost. Set plants 38cm (15in) apart and grow them in groups of at least three.

Begonias grow happily in light shade or sun, provided the soil is enriched with humus. Water them regularly during dry weather – erratic watering will cause the flowers to fall off. Give begonias in containers a dilute liquid foliar feed every week until the last flowers fade.

Lift the tubers before the first frosts. Dry the plants off thoroughly, remove the stems and clean any soil off the tubers. Store them in boxes of dry compost in a frost-free place over winter. Water lightly now and then to prevent the tubers shrivelling.
Propagation In mid spring take 7.5-10cm (3-4in) basal cuttings, preferably with a heel of the parent tuber attached. Root the cuttings in a proprietary cuttings compost in a propagating case at 18-20°C (64-70°F). When the cuttings have rooted, pot them up in compost for planting out in early summer. Alternatively, divide the tubers in mid spring when the shoots are small.
Pests and diseases Weevils can be a problem tunnelling into the begonia tubers.

BLUEBELL – see *Scilla*

BUTTERCUP – see *Ranunculus*

Camassia

quamash

Camassia leichtlinii

- ☐ Height 60-90cm (2-3ft)
- ☐ Planting distance 15cm (6in)
- ☐ Flowers early to mid summer
- ☐ Moist humus-rich soil
- ☐ Lightly shaded or sunny site
- ☐ Bulbs available in autumn

As they thrive in moist and shady conditions, an ideal site for these spiky-looking plants is a spot beside a garden pool. They will also grow in herbaceous borders and naturalize happily in semi-wild grassy areas provided the soil isn't too light. The star-like flowers come out in early to mid summer – large scilla-like spikes in various shades of blue and violet or white on 90cm (3ft) tall stems. All the species are hardy and require very little attention once they have been planted.

Popular species

Camassia cusickii has wisteria-blue flowers on stems 60cm (2ft) high. Plant the bulbs 7.5cm (3in) deep and 15cm (6in) apart and they will spread freely.

Camassia leichtlinii is the most striking species with creamy-white or aster-blue flowers. These appear in mid summer. The plants are 90cm (3ft) high; set the bulbs 15cm (6in) apart.

Camassia quamash (syn. *esculenta*) is 75cm (2½ft) high. Its violet-blue flowers are clustered together densely at the tops of the stems.

Cultivation

Plant the bulbs 7.5-10cm (3-4in) deep in early or mid autumn in humus-rich, heavy, moist soil which is unlikely to dry out in the spring and early summer. (Covering the bulbs with plenty of leaf-mould will help keep the soil damp.) Arrange the bulbs 15cm (6in) apart in large groups in light shade or full sun for the best effect. Dead-head after flowering in early and mid summer.

Propagation When the clumps become too dense, lift the bulbs in early autumn, remove any offsets and replant immediately. These offsets take between one and three years to produce flowers.

Pests and diseases Trouble free.

Camassia leichtlinii

Canna

canna

Canna × hybrida 'Denmans'

- ☐ Height 75-120cm (2½-4ft)
- ☐ Planting distance 45-60cm (1½-2ft)
- ☐ Flowers late summer and early autumn
- ☐ Moist, humus-rich soil
- ☐ Sunny sheltered position
- ☐ Rhizomes available in autumn and winter

For many years it was difficult to buy the rhizomes of these tropical plants, but recently they have become more readily available. They are excellent for summer bedding with their brightly coloured blooms resembling a cross between an orchid and a gladiolus. They can reach 1.2m (4ft) high, so plant them at the back of a border. The leaves are very large, at least 45cm (1½ft) long and 30cm (1ft) wide, with colours ranging from pale green, deep green and bronze to purple according to variety.

The varieties available have all been developed from *C. indica* but they are usually referred to as *C. × hybrida* or horticultural cannas. Green-leaved varieties include: 'Bonfire' with orange-scarlet flowers; 'Denmans' with yellow flowers; 'Evening Star' with dull carmine-pink flowers; 'Humbert's Seedling' with scarlet flowers; 'J B van der Schoot' with lemon-yellow flowers speckled with purple-red; 'Orange Perfection', a soft orange; 'President', a vivid scarlet. Bronze

Cardiocrinum

giant lily

Canna × hybrida 'Humbert's Seedling'

and purple-leaved varieties include: 'America' has red flowers; 'Di Bartolo' has deep pink flowers; 'Wyoming' is bronze-yellow; 'Lucifer' has red petals with yellow edges; and 'Verdi' is orange blotched yellow and purple.

Cultivation

Plant the rhizomes 2cm (1in) deep in pots of moist compost in early spring. Place them in the greenhouse at a minimum temperature of 16°C (61°F). If more than one shoot appears on a rhizome, divide the rhizome into sections, each with a shoot and some roots, and repot. Plant out from early summer onwards in well-manured soil in a sheltered sunny position.

Alternatively, transfer young plants to tubs in mid spring and move these outside after risk of frost has passed. Bring the plants inside again before autumn frosts.

Partially dry plants lifted from beds, then cut off the leaves and roots and store them in just moist compost or leaf-mould in a frost-free place for the winter. If kept too dry, the rhizomes will shrivel and die; too wet and they rot.

Propagation In early spring, divide recently potted rhizomes which produce more than one shoot. Make sure each new division has some roots as well as a shoot. Pot them in moist compost and plant out in early summer.

Pests and diseases Slugs, leatherjackets and cutworms eat the rhizomes.

Cardiocrinum giganteum

☐ Height 1.8-3m (6-10ft)
☐ Planting distance 90-120cm (3-4ft)
☐ Flowers in mid and late summer
☐ Deep rich, moist soil
☐ Partial shade
☐ Bulbs available late autumn

There are few more majestic sights than the giant lily (*Cardiocrinum giganteum*) when it raises its robust 1.8-3m (6-10ft) tall flower stems topped with clusters of long trumpet flowers in mid and late summer. The fragrant flowers are creamy-white, streaked with purple or crimson inside the trumpet and up to 15cm (6in) long. The leaves are equally impressive – dark green and heart-shaped and as much as 50cm (20in) long; they are arranged in a spiral along the flower stem.

Giant lily is monocarpic which means that it dies after flowering, but it leaves behind two or more offset bulbs which in turn will reach flowering size after about three years.

Cultivation

Giant lilies thrive at the edge of woodland or planted among low-growing shrubs which will offer protection against spring frost and excessive summer heat; they will also grow in any cool, lightly shaded position where the soil is deep and moist but well-drained and rich in organic matter. Set the bulbs, shallowly, with their tops just level with the surrounding soil; space them 90cm (3ft) apart.

Propagation

Lift the flowered bulbs in mid autumn, discard the old collapsed bulbs and replant the offsets immediately. Leave undisturbed until they reach flowering size.

Pests and diseases Trouble free.

Cardiocrinum giganteum (growth habit)

Chionodoxa

glory-of-the-snow

Chionodoxa sardensis

Chionodoxa luciliae

- ☐ Height 10-20cm (4-8in)
- ☐ Planting distance 5-10cm (2-4in)
- ☐ Flowers late winter to late spring
- ☐ Ordinary well-drained garden soil
- ☐ Sunny or slightly shaded site
- ☐ Bulbs available in late summer and autumn

Chionodoxa luciliae 'Pink Giant'

Glory-of-the-snow casts swathes of brilliant star-like flowers over the ground from late winter and throughout spring, in northern gardens raising their blue stars above the melting snow. These little plants are among the easiest of bulbs to grow and left to their own devices they will spread and colonize readily. They are ideal for brightening up the rock garden in early spring, for planting at the front of borders and for naturalizing in short grass.

Chionodoxas grow equally well in full sun and light shade and look stunning as a carpet below deciduous shrubs and trees.

Popular species

Chionodoxa gigantea is the tallest member of its genus at 20cm (8in) high. The flower spikes are violet-blue with white centres and appear from late winter to mid spring. 'Blue Giant', 15cm (6in) tall, is bright blue with large white centres. Plant 7.5-10cm (3-4in) apart.

Chionodoxa luciliae, the most popular species, has porcelain-blue flowers with white centres, and a pure white form, 'Alba', is also available. The variety 'Pink Giant' is outstanding, with robust flower spikes of rosy-pink. All flower from late winter to mid spring on stems 15cm (6in) high. Set the bulbs 5-10cm (2-4in) apart. *Chionodoxa sardensis* is the smallest species, 10-15cm (4-6in) high. Its nodding sky-blue flowers with tiny white centres appear slightly later than the other chionodoxas, from early spring to late spring. Plant 5-10cm (2-4in) apart.

Cultivation

Plant the bulbs as soon as they are available in autumn, setting them 5-7.5cm (2-3in) deep and about 10cm (4in) apart in large groups. They do well in any ordinary well-drained garden soil in a sunny or lightly shaded site. They need little attention apart from removing the foliage as it dies down and lifting and dividing the clumps as they become crowded. Replant the divisions immediately, 10cm (4in) apart.

Propagation Division is the easiest method, in late spring when the leaves are turning yellow. Many chionodoxas also spread rapidly by self-sown seed; the round seed pods can be gathered in late spring when they are ripe and the seeds sown in an outdoor nursery bed. Transplant the seedlings to their flowering positions during the second summer. Named varieties do not breed true to type from seed and should be propagated from divisions.

Pests and diseases Slugs sometimes eat the leaves and flowers.

Colchicum
autumn crocus

Colchicum speciosum 'William Dykes'

Colchicum autumnale

- ☐ Height 15-20cm (6-8in)
- ☐ Planting distance 15-23cm (6-9in)
- ☐ Flowers early to late autumn
- ☐ Well-drained soil
- ☐ Sunny or partially shaded site
- ☐ Corms available in mid and late summer

Colchicums are renowned for the lovely colours they introduce to the garden in autumn – muted lilacs, purples and pinks that seem to blend perfectly with fallen leaves covering the ground. An ideal site is among rough grass which supports the 15-20cm (6-8in) high leafless stems during flowering time and hides the mass of coarse, untidy leaves that develop in spring. All colchicums are hardy, so can be left undisturbed for years. Don't confuse them with the genuine crocus.

Popular species
Colchicum autumnale has lilac-pink goblet-shaped flowers that appear in early and mid autumn. The stems are particularly fragile so ideally this species should be grown among rough grass that can be left uncut in spring and autumn. Plant 10cm (4in) deep and 20cm (8in) apart. A double-flowered white form 'Album-plenum' and a single white form 'Album' are also available.

Colchicum speciosum has flowers which are varying shades of mauve. They appear from early to late autumn. It is a more robust species with a stronger stem, so can be grown in a border, preferably a shrub border where the 40cm (16in) high leaves that appear in spring can't smother other plants. Plant in a group of at least 10 corms in the dappled shade of a shrub or a small tree. Set them about 10cm (4in) deep and 15cm (6in) apart. Varieties include 'Album', a pure white form.

Dutch hybrids have stronger coloured flowers, appearing between early and late autumn. They are more robust and easier to grow. Popular varieties include 'The Giant' (rosy-lilac), 'Lilac Wonder' (lilac-rose), 'Waterlily' (mauve with double flowers) and 'William Dykes' (lilac-pink).

Cultivation
Colchicums grow in any soil provided it is well drained, but they are more likely to spread in fertile soil. A site in sun or partial shade is suitable. Plant in mid to late summer or as soon as they're available, setting them in small clumps. Remove dead foliage.

Propagation Every third year, when the leaves die down in summer, dig up the corms and separate any small cormlets and replant them.

Pests and diseases Slugs may eat the leaves and corms.

Convallaria
lily-of-the-valley

Convallaria majalis

☐ Height 15-20cm (6-8in)
☐ Planting distance 15cm (6in)
☐ Flowers mid and late spring
☐ Good moist soil
☐ Shady site
☐ Rhizomes available in late and mid autumn

Convallaria majalis is the only species in this genus. It has delicate white bell-shaped flowers, arranged in loose spikes. These appear in mid and late spring and have a magnificent heady scent that makes them popular as cut flowers. The berries that appear in autumn, and the roots, are poisonous.

Lily-of-the-valley is best planted in large clumps in a cool shady corner or in a wild garden; it spreads rapidly, so avoid confined spaces or borders where it can overcome more delicate plants. When you choose the site, bear in mind that the broad green leaves which provide such deceptively good ground cover in late spring and early summer become an untidy decaying yellow and brown mass towards the autumn. This problem is made worse if the plants are growing in a bright, sunny site.

Cultivation
Grow lily-of-the-valley in ordinary garden soil containing plenty of leaf-mould or compost. The site should be shady. Plant the crowns singly in early and mid autumn at least 15cm (6in) apart, pointed end upwards, and just below the soil surface. When the leaves die down in summer, top-dress with leaf-mould, compost or shredded forest bark – this encourages continuous flowering the following year. Avoid disturbing the roots except for propagation.
Propagation Lift and divide the rhizomes any time between mid autumn and early spring. Replant 15cm (6in) apart just below the surface, then apply a top-dressing of compost and leaf-mould and water well.
Pests and diseases Swift moth caterpillars sometimes eat the rhizomes of established plants. In wet sites, a grey mould fungus can develop on the plants.

CORN LILY, AFRICAN – see *Ixia*

Crinum
crinum

Crinum × powellii

☐ Height 45-60cm (1½-2ft)
☐ Planting distance 30-45cm (1-1½ft)
☐ Flowers late summer to early autumn
☐ Rich well-drained soil
☐ Sunny sheltered site
☐ Bulbs available from late winter to late spring

Any gardener wanting to introduce a subtropical feel to a sunny part of the garden should consider planting *Crinum × powellii*, the hardiest member of the crinum genus. It is not the easiest bulb to grow, demanding mild conditions, and frequent tidying up if it is to look at all presentable. But perseverance is rewarded with an exotic display of white or pink lily-like flowers.

Cultivation
Grow crinums in clumps in a sunny position protected from north and east winds – perhaps the base of a south-facing wall. They also flourish in containers on sunny terraces in summer. Plant in late spring in rich, moisture-retentive, but well-drained soil. Set them 30-45cm (1-1½ft) apart with their necks just below soil level. Water freely during the summer, then ease off in autumn. Keep those in containers almost dry during the winter. Protect young shoots from frost with a light mulch of bracken, coarse sand or straw. Move container-grown crinums into a frost-free greenhouse during winter.
Propagation Crinums prefer not to be disturbed. You can propagate them by removing offsets in early spring and replanting. However, these will take three years to develop into flowering plants.
Pests and diseases Trouble free.

Crocosmia

crocosmia

Crocosmia × *crocosmiiflora*

Crocosmia × *crocosmiiflora* 'Citronella'

- ☐ Height 60-75cm (2-2½ft)
- ☐ Planting distance 10-15cm (4-6in)
- ☐ Flowers mid summer to early autumn
- ☐ Well-drained soil
- ☐ Sunny sheltered location
- ☐ Corms available from early to late spring

A clump of crocosmias presents a cheerful sight in summer and early autumn with their sword-shaped green leaves and profuse sprays of orange flowers. They like well-drained soil and sun, and spread rapidly, so give them plenty of room – sunny banks are a favourite spot, but they also look attractive planted in clumps among shrubs or herbaceous perennials. The tubular flowers are held on wiry stems 60cm (2ft) tall. They come in varying shades of orange or yellow, depending on variety, and are excellent for flower arranging.

Popular species

Crocosmia × *crocosmiiflora*, popularly known as montbretia, has orange flowers opening from mid summer to late autumn. In the milder parts of Britain it has naturalized on banks, in hedges and on rough ground. Being the

Crocosmia masonorum

hardiest member of the genus, it will survive all but the harshest winters, if it is given a warm sheltered position. It spreads rapidly, so allow plenty of room. Several varieties, which are less rampant, have been developed from *C.* × *crocosmiiflora*. They offer the gardener almost every shade of orange, as well as yellow and red: 'Bressingham Blaze' and 'Ember-glow' are orange-red; 'Emily McKenzie' is deep orange with

crimson-brown markings; 'Jacka-napes' is yellow or orange; 'Lucifer' (90cm/3ft) is brilliant flame red and early flowering; 'Solfatare' is apricot yellow with bronze-flushed leaves; 'Spitfire' is fiery orange; and 'Vulcan' is orange-red. Mixed collections of these varieties are available from some nurseries.

Crocosmia masonorum has bright orange blooms that appear in succession in mid and late summer. These are smaller than those of the hybrids and packed together more densely on arching stems.

Cultivation

Plant the corms about 10-15cm (4-6in) apart and 7.5cm (3in) deep in clumps in early spring. They need open, well-drained soil and full sun. *C. masonorum* prefers a site where it can be left undisturbed. Water regularly in the summer. In mid autumn, cover the root area with a winter mulch – bracken or dry leaves. If your garden is in a frost pocket, lift the corms, dry them off and store in a frost-free place. Remove the dead leaves of plants left in the ground in early spring, before the new foliage appears.

Propagation Divide clumps every three years, either just after flowering or before the new growth starts in spring.

Pests and diseases Trouble free.

Crocus

crocus

Crocus medius

Crocus chrysanthus 'EA Bowles'

□ Height 7.5-12cm (3-5in)
□ Planting distance 7.5-10cm (3-4in)
□ Flowers late winter to early spring;
  also autumn
□ Any well-drained soil
□ Full sun or dappled shade
□ Corms available in mid summer for
  autumn flowering, and autumn for
  spring flowering

Crocuses come from the mountainous regions of southern and eastern Europe, so they are remarkably hardy. In gardens they provide some of the earliest spring colour at ground level, though there are several species that are autumn-flowering. Most species stand about 7.5cm (3in) high – the Dutch hybrids are slightly taller at 10-12cm (4-5in). The flower colours vary enormously, coming in shades of yellow, blue, purple, lilac and white according to the species and variety. Some are only one colour, some are bicoloured, others are striped. All have thin green leaves with a faint white stripe. The leaves of spring-flowering crocuses appear with the flowers.

Crocuses are happy in sun or dappled shade. They are best grown in clumps in rockeries or sink gardens, but they also look attractive edging flower or shrub borders. The more robust species are ideal for naturalizing in short grass, provided it is not mown before the leaves turn yellow in late spring. Try planting autumn-flowering crocuses among low ground cover.

Crocus chrysanthus 'Ladykiller'

Popular species and varieties
Crocus ancyrensis, often listed as 'Golden Bunch', has 5cm (2½in) high rich yellow flowers in late winter and early spring.
Crocus chrysanthus has 7.5cm (3in) high golden yellow flowers in late winter. It is suitable for rockeries, borders and containers. Popular varieties are 'Advance' (yellow and violet), 'Blue Bird' (violet and white), 'Blue Pearl' (blue and white), 'Cream Beauty' (cream), 'EA Bowles' (yellow with bronze base), 'Elegance' (bright golden-yellow, brown markings), 'Fuscotinctus' (striped and feathered plum-purple on pale yellow ground), 'Ladykiller' (purple and lilac-white), 'Princess Beatrix' (clear blue with yellow base), 'Prins Claus' (deep violet-blue flushed with white), 'Snow Bunting' (white), and 'Zwanenburg Bronze' (garnet-brown and yellow).

Crocus imperati has 7.5-10cm (3-4in) high flowers with buff outer petals streaked purple, and bright purple satiny inner petals. It is another early-flowering species appearing in mid to late winter.
Crocus medius has 7.5cm (3in) high, lightly scented lilac blooms with deep orange stigmas. It is one of the autumn-flowering species. Grow in a sunny spot.
Crocus sieberi has 7.5cm (3in) high pale mauve flowers with yellow bases. These appear in late winter and early spring. Two garden hybrids have been developed: 'Hubert Edelsten' (rose-lilac) and 'Violet Queen' (violet-blue).
Crocus speciosus has flowers 10-12cm (4-5in) high. They are bright lilac-blue with yellow anthers and red stigmas, and open in mid autumn. This species multiplies freely, making it the most popular autumn-flowering crocus. 'Aitchisonii' (pale lavender-blue) and 'Conqueror' (deep sky-blue) are varieties. A white form 'Albus' is sometimes also available.
Crocus susianus has star-shaped flowers standing 5-7.5cm (2-3in) high. They are bronze outside, and yellow inside, and appear in February. It is one of the oldest crocuses in cultivation.
Crocus tomasinianus has lilac flowers that appear in late winter, 7.5cm (3in) above ground. For a deeper mauve try 'Whitewell Purple'. It is one of the best crocuses for naturalizing in grass.

Crocus tomasinianus 'Whitewell Purple'

Dutch crocus 'Pickwick'

Crocus vernus

Dutch hybrids have been developed from the species *Crocus vernus* and have large robust flowers in an enormous choice of colours. The flowers are goblet-shaped; they stand 10-12cm (4-5in) high, and open in early spring. Plant them in rough grass or a border where, left undisturbed, they will develop into dense clumps. Well-known varieties are 'Enchantress' (light blue), 'Joan of Arc' (white), 'Pickwick' (pale lilac), 'Purpureus Grandiflorus' (purple-blue), 'Queen of the Blues' (blue), 'Remembrance' (soft violet-blue), 'Striped Beauty' (white striped violet) and 'Yellow Mammoth' (golden yellow).

Cultivation

Plant crocuses as soon as the corms are available in early autumn, although the Dutch hybrids can wait until late autumn. Choose a sunny or partially shaded site with well-drained soil. Set the corms 5-7.5cm (2-3in) deep and 7.5-10cm (3-4in) apart in small clumps.

When the flowers are over, don't dead-head. And avoid the temptation to remove the leaves – wait until they are yellow and can be pulled off easily without disturbing the corms in the soil.

Propagation When the leaves die down, lift the corms, remove any small cormlets and replant. Under good conditions *C. tomasinianus* and the Dutch hybrids multiply naturally.

Pests and diseases Mice and leatherjackets sometimes eat corms in the soil. Watch out for birds pecking at young flower buds – especially yellow varieties.

CROWN IMPERIAL – see *Fritillaria*

Crocus sieberi 'Hubert Edelsten'

131

Curtonus

aunt Eliza, pleated leaves

Curtonus paniculatus

☐ Height 1.2m (4ft)
☐ Planting distance 23cm (9in)
☐ Flowers in late summer and early autumn
☐ Rich, well-drained soil
☐ Sunny site
☐ Corms available in autumn

Curtonus paniculatus (syn. *Antholyza paniculata*) is the only species in this South African genus. It is closely related to *Crocosmia* species, but is taller, up to 1.2m (4ft), and distinguished by its pleated, sword-shaped and mid green leaves and by the zigzagging flower stems that carry orange-red trumpets in late summer and autumn.

Once established, curtonus is hardy in all but the coldest regions and naturalizes well. Grow it in sunny mixed borders, among low shrubs or at the foot of a south-facing wall. The flowers are good for cutting.

Cultivation

Plant the corms in early autumn, setting them 15cm (6in) deep in groups of three or five spaced 23cm (9in) apart. They will grow in any well-drained soil but thrive on plenty of organic matter and in full sun, with some shelter. After flowering, trim the faded stems back but leave the foliage as protection during winter. Cut it back to the ground in spring.

Propagation Lift crowded clumps in mid autumn, separate and replant the corms, taking care that each division is complete with corm, roots and leaf cluster.

Pests and diseases Trouble free.

Curtonus paniculatus (growth habit)

Cyclamen

cyclamen

Cyclamen hederifolium 'Album'

☐ Height 7.5-10cm (3-4in)
☐ Planting distance 15cm (6in)
☐ Flowers mid summer to late winter
☐ Well-drained humus-rich soil
☐ Shaded sheltered site
☐ Corms available in mid summer for autumn flowering, and autumn for winter and spring flowering

The pretty pink or white flowers of cyclamen present a charming sight in a shaded rockery, beneath a tree, or around the base of a shrub – they are one of the few bulbous plants to flourish under conifers.

Closely related to the florist's cyclamen, several species are hardy enough to be grown outdoors, in well-drained but moisture-retentive soil. As natural woodland plants, they prefer a soil rich in leaf-mould or well-decayed garden compost and need a site shaded from hot summer sun and protected from cold winds. Sometimes slow to establish themselves, cyclamens when happy will colonize to form carpets of colour from mid summer right through to mid spring.

Popular species

Cyclamen cilicium, height 10cm (4in), is hardy in most winters and produces its honey-scented flowers in early and mid autumn, usually before the silver-speckled leaves appear. Flower colour varies from near white to deep rose-pink.
Cyclamen coum has purplish pink, rose-pink ('Roseum') or, more rarely, pure white flowers ('Album') that usually appear in mid winter. The 'Pewter' selection ranges from pale to deepest pink. In a mild year, they might just come out in time for Christmas. The plants are only 7.5cm (3in) high with round green leaves

Cyclamen hederifolium

Cyclamen coum

marbled with silver. This species does best under trees and self-seeds freely.

Cyclamen europaeum (syn. *C. pur-purascens*) has strongly scented rose-pink to purple blooms standing 10cm (4in) high. They begin to appear in mid and late summer and continue in succession until Christmas. The green, rounded to kidney-shaped leaves have faint silver markings. This is one of the hardiest cyclamens.

Cyclamen hederifolium (syn. *C. neapolitanum*) has delicate pink or white flowers on stalks 10cm (4in) high. These open in early and mid autumn. The deep green leaves are variegated with silver and form an attractive carpet through the winter and spring months, until they die down in late spring. Plant in a rock garden

or beneath shrubs, where the soil is rarely disturbed. The variety 'Album' is pure white, sometimes with a hint of pink around the mouth.

Cyclamen libanoticum grows in mild regions only, producing its scented pale pink flowers in early spring. The ivy-shaped, toothed leaves are dark green and white-marbled above, red on the under-sides. It grows to 15cm (6in) tall.

Cultivation

Cyclamen do best under woodland conditions, in shady sites, sheltered from the wind, with well-drained, humus-rich soil. Choose a spot where the plants can be left undisturbed. Plant the corms in late summer and early autumn, setting them 15cm (6in) apart in clusters. Place *C. coum* and *C.*

europaeum 2-5cm (1-2in) deep, or more in light soil. With *C. hederi-folium* barely cover the corms, but add a 2cm (1in) mulch of leaf-mould annually after flowering.

Propagation The corms do not divide or produce offsets and seed propagation is the only means of increase. Many cyclamens will seed themselves, and bought seed can be sown in late summer or early autumn in pans or pots of a proprietary seed compost. Leave the seeds to germinate in a cold frame or, preferably, place the pans outdoors against a north wall for sturdier seedlings.

Prick off the seedlings singly into 6cm (2½in) pots of compost and grow them on in a cold frame before planting them out in their flowering sites in late spring or summer. They will usually flower in their second year.

Pests and diseases Mice sometimes eat the corms in the ground. A disease, black root rot, can kill the roots and discolour the foliage.

DAFFODIL – see *Narcissus*

Dahlia
dahlia

Giant decorative 'Inca Blaze'

☐ Height 25cm-1.5m (10in-5ft)
☐ Planting distance 45-120cm
(1½-4ft)
☐ Flowers mid summer till the first
severe frost
☐ Any well-drained garden soil
☐ Sunny site or light shade
☐ Tubers available mid winter until late
spring

Dahlias come in a range of forms,
sizes and colours unmatched by
any other garden plants. Their
glorious flower heads appear from
late summer until mid autumn or
the first severe frosts, filling the
garden with colour when most
other plants are past their best.

Garden dahlias are grown from
tubers or cuttings, but dwarf bedding dahlias are grown from seed
as well so they are treated as true
annuals. (For bedding dahlias, see
page 42).

The bold flower heads and
strong colours of dahlias make
them outstanding plants for garden decoration and cutting.
Depending on their size, they can
be grown in a bed of their own, in
perennial borders, open shrubberies or along walls. They prefer a
sunny bed but will tolerate shade.
As they are only half-hardy, the
tubers should be lifted in autumn
and stored in a frost-free place
over winter. They are easy to grow

Anemone-flowered 'Comet'

if you merely want bright splashes
of colour in late summer and
autumn. If you're aiming for the
perfect exhibition flower head,
however there's a host of refining
techniques.

Popular varieties
Border dahlias are organized into
nine divisions or groups, determined by the shape of the flower
heads.

Single-flowered dahlias have
blooms up to 10cm (4in) across
with a single outer ring of florets
and a central disc. The plants are
30-50cm (12-20in) tall and should
be grown 30-45cm (1-1½ft) apart.
Varieties in this group can be
cultivated in beds or mixed

Single-flowered 'Cosmos'

borders as they don't require support. Their flowers are abundant
and they will last a long time if
dead-headed regularly. Popular
varieties include 'Cosmos' (pink),
'Nellie Geerling's' (red), 'Yellow
Hammer' (yellow) and 'Princess
Marie José' (pink).

Anemone-flowered dahlias have
blooms up to 10cm (4in) across, resembling anemones: double
flowers with flat outer florets surrounding a densely packed group
of shorter, tubular florets – often of
a different colour. The plants
reach 25-45cm (10-18in) high and
should be grown 30-45cm (1-1½ft)
apart in beds, borders, tubs or deep
window-boxes. This is one of the
rarer groups; it includes several
varieties in pastel shades. Varieties available are 'Comet'
(maroon), 'Jazz' (scarlet) and 'Thalia' (lavender-pink).

Collerette dahlias also have
blooms 10cm (4in) across. They are
single-flowered with an inner ring
or collar (often of another colour)
and a central disc. This group includes varieties reaching 75-
100cm (30-40in) high. Set the
plants 60-75cm (2-2½ft) apart.
Collerette dahlias have especially
strong stems, making them
favourites among flower arrangers. Popular varieties are 'Grand
Duc' (red and gold), 'Can-Can'
(pink and yellow), 'Claire de Lune'
(yellow), and 'Kaiserwalzer' (fiery
red and yellow).

Peony-flowered dahlias have
blooms up to 12cm (5in) across.
These consist of two or more rings
of flat ray florets and a central
disc. The plants reach 100cm
(40in) high and should be grown
60-75cm (2-2½ft) apart. Only a
few varieties are available. They

Collerette 'Grand Duc'

Peony-flowered 'Bishop of Llandaff'

Small decorative 'Heidilandlied'

include 'Gerrie Hoek' (pink), 'Bishop of Llandaff' (scarlet) and 'Orange Flora' (orange).

Decorative dahlias have double blooms consisting of broad flat ray florets without a central disc. They form a large group which, like both the cactus and the semi-cactus groups, is sub-divided into sections according to flower size. GIANT varieties are 1.2-1.5m (4-5ft) high with flowers 25cm (10in) or more wide; plant 1.2m (4ft) apart. LARGE varieties are 1-1.5m (3½-5ft) tall with blooms 20-25cm (8-10in) wide; plant 1.2m (4ft) apart. MEDIUM varieties reach 1-1.2m (3½-4ft) high and have blooms 15-20cm (6-8in) across; plant 90cm (3ft) apart. SMALL varieties are 1-1.2m (3½-4ft) tall with blooms only 10-15cm (4-6in) across; plant 75cm (2½ft) apart. MINIATURE varieties are 90cm-1.2m (3-4ft) tall with blooms up to 10-15cm (4-6in) across; plant 75cm (2½ft) apart. Decorative dahlias have an extensive colour range. They are good for both exhibiting and cutting. Popular varieties are 'Arabian Night' (maroon-red), 'Eveline' (white, lilac tint), 'Inca Blaze' (golden yellow), 'Patty' (coral pink overlaid with salmon-pink), and 'Trendy' (rose and yellow).

Ball dahlias have fully double, ball-shaped blooms sometimes flattened on top. Reaching 90-120cm (3-4ft) high, they are suitable for growing in mixed borders, for cutting and for exhibiting. Plant the tubers 75cm (2½ft) apart. The varieties are sub-divided into two groups: small ball with blooms 10-15cm (4-6in) wide, and miniature ball with blooms up to 10cm (4in) across. Popular vari-

Ball 'Alltami Melody'

eties are 'Rokesley Rocket' (scarlet), 'Nettie' (primrose yellow), 'Opal' (pink and white) and 'Alltami Melody' (mauve-pink).

Pompon dahlias have flowers similar to ball varieties, but they are more globular and much smaller – only 5cm (2in) across. The free-flowering plants reach 90-120cm (3-4ft) high and should be grown 60cm (2ft) apart. Their selling point is their long-lasting cut flowers. Popular varieties are 'Moor Place' (purple), 'Andrew Lockwood' (lilac) and 'Stoneleigh Cherry' (red).

Cactus dahlias have fully double blooms with pointed ray florets. This is another group divided into

sections, determined by the size of the blooms. GIANT varieties reach 1.2-1.5m (4-5ft) high with blooms over 25cm (10in) across; plant 1.2m (4ft) apart. Their flowers don't appear until early autumn. LARGE varieties are also 1.2-1.5m (4-5ft) high with slightly smaller blooms at 20-25cm (8-10in) across; plant 1.2m (4ft) apart. MEDIUM varieties are 1-1.35m (3½-4½ft) high with blooms 15-20cm (6-8in) across; plant 90cm (3ft) apart. SMALL varieties are 1-1.2m (3½-4ft) high with blooms 10-15cm (4-6in) across; plant 75cm (2½ft) apart. MINIATURE varieties are 90-120cm (3-4ft) high with blooms up to 10cm (4in) across; plant 75cm

Pompon 'Stoneleigh Cherry'

Large semi-cactus 'Reginald Keene'

(2½ft) apart. All cactus varieties are easy to grow well and make impressive cut flowers. Popular varieties are 'Golden Explosion' (yellow-golden), 'Rokesley Mini' (white) and 'Star's Favourite' (rose-pink).

Semi-cactus dahlias have flowers similar to the cactus varieties, but the ray florets are wider. They are divided into the same sections as the cactus group, determined by flower size. Semi-cactus dahlias are excellent for exhibiting. Popular varieties include 'Reginald Keene' (orange and flame) and 'Hamari Sunset' (orange-yellow).

Cultivation

Dahlias will grow in any well-drained soil enriched with compost, manure or other organic material. Rake in some bone-meal at planting time. Plant the tubers in mid spring; leave any that have sprouted until late spring. If it is cold and wet, delay planting until the weather improves. Dig holes 10-15cm (4-6in) deep for the tubers, insert stout supporting stakes 30cm (1ft) shorter than the final height of the dahlia, and then place the tuber in the hole and cover with soil. As the stems grow, tie them loosely to the stakes. Water well after planting.

Three or four weeks after planting, pinch out the tips on the main stems to encourage strong side-growths. To grow large flowers on long stems suitable for cutting or exhibiting, disbud regularly and dead-head as necessary.

A week after frosts have blackened the leaves in autumn, cut down the stems to 15cm (6in) above ground. Using a spade, make a cut one spade's depth around each plant, 30cm (1ft) from the main stem. Holding the stems, gently ease the tubers from the soil with a fork. Take care not to damage the point at which the stem joins the tuber – this is where new growth begins. Discard any broken and rotting tubers. Place the tubers upside down and under cover for a week to drain off water that has accumulated in the hollow stems.

Put tubers in shallow boxes of dry compost, keeping the crowns free. Store in a frost-free place at 5-8°C (41-43°F). Inspect the tubers every few weeks for signs of shrivelling or disease. Place any shrivelled tubers in a bucket of water overnight, then dry thoroughly before returning to storage.

Propagation Division is the simplest method for propagating dahlias. In early spring, begin watering stored dahlia tubers, but avoid watering the crowns. Two to three weeks later the eyes on the crowns of the tubers should swell. Divide the tubers with a sharp knife, making sure each division has an undamaged eye. Dust the cut parts of the tubers with flowers of sulphur to prevent fungal attack. Then plant out when weather permits.

Mini cactus 'Rokesley Mini'

If planting outdoors has to be delayed, the tubers may be potted up singly in potting compost and kept in a frost-proof frame until conditions improve.

Pests and diseases Slugs sometimes attack young plants in wet weather and aphids may infest dahlias at any stage of growth. Earwigs often hide in the flowers and eat the leaves. Grey mould may be troublesome on flower stalks and tubers in a wet summer.

Dierama

wand flower or angel's fishing rod

Dierama pulcherrimum

☐ Height 90-180cm (3-6ft)
☐ Planting distance 23-60cm (9-24in)
☐ Flowers late summer to mid autumn
☐ Well-drained fertile soil
☐ Sunny sheltered site
☐ Corms available in early spring or
   autumn

Two *Dierama* species are commonly available – *Dierama pulcherrimum* and the smaller *D. pendulum*. They have long narrow grass-like leaves, joined in late summer and autumn by graceful curving stems bearing drooping heads of purple-red flowers. The plants, which are hardy in all but the coldest districts, look superb grown in gaps in paving surrounding a garden pool.

Cultivation

Grow in well-drained soil enriched with organic matter. Choose a sunny sheltered site, although partial shade is tolerated. Plant the corms in early or mid spring (mid spring in a cold garden), or in autumn, 7.5-10cm (3-4in) deep and 23-60cm (9-24in) apart. After flowering, remove the stems and

Dierama pendulum

cut back damaged or dying leaves. In cold districts protect with a winter mulch but otherwise leave them alone.

Propagation Plants may be increased by lifting and separating the offsets in mid spring. Plant them in a nursery bed and grow on until they reach flowering size.

Pests and diseases Trouble free.

DOG'S TOOTH VIOLET – see *Erythronium*

Eranthis

winter aconite

Eranthis hyemalis

☐ Height 10cm (4in)
☐ Planting distance 7.5cm (3in)
☐ Flowers mid winter to mid spring
☐ Well-drained, moisture-retentive soil
☐ Sun or partial shade
☐ Tubers available in early and mid
   autumn

These small hardy perennials are some of the earliest plants in the garden, sometimes appearing in mid and late winter. Their enchanting buttercup-like flowers stand 10cm (4in) above ground, surrounded by deep green ruffs. For greatest impact, plant them in large groups to form a carpet. A sunny or partially shaded site with plenty of humus-rich soil is best.

Popular species
Eranthis hyemalis has lemon-yellow flowers that appear in late winter; flowering time can be earlier in mild areas. It stands 10cm (4in) high and its tubers should be planted 7.5cm (3in) apart. As a woodland species thriving in dappled shade, it is best grown in a semi-wild setting below deciduous trees or in between shrubs.
Eranthis × *tubergenii* has robust, slightly larger rich golden-yellow flowers that emerge in early spring. It tolerates sunnier conditions than *E. hyemalis* and can be grown in a rock garden or at the front of a border, provided there is plenty of humus in the soil. Two varieties are available: 'Guinea Gold' with bronze leaves and stems and large deep yellow

137

Erythronium
erythronium

Eranthis × tubergenii

fragrant flowers that appear in early and mid spring, and 'Glory' with slightly less fragrant flowers appearing in late winter and early spring, and with bronze-tinted young foliage.

Cultivation
Plant the tubers as soon as they are available in early autumn, setting them 5cm (2in) deep, and 7.5cm (3in) apart in groups. Some nurseries offer plants 'in the green' in mid spring; these establish themselves quicker than dormant corms. They grow best in well-drained moisture-retentive soil, preferably a heavy loam. Incorporating leaf-mould into the soil at planting time is often a good idea. An ideal site for winter aconites would be below deciduous trees or between shrubs where the ground will be cool and moist in summer, but where the sun will reach the plants in winter and spring. Avoid too much disturbance after planting and water, if necessary, during the growing season, until the leaves die down.
Propagation When the plants die down, lift the tubers, divide the large knobbly ones into several pieces and replant immediately. Original tubers should not be propagated from for three to four years to allow them to swell in size. Winter aconites will also spread rapidly to form colonies by self-seeding.
Pests and diseases Birds sometimes damage opening flowers.

Erythronium revolutum

- Height 10-30cm (4-12in)
- Planting distance 10-15cm (4-6in)
- Flowers mid to late spring
- Moist humus-rich soil
- Shady or sunny site
- Corms available in early and mid autumn

Erythroniums are among the most attractive spring-flowering plants with their delicate white, yellow or purple-pink flowers that resemble little Turk's-cap lilies, and their broadly lance-shaped marble-patterned leaves. All three common species are natives of woodland, requiring some shade and moist, humus-rich soil. The best situation for them in the garden would be a semi-wild wooded corner or a cool shady patch among shrubs. If you have a peat garden or a border full of rhododendrons, erythroniums are the ideal bulbs for providing ground interest in spring.

Popular species
Erythronium dens-canis, often referred to as dog's tooth violet, has pink-purple flowers on 10-15cm (4-6in) high stems, and green leaves blotched grey or brown. It is the only European species and the one most commonly cultivated. Named varieties include 'Frans

Erythronium dens-canis

Hals' (rosy purple), 'Lilac Wonder' (pale purple with brown blotches at the base of the flowers), 'Pink Perfection' (clear pink with yellow centres) and 'Snowflake' (white). These varieties are often sold as a mixed selection.
Erythronium revolutum, or American trout lily, is the parent of a number of garden varieties with yellow or white flowers. 'White Beauty' (white flowers with yellow centres) is the free-flowering form most often found in gardens. It has two beautiful brown and white mottled leaves and 30cm (1ft) high stems carrying one or two flowers. Other garden forms range in colour from pink to

Eucomis
pineapple lily

Erythronium tuolumnense

purple with deeper markings. The yellow 'Kondo' and creamy-yellow, pink flushed 'Joanna' are hybrids of *E. revolutum* and *E. tuolumnense.*

Erythronium tuolumnense has bright yellow drooping flowers and pale green leaves on 23-30cm (9-12in) high stems. It is named after California's Tuolumne River, on whose banks it grows wild. The plants have taken readily to garden cultivation and quickly form clumps. The hybrid 'Sundisc' has golden-yellow flowers with red centres, and bronze foliage.

Cultivation
Erythroniums should be planted in moist, but not water-logged,soil rich in organic matter. A shady site or north-facing slope is best as the soil there is less likely to dry out. Avoid any site that will become hot and dry in summer. Plant the corms in early autumn, immediately after purchase. Arrange them 10-15cm (4-6in) deep and 10-15cm (4-6in) apart, in groups of at least twelve. Top-dress annually in late summer with forest bark chips or leaf-mould. Once in the ground, erythroniums are best left undisturbed. If you have to move them, do so after flowering when the leaves die down.

Propagation As the plants dislike disturbance, it's best to buy fresh corms to increase stock. Left undisturbed, and grown under suitable conditions, erythroniums will sometimes seed themselves.

Pests and diseases Trouble free.

Eucomis comosa

- ☐ Height 45-60cm (1½-2ft)
- ☐ Planting distance 30cm (12in)
- ☐ Flowers in late summer and early autumn
- ☐ Any good, well-drained soil
- ☐ Sunny and sheltered site
- ☐ Bulbs available in spring

The South African pineapple lily takes its common name from the small tuft of pineapple-like leaf bracts on top of the robust flower stem. This rises as a dense spike of starry flowers above a basal rosette of arching, bright green strap-shaped leaves.

The species are not reliably hardy in Britain but make unusual and exotic additions to late-summer beds; they are also suitable for growing in deep pots or tubs on a sunny patio or in a conservatory.

Popular species
Eucomis autumnale (syn. *E. undulata*) grows 45cm (1½ft) tall and has wavy margins to the leaves. The flower spikes, in early autumn, are creamy-white, sometimes tinged green, and the individual flowers expand to wide stars. *Eucomis bicolor* is of similar height, with crimped leaf margins and flower spikes of palest green, with purple edges to the petals.

Eucomis comosa (syn. *E. punctata*) is the tallest species, 60cm (2ft) or more high, with purple-spotted leaves and stems. The dense greenish-yellow flower spikes, with lilac throats, are scented.

Cultivation
Plant the bulbs in mid spring, setting them 10-15cm (4-6in) deep. They need fertile and very well-drained soil and a sheltered position, such as the foot of a warm wall, in full sun. Alternatively, grow the bulbs singly in 15cm (6in) pots of compost in a greenhouse or conservatory.

Outdoors, lift the bulbs in mid autumn as the foliage dies down; store in a frost-free place during winter.

Propagation Detach offset bulbs when the plants are lifted and grow on in 7.5cm (3in) pots of compost. They should reach flowering size in a couple of years.

Pests and diseases Slugs and snails eat holes in the leaves.

Freesia

freesia

Freesia × *hybrida* (single)

☐ Height 20-45cm (8-18in)
☐ Planting distance 10cm (4in)
☐ Flowers mid summer to early autumn
☐ Well-drained good soil
☐ Sunny sheltered site
☐ Corms available late winter to mid spring

Freesias can now be grown out-doors in mild districts, thanks to the development of specially pre-pared corms (sold as *Freesia* × *hybrida*). The colourful flowers (white, pink, yellow, orange, red, mauve, purple and blue) come in a single or double form, carried on 20-45cm (8-18in) high wiry stems. They appear in late summer and have a magnificent fragrance and are excellent for cutting. Usually freesias are sold as mixed collec-tions of single or double flowered forms.

Cultivation
In mid and late spring, plant pre-pared corms in any good well-drained soil. They thrive in sandy soils. Choose a bed in a sunny, sheltered position: as freesias are primarily grown for cutting, a spot in the vegetable patch would be ideal. Set the corms 5-7.5cm (2-3in) deep and 10cm (4in) apart and give each one a twiggy stick

Freesia × *hybrida* (double)

for support. Water frequently during the growing period.

Freesias will not survive the winter outdoors. Lift after the foliage has turned yellow. It's generally not worth storing the corms over winter – often they fail to flower the following year. Buy fresh ones every spring.

Propagation Prepared corms for outdoor cultivation are usually ex-hausted after flowering so propa-gation is difficult.

Pests and diseases Aphids some-times infest the stems and leaves.

Fritillaria

fritillary

Fritillaria imperialis 'Lutea'

☐ Height 20-90cm (8-36in)
☐ Planting distance 10-20cm (4-8in) unless otherwise stated
☐ Flowers in spring and early summer
☐ Fertile well-drained soil
☐ Sun or partial shade
☐ Bulbs available in early and mid autumn

Fritillaries are a large group of mainly spring-flowering bulbous plants whose exquisite flowers add charm to any garden. Bell-shaped and nodding, these are borne either in clusters atop robust stems or singly at intervals along thin but wiry stalks. Fritillaries range from the majestic crown im-perial to the beguiling little snake's head fritillary and more than repay the extra care they re-quire. Sometimes difficult to establish and maintain, the species and varieties described here are among the easiest to cultivate.

Popular species
Fritillaria acmopetala is one of the easier species. It grows 30-45cm (12-18in) tall and has narrow grey-green leaves. Each flower stem bears two or three solitary flowers in mid spring; they are pale green with maroon on the inner petals.
Fritillaria imperialis, commonly known as crown imperial, carries clusters of large red, orange or yellow flowers. These appear in mid spring on 60-90cm (2-3ft) high stems. Each cluster of flowers has a crowning tuft of leaves to com-

Fritillaria imperialis

Fritillaria meleagris

plete the beauty of a plant which has only one fault – an unpleasant foxy smell when the new growth appears in spring.

Crown fritillary looks best grown in groups among other herbaceous plants in a border, or in clumps on its own at focal points in the garden. Popular named varieties include 'Aurea-marginata' (orange-red flowers, and green leaves with distinct yellow margins); 'Aurora' (orange-yellow); 'Lutea' (golden-yellow); and 'Rubra' (deep red). Plant the bulbs 20-25cm (10-12in) apart.

Fritillaria meleagris, commonly known as snake's-head fritillary, has pairs of flowers resembling large drooping white bells heavily overlaid with purple chequering. They come out in late spring on 25-30cm (10-12in) high stems, accompanied by a few narrow grey-green leaves that contribute to the plants' particularly delicate appearance.

Snake's-head fritillary inhabits moist meadows in the wild, so in the garden it looks at home growing among rough grass. Other possible planting sites might be an undisturbed border, a peat garden, or bordering a garden pool. A white form ('Alba') with green or pink chequering is also available and excellent for naturalizing. The two frequently cross-breed.

Fritillaria michailovskyii grows about 20cm (8in) tall and is ideal for a cool shady position in the rock garden. It has solitary bell flowers in early to mid spring, maroon-purple with striking golden yellow rims.

Fritillaria persica has loose spikes of small reddish or purple bells that appear in late spring. It has grey leaves and a twisted stem that reaches 60cm (2ft) high.

Fritillaria pontica thrives in most gardens. It is 30cm (12in) tall and in late spring and early summer produces single flowers, lemon green suffused with brownish purple.

Cultivation

Plant all fritillaries immediately after purchase; handle the fleshy bulbs carefully as they deteriorate if bruised or damaged. Set them 10-15cm (4-6in) deep, except for *F. imperialis* whose large bulbs should be planted 20cm (8in) deep, and on their sides so that the hollow crowns do not collect water – a layer of coarse sand beneath the bulbs improve drainage.

Fritillaries are best grown in fertile, well-drained soil in a sunny or lightly shaded position where they can be left undisturbed for several years. *F. meleagris* prefers moist soil. Cut all stems back to the ground as they die back in early summer.

Propagation This can be done from seed but, as it takes six years to produce flowers, it is better to increase stock with new bulbs. Left undisturbed, snake's-head fritillary seeds itself.

Pests and diseases Trouble free.

Galanthus

snowdrop

Galanthus nivalis

☐ Height 10-18cm (4-7in)
☐ Planting distance 5-15cm (2-6in)
☐ Flowers mid winter to early spring
☐ Moist heavy soil
☐ Partial shade
☐ Bulbs available in early and mid autumn

The delicate, drooping white flowers of the snowdrop are always a welcome sight in spring. As natural plants of mountain and woodland, they thrive under cool moist conditions. They look most effective planted in drifts beneath deciduous trees to flower among the fallen brown leaves.

Popular species
Galanthus elwesii has larger flowers than the common snowdrop, with deep green on the inner petals. The flowers appear in late winter and early spring on stems 15-18cm (4-7in) high.
Galanthus nivalis, the common snowdrop native to Britain, flowers from mid winter onwards. Its height varies from 10-15cm (4-6in), depending on growing conditions, reaching its tallest in rich soil in partial shade. Single and double-flowered forms are available as well as a named variety, 'S. Arnott', with large scented flowers on 25cm (10in) high stems.

Cultivation
Plant in early autumn, 5-10cm (2-4in) deep – 5-7.5cm (2-3in) apart for *G. nivalis* and 10-20cm (4-8in) apart for *G. elwesii*. They do best in heavy, moist loam in a shady site with a northerly aspect. Snowdrops can be difficult to establish, but once started they need little attention.
Propagation Divide clustered plants at, or just after, flowering time. Lift and divide carefully so that each bulb is separated with its roots and leaves intact. Replant immediately at the same depth.
Pests and diseases Stem and bulb eelworms may invade the bulbs, and grey mould can affect the leaves and stalks, destroying them as the growth spreads.

Galtonia

summer hyacinth

Galtonia candicans

☐ Height 1.2m (4ft)
☐ Planting distance 20-25cm (8-10in)
☐ Flowers mid summer to early autumn
☐ Any well-drained soil
☐ Full sun
☐ Bulbs available late winter to mid spring

Pure white, hanging, bell-shaped flowers, tinged green at the base, make the summer hyacinth a particularly beautiful plant for a border. Its slightly scented flowers appear from mid summer to early autumn, in clusters of 10-30 at the top of a single, leafless stem, up to 1.2m (4ft) high. *Galtonia candicans* is the only readily available species. It looks best at the back of a herbaceous border, among shrubs, or in large outdoor containers.

Cultivation
Cover the bulbs with 15cm (6in) of soil and set them 20-25cm (8-10in) apart in early or mid spring. Place three or five bulbs together, or scatter them among early flowering herbaceous plants or annuals. Leave undisturbed once established. Remove the flower stems when tidying the border in autumn.
Propagation Every four years, divide offsets in early autumn and replant. They will produce flowers two to three years later.
Pests and diseases Generally trouble free, though grey mould may sometimes affect newly planted bulbs.

GIANT LILY – see *Cardiocrinum*

Gladiolus

sword lily

Mixed large-flowered hybrids

Large-flowered hybrid 'Sweepstake'

Miniature hybrid 'Greenbird'

☐ Height 30-120cm (1-4ft)
☐ Planting distance 10-20cm (4-8in)
☐ Flowers mid summer to mid autumn
☐ Humus-rich well-drained soil
☐ Sunny sheltered position
☐ Corms available late winter to mid spring

The showy flower heads of gladioli make them popular for cutting and exhibiting. Growing them as decorative plants in a border does have some drawbacks – the individual flower spikes last only two weeks and the plants often need staking. However, their bold form and colour compensate for this.

The original gladiolus species have now mostly been replaced by half-hardy hybrids. These showy hybrids are planted in spring, then lifted in autumn and stored in a frost-free place over winter. The few species gladioli still avail-able are hardy and can be planted in autumn and left in the ground right through the year.

Popular hybrids and species
The half-hardy hybrids are organized into four groups, according to size and flower shape.

Large-flowered hybrids have 50cm (20in) long flower spikes consisting of roughly triangular florets. Coming in an enormous range of colours, they appear from mid summer to early autumn on 1-1.2m (3½-4ft) high stems. Gladioli in this group are best grown for general garden display and cutting. Popular hybrids include 'Early Yellow' (deep yellow), 'Flowersong' (bright golden-yellow), 'Oscar' (scarlet), 'Peter Pears' (soft-orange), 'Shake-speare' (lilac), 'Sweepstake' (sal-mon-pink) and 'Traderhorn' (scarlet with white blotches).

Primulinus hybrids have 38cm (15in) long flower spikes composed of loosely arranged florets that bloom in mid and late summer. The top petal of each floret is hooded. They are free-flowering but less vigorous and smaller than the large-flowered varieties. These hybrids reach 60-100cm (2-3½ft) high and are usually grown for cutting. Popular hybrids include 'Columbine' (shell-pink), 'Robin' (pink-red), 'White City' (white) and 'Yellow Special' (yellow).

Butterfly hybrids have 45cm (18in) long spikes of closely packed florets. Their petals are ruffled and they often have distinctive throat markings and blotches. They flower in mid and late summer on 60-90cm (2-3ft) high stems. Popular hybrids include 'Bambino'

Butterfly hybrid 'Prelude'

Butterfly hybrid 'Summer Fairy'

Large-flowered hybrid 'Shakespeare'

Large-flowered hybrid 'Peter Pears'

(carmine-pink), 'Melodie' (salmon-pink), 'Prelude' (red and white) and 'Summer Fairy' (salmon-red).

Miniature hybrids have florets similar in arrangement to those of the primulinus hybrids, but smaller. The florets are usually ruffled and arranged on 38cm (15in) long spikes. They appear in mid and late summer on 45-75cm (1½-2½ft) high stems. The shorter hybrids are suitable for growing in mixed borders since they don't require staking. All make excellent cut flowers. Popular hybrids include 'Bo Peep' (apricot-salmon), 'Dancing Doll' (cream with salmon and scarlet blotches) and 'Greenbird' (sulphur-green florets with crimson throats).

Gladiolus byzantinus, a hardy species, has 38cm (15in) long spikes of loosely arranged wine-red flowers which appear in early summer, sooner than most other gladioli. They stand 60cm (2ft) high.

Gladiolus × colvillei hybrids have loosely arranged white florets. 'The Bride' is pure white. Only 30-50cm (1-1½ft) high, these delicate gladioli flower in mid and late summer.

Gladiolus nanus hybrids – which have been developed from species gladioli – come in shades of pink, rose or scarlet with violet to purple blotches. They stand 45-60cm (1½-2ft) high and flower in mid and late summer.

Hermodactylus

snake's-head iris

Gladiolus byzantinus

Primulinus hybrid 'Columbine'

Hermodactylus tuberosus

☐ Height 25-30cm (10-12in)
☐ Planting distance 15cm (6in)
☐ Flowers mid to late spring
☐ Well-drained alkaline soil
☐ Sheltered sunny position
☐ Tubers available in early autumn

Cultivation

Gladioli grow best in well-drained soil in a sunny position. As soon as the ground is workable, prepare it for planting. Dig in well-rotted manure, rake in some bone-meal and, if the soil is too heavy or too light, work in plenty of strawy manure. Cover the corms with 10cm (4in) of soil – slightly more on light soil – in early to mid spring. Make sure the base of each form is settled firmly in the soil – in heavy soil, set them on a base of sharp (gritty) sand to aid drainage. For a succession of blooms through the summer, make three or four plantings at fortnightly intervals.

Gladioli for garden decoration in a mixed border should be planted in clumps; set the corms 10-15cm (4-6in) apart. Gladioli grown for cutting are best planted in single or double rows, 30-38cm (12-15in) apart.

Eight to ten weeks after planting, begin to water generously, particularly during dry periods after the flower spikes have appeared. Start to give liquid feeds regularly. Stake large-flowered hybrids and plants grown for exhibition in an exposed position. Arrange the stake on the side opposite to that of the developing flower spike. Secure the stem with raffia or wire rings.

When the foliage begins to turn yellow-brown in mid autumn, and before the first frost, lift gladioli corms with a fork. Clean soil off the corms, and cut off the main stem 1cm (½in) above each corm. Take care not to bruise them. Dry off the corms for 7-10 days, then store in trays or shallow boxes in a cool, but frost-free place.

Break away and discard old shrivelled corms at the base of the new corm as soon as they will come away easily in your fingers. Pull off the tough outer skin on large corms and remove and store small cormlets for propagation. Check all corms during the winter and throw out any that show signs of disease. *G. byzantinus, G. colvillei* hybrids and *G. nanus* hybrids need not be lifted.

Propagation In winter, remove cormlets (resembling the size of a pea) produced at the base of the new corm. Plant in early spring in an outdoor nursery bed, setting them close together in drills 5-7.5cm (2-3in) deep, with a layer of sand below and above to help growth and make lifting easier in autumn. Keep the young plants weed-free and well watered.

When the leaves become discoloured in autumn, lift the cormlets and store them in the same way as adult corms. The following spring plant out and tend as before. Most cormlets reach flowering size in the second year; if they don't, repeat storing and growing cycle for another year.

Pests and diseases Thrips and aphids may infest corms in store, producing rough brown patches. Thrips may also infest growing plants, mottling the leaves and flowers. Stored corms may be affected by storage rot.

GLORY-OF-THE-SNOW – see *Chionodoxa*
GRAPE HYACINTH – see *Muscari*
GUERNSEY LILY – see *Nerine*
HARLEQUIN FLOWER – see *Sparaxis*

Hermodactylus tuberosus (syn. *Iris tuberosa*) is the only species in this genus of iris look-alikes. It is an interesting plant to have in the garden, with its greenish-yellow flowers tipped dark brown at the tips of the lower drooping petals. To ensure that the delicately scented flowers appear in mid and late spring, give the plants a warm sunny situation.

Cultivation

Plant the tubers in early autumn, 5-7.5cm (2-3in) deep and 15cm (6in) apart. They grow particularly well on chalk but tolerate other soil, provided it is warm, well-drained and doesn't dry out in summer.

Propagation Lift and divide established clumps in autumn.

Pests and diseases Slugs may attack flower buds as they emerge.

Hyacinthus
hyacinth

Hyacinthus orientalis

☐ Height 23-30cm (9-12in)
☐ Planting distance 7.5-15cm (3-6in)
☐ Flowers late winter to late spring
☐ Any light or well-drained soil
☐ Full sun
☐ Bulbs available early to late autumn

The large-flowered Dutch hya-cinths have largely replaced the wild species, *Hyacinthus orienta-lis*, from which they are des-cended. They have deliciously scented spikes of flowers that make them popular for window-boxes and containers in late winter and early spring, or for bed-ding schemes in sunny formal borders in late spring. The com-pact flowers, on stems 23-30cm (9-12in) high, have a long flowering period, from late winter until late spring.

A substantial number of Dutch hyacinth varieties are available. Early garden flowering varieties include 'Pink Pearl' (pink) and 'Jan Bos' (red). Popular mid-sea-son varieties include 'Lady Derby' (pink), 'Blue Jacket', 'Delft Blue' and 'Ostara' (blue) and 'Yellow Hammer' (cream). Late season varieties include 'Carnegie' (white) and 'City of Haarlem' (yellow).

Dutch hyacinth 'City of Haarlem'

Cultivation
Plant 12-15cm (5-6in) deep in autumn in any light well-drained soil; a sunny location is best. Set them 7.5-15cm (3-6in) apart if they are being grown alone in a group, and a few centimetres further apart if they are among other plants. Dead-head after flowering. Allow leaves and stems to die down naturally.
Propagation Propagation by division is rarely successful, and stock is best increased by planting new bulbs or leaving the hybrids to increase naturally.
Pests and diseases Grey bulb rot can occur if the bulbs are planted too soon, in warm soil.

Ipheion
ipheion

Ipheion uniflorum

☐ Height 10-15cm (4-6in)
☐ Planting distance 5-7.5cm (2-3in)
☐ Flowers mid to late spring
☐ Well-drained soil
☐ Sheltered, sunny or partially shaded site
☐ Bulbs available in early and mid autumn

This pretty flower is one of the few truly hardy bulbous plants to have come to Britain from South America. Its narrow pale green leaves clothe the ground from autumn onwards, and the scented lilac-blue flowers appear in mid and late spring. Only one star-like flower is carried on each 10-15cm (4-6in) high stem, but a bulb pro-duces several stems, so a notice-able clump is soon formed.

Ipheion looks most effective planted in groups in a rock garden, or at the front of a border. It tolerates full sun or partial shade, and is a useful addition to any gar-den by the sea. *Ipheion uniflorum* (also known as *Brodiaea uniflora* and *Triteleia uniflora*) is the only species available; 'Album' is a pure white form, and 'Wisley Blue' is violet-blue.

Cultivation
Plant bulbs 5-7.5cm (2-3in) deep, and 5-7.5cm (2-3in) apart in early to mid autumn. Choose a sheltered position in sun or partial shade, with well-drained soil. Keep the site free of weeds. In late summer remove the dead leaves and flower stems.
Propagation Divide in autumn and replant immediately.
Pests and diseases Trouble free.

Iris (bearded)
iris

Tall bearded iris 'Kent Pride'

Tall bearded iris 'Desert Song'

☐ Height 7.5cm-1.5m (3in-5ft)
☐ Planting distance 15-38cm (6-15in)
☐ Flowers mid spring to mid summer
☐ Any good garden soil
☐ Open sunny position
☐ Rhizomes available early to late
   summer

Bearded irises are a large group of irises that spread underground by means of rhizomes. Above ground, they are characterized by thick leaves arranged in a flat fan shape, and flowers with tufts of hair (beards) on the three outer petals (falls). The flowers, some of which are scented, come in a mass of colours. They are carried on strong stems above the spears of foliage between mid spring and mid summer.

All species and hybrids are fully hardy, so you can leave them in the ground over winter. They grow in most garden soils, but must be given an open sunny position. The most widely grown bearded irises belong to the Eupogon group, recognized by their grey-green leaves which die down to small fans in winter.

Popular species and hybrids
Bearded irises are divided into three groups, according to height.
Dwarf bearded irises have flowers in mid and late spring on 7.5-25cm (3-10in) high stems. Plant the rhizomes in small clumps 15-20cm (6-8in) apart in well-drained soil in a rockery or at the edge of a raised border. Replant every two to three years.
Iris pumila has flowers in shades of purple, white, yellow, and yellow with brown tints in mid spring. It stands only 10cm (4in) high and has no stem. As it grows naturally on mountains, well-drained soil in a rockery provides an ideal site. It's advisable to divide the rhizomes every two years after flowering.
Hybrids come in similar colours to *I. pumila* but tend to be taller – some reaching 25cm (10in) high. Popular varieties include 'Bee Wings' (yellow with brown spots on the falls), 'Blue Denim' (lilac-blue) and 'Bright White' (white).
Intermediate bearded irises flower in late spring. They reach 25-70cm (10-28in) high. Plant 30cm (12in) apart at the front of a herbaceous border or in a large pocket in a rockery. Divide and re-plant every third year.
Iris germanica, often called London flag or purple flag, has rich blue-purple falls with a white beard and light purple standards (upright inner petals). The sweetly scented flowers appear in early summer, 60-90cm (2-3ft) above ground. The foliage is evergreen.
Hybrids have well-shaped flaring flowers throughout late spring. They are vigorous, free-flowering and come in a range of yellows, creams, whites, purples and blues. Popular hybrids include 'Arctic Fancy' (purple and white), 'Golden Fair' (deep yellow), 'Green Spot' (pale cream with green 'thumb' marks on the falls) and 'Langport Star' (white).
Tall bearded irises flower in early summer on 75-150cm (2½-5ft) high stems. The tallest varieties sometimes need staking. Plant the rhizomes 38cm (15in) apart. An enormous variety of hybrids is available in a range of colours. The most popular include 'Amethyst Flame' (amethyst), 'Berkeley Gold' (rich yellow), 'Black Taffeta' (black), 'Desert Song' (pale yellow), 'Jane Phillips' (pale blue), 'Kent Pride' (chestnut-brown), 'Party Dress' (flamingo-pink), 'St Crispin' (golden yellow) and 'Staten Island' (gold and red brown).

Cultivation
Plant the rhizomes from early to late summer in beds prepared

147

Tall bearded iris 'Raja'

Tall bearded iris 'Silver Tide'

Dwarf bearded iris 'Blue Denim'

Intermediate bearded iris 'Copper Pot'

Tall bearded iris 'St Crispin'

Iris (beardless Pacific coast)
iris

Pacific coast hybrid

Intermediate bearded iris 'Arctic Fancy'

with well-rotted manure, compost, bone-meal and a little lime. Arrange the rhizomes so they all face the same way – leaf-shoot end away from the sun. Plant so that the top of the rhizome is just visible above ground. Make sure the soil around them doesn't dry out for the first two or three weeks after planting. Keep the weeds down and peel off any dead leaves. In winter cut back foliage to discourage slugs. In early spring apply a dressing of general fertilizer. Dead-head during the flowering season.

Propagation Every three years after flowering, divide the rhizomes by cutting off pieces from the outer part of the clump and discarding the centre. Make sure each piece has one or two strong foliage fans; replant immediately.

☐ Height 15-45cm (6-18in)
☐ Planting distance 23-60cm (9-24in)
☐ Flowers late spring to early summer
☐ Neutral or acid soil
☐ Sun or partial shade
☐ Rhizomes available in autumn

This North American group of irises is also rhizomatous, but the species in the group have no beards – the falls are perfectly smooth. Their evergreen foliage is narrow, tough and dark green. All the species and hybrids are hardy and all flower in late spring to early summer and make good cut flowers. They grow best in neutral to acid soils, making excellent companions for rhododendrons.

Popular species and hybrids
Iris douglasiana usually has flowers in shades of blue-purple or lavender with veining on the falls. Each stem carries four or five blooms, 30-45cm (12-18in) above ground. Plant the rhizomes 60cm (24in) apart. Unlike other Pacific coast irises, this species tolerates lime.

Iris innominata usually has cream, buff, yellow or orange flowers with rich brown veins, though there are also orchid-pink and blue-purple forms. Each stem carries one flower or occasionally two, 15cm (6in) above ground, accompanied by grass-like ever-

Iris innominata

green leaves. Grown under favourable conditions – humus-rich soil – it soon forms small clumps. Plant the rhizomes 23cm (9in) apart.

Hybrids look like crosses between *I. douglasiana* and *I. innominata*. The flowers vary in colour from white through yellow and orange to pale blue and purple. They are free-flowering and reach between 23-45cm (9-18in) high. Plant 30cm (12in) apart.

Cultivation
Plant the rhizomes of species irises and hybrids in late autumn in sun or partial shade. *I. douglasiana* tolerates lime; *I. innominata* and the hybrids prefer neutral or acid soil.

Propagation In early autumn, when new roots start to grow, divide and replant rhizomes. Water well – the soil must not be allowed to dry out.

Iris (beardless laevigata)
bog iris

Iris pseudacorus

☐ Height 45-120cm (1½-4ft)
☐ Planting distance 23-90cm (9-36in)
☐ Flowers late spring and summer
☐ Humus-rich soil at water margins
☐ Full sun
☐ Rhizomes available in autumn

These are the irises seen growing around the edge of pools and in ornamental bog gardens. They form another section in the group of beardless rhizomatous irises. All are hardy and prefer moist growing conditions and should be planted in full sun.

Popular species
Iris kaempferi, often called the bog iris, has white, blue or purple flowers with yellow streaks on the falls. The flowers appear in early and mid summer, three to four, single or double, flat or peony-shaped blooms on each stem. They stand 60-90cm (2-3ft) high; the rhizomes should be planted 30-45cm (12-18in) apart in moist soil. This species and its varieties will not tolerate lime.

Iris laevigata has three blooms per stem – deep royal blue flowers with white streaks on the falls. The deciduous leaves are pale green. It flowers in early summer and is a true water and waterside plant, growing best in a water depth of up to 15cm (6in). Each plant reaches 45-60cm (18-24in) high, and should be set 23-45cm (9-18in) apart.

Iris pseudacorus, also known as yellow flag or flag iris, has five or more yellow flowers – sometimes pale orange with brown veins – and attractive yellow and green leaves. The flowers appear in late spring and early summer. This is another true water iris that will grow at the water edge and thrives in a water depth of 45cm (18in) – here the plants can reach 90-150cm (3-5ft) high.

Cultivation
Plant the rhizomes from mid summer to early autumn, in full sun, beside streams and in pools.
Propagation Divide the rhizomes after flowering every three years and replant at once.

Iris kaempferi

Iris (beardless sibirica)
iris

Iris sibirica hybrid

☐ Height 60-110cm (2-3¾ft)
☐ Planting distance 45-60cm (18-24in)
☐ Flowers in early summer
☐ Good moisture-retentive soil
☐ Sun or partial shade
☐ Rhizomes available late spring to early summer

The species and hybrids in this section of the rhizomatous beardless iris group are hardy and easy to cultivate, provided the soil is moisture-retentive. Grow them in herbaceous borders for garden decoration and cutting, or along the edges of garden pools. A sunny site is preferable but these summer-flowering irises will tolerate partial shade.

Popular species and hybrids
Iris sibirica has flowers in varying shades of blue with white veins on the falls. It stands 60-110cm (2-3¾ft) high and has a well-branched stem. Plant the rhizomes 60cm (24in) apart.
Hybrids come in shades of blue, or white, and have larger flowers. The plants reach 90cm (3ft) high and have a less branching habit. Set the rhizomes 45-60cm (18-24in) apart.

Cultivation
Plant from mid summer to autumn or in mid spring, in good moist soil in a sunny or partially shaded site. Set 2.5cm (1in) deep in groups. If growing them near water, make sure the rhizomes are at least 15cm (6in) above water level. Avoid hoeing or cultivating around plants.
Propagation Divide large clumps every five years into four to eight pieces. Replant 2.5cm (1in) deep, after flowering, in autumn, or in spring when growth restarts.

Iris (miscellaneous beardless)
iris

Iris unguicularis

☐ Height 23-75cm (9-30in)
☐ Planting distance 30-45cm (12-18in)
☐ Flowers early summer; mid autumn to mid spring
☐ Moist humus-rich or well-drained soil
☐ Shady or sunny site
☐ Rhizomes available in spring

Some of the beardless rhizomatous irises have a character or uniqueness of their own which makes them well worth considering.

Popular species
Iris foetidissima, called stinking iris, gladdon or gladwyn iris, is renowned for its seed pods which split open and peel back to reveal striking scarlet seeds in autumn. These are far more attractive than the insignificant pale purple flowers that appear in early summer. They can be dried and used in winter arrangements. The plants stand 75cm (30in) high and give off a rank smell when bruised. Several forms are available: *I. foetidissima lutea* has yellow flowers with brown veining and orange red seeds, and 'Variegata' has attractive variegated leaves.
Iris unguicularis (syn. *I. stylosa*), sometimes called the Algerian iris, is a winter-flowering species with soft lavender or lilac flowers marked by a yellow blaze on the falls. Flowering begins in mid autumn and continues until mid

Iris foetidissima

spring. The plants are 23cm (9in) high with dark green, evergreen foliage.

Cultivation
Plant *I. foetidissima* rhizomes in summer in moist humus-rich soil. Set the rhizomes 30-45cm (12-18in) apart in clumps and 3cm (1½in) deep. This species does well in shade.

Plant *I. unguicularis* rhizomes in summer, 38cm (15in) apart and 2.5cm (1in) deep, in small clumps. The site must be sunny, with well-drained even poor soil.
Propagation Divide and replant the rhizomes in early and mid autumn.

Iris (bulbous)
iris

Iris danfordiae

☐ Height 10-67cm (4-27in)
☐ Planting distance 5-20cm (2-8in)
☐ Flowers early winter to mid spring; early to mid summer
☐ Well-drained soil
☐ Sheltered sunny site
☐ Bulbs available early to mid autumn

The irises in this group all grow from bulbs, unlike bearded and beardless irises which are rhizomatous. The species bulbous irises, which flower in winter and spring, are the smallest and ideal for soil pockets in a rockery, the front of a border, or bare ground beneath deciduous shrubs. The hybrids, which appear in early and mid summer, make good cut flowers as they are taller and larger flowered. Most bulbous irises are hardy and prefer light well-drained soil (ideally chalk or limestone), and a sheltered, sunny position.

Popular species and hybrids
Iris bucharica has up to seven sweetly scented cream and yellow flowers on 45cm (18in) high stems. These appear in mid and late spring. It grows best in a light well-drained soil containing humus and some lime. An ideal position would be below deciduous shrubs or trees, which will shelter the plants and keep them dry in summer. Plant the bulbs 15cm (6in) apart in early autumn.
Iris danfordiae has vivid lemon yellow flowers that appear in mid and late winter. The plants stand only 10cm (4in) high and the flowers have an attractive honey-like scent. Hardly any leaves are evident at flowering time. The bulbs should be planted 5-10cm

Spanish hybrid

Dutch hybrid

Iris histrioides 'Major'

(2-4in) apart in light well-drained chalky soil and in full sun.

Iris histrioides 'Major' has bright royal blue flowers with a yellow central ridge on the falls. It is one of the earliest bulbous irises to appear, flowering in early to mid winter. The plant is extremely hardy, with blooms remaining unscathed through the severest frosts and snow. At flowering time the leaves are only 2.5cm (1in) high, but by spring they may have reached 45cm (18in). As the flower stems are just 12.5cm (5in) high they look most effective grown as a mass in a rockery. It's a useful species for the garden, being one of the few small bulbous irises to tolerate dappled shade. Set the bulbs 5-10cm (2-4in) apart in light, well-drained chalky or limy soil.

Iris reticulata has deep violet-blue flowers with a gold spot in the centre of each fall. The flowers appear in late winter and early spring and are accompanied by taller leaves. This species and its varieties are 15cm (6in) high and should be planted 5-10cm (2-4in) apart. 'Joyce' (sky blue), 'Katharine Hodgkin' (large, pale blue and yellow), 'Natasha' (white and blue, yellow markings), and 'Pauline' (violet, white and blue variegated blotches) are popular varieties.

Three types of hybrid bulbous irises have been developed, primarily from the *xiphium* species which are tender Mediterranean plants.

Dutch hybrids flower in early summer. Their colours range from white, yellow and blue to purple. The plants reach 38-60cm (15-24in) high. Set the bulbs 10-15cm (4-6in) apart in light fertile soil in a sunny site.

English hybrids are the last of the bulbous irises to flower, coming out in mid summer. They have the largest flowers, but the smallest colour range: whites, blues, pinks and purples that are often flecked. The plants reach 38-68cm (15-27in) high and should be set 15-20cm (6-8in) apart in rich soil.

Spanish hybrids flower between the Dutch hybrids and English hybrids in early to mid summer. The fragrant blooms come in a good colour range, including smoky shades: whites, browns,

blues, purples and mauves. The plants stand 30-45cm (12-18in) high. The bulbs should be set 15-20cm (6-8in) apart in light soil in a sunny position.

Cultivation
Plant the species and hybrid bulbs in early and mid autumn. Set species bulbs 5-7.5cm (2-3in) deep and hybrids 10-15cm (4-6in) deep. Feed species bulbs with a general liquid fertilizer once a month for three months. On heavy and wet soils, lift Dutch and Spanish hybrids after the leaves have died down and replant in early autumn. Protect them in winter with cloches.

Propagation After the foliage has died down, lift, divide and store the bulbs until planting time in autumn. The large bulbs will flower the following year, but small offsets may take two years.

Pests and diseases Stored bulbs may be attacked by aphids and stem and bulb eelworms. Narcissus fly larvae can also be a problem. Leaves and stems, particularly those of *I. unguicularis*, may be eaten by slugs and snails. Rust occasionally occurs on rhizomatous irises. Blue mould may cause the bulbs of Spanish, English and Dutch hybrids to rot, and grey bulb rot attacks the bulbs' necks. Black spots appearing on the leaves during wet periods are a result of ink disease, a fatal fungus disease.

Ixia

African corn lily

Ixia hybrid 'Panorama'

☐ Height 30-45cm (12-18in)
☐ Planting distance 10cm (4in)
☐ Flowers early to mid summer
☐ Full sun
☐ Well-drained soil
☐ Corms available in autumn

The species in this South African genus will grow outdoors only in the mildest parts of Britain. Here, hybrids developed from them can be planted in mid autumn for flowering during early and mid summer. Their starry flowers gather in dense clusters on wiry stems, 30-45cm (12-18in) high. They come in a mass of different colours – orange, yellow, pink, red, purple and white – and are usually sold as a mixed collection. Since the flowers open only in bright sunlight, a sunny site is essential. Grow them in herbaceous borders for garden decoration and cutting.

Cultivation

Plant the corms in autumn. Set them 10cm (4in) apart and 7.5cm (3in) deep in well-drained sandy soil in full sun.

Propagation Buy fresh corms every year.

Pests and diseases Trouble free.

KAFFIR LILY – see *Schizostylis*

Leucojum

snowflake

Leucojum aestivum 'Gravetye Giant'

☐ Height 20-45cm (8-18in)
☐ Planting distance 7.5-10cm (3-4in)
☐ Flowers winter and spring
☐ Moisture-retentive fertile soil
☐ Full sun or partial shade
☐ Bulbs available in autumn

The delicate white bell-shaped flowers of snowflakes are similar to those of snowdrops, except that they are more rounded and are carried on taller stems. Their foliage is like that of a daffodil – long, narrow and green. Two species are hardy enough to grow outdoors. They like full sun or partial shade.

Popular species

Leucojum aestivum, commonly known as the summer snowflake, has nodding white green-tipped, bell-shaped flowers that appear in clusters at the top of 45cm (1½ft) high stems. They bloom in mid to late spring among clumps of spiky fresh green leaves. Summer snowflake thrives in moist conditions – the ground around a garden pool is an excellent site for them. 'Grave-tye Giant' is a large, robust form suitable for a shady site.

Leucojum vernum has similar flowers to *L. aestivum* but they appear in late winter and early spring. The 20cm (8in) high plants naturalize well in damp grassy places – they're also useful for cheering up a rockery when little else is in flower. Bear in mind that they tolerate partial shade as well as full sun.

Cultivation

Plant the bulbs as soon as they are available in late summer or early autumn. Plant 7.5-10cm (3-4in) deep in moisture-retentive, humus-rich soil. Leave undisturbed for several years.

Propagation When the groups become overcrowded, producing too many leaves and too few flowers, lift and divide as the leaves die down. Replant at once, giving the offsets the same spacing and depth as you would fresh new bulbs.

Pests and diseases Trouble free.

Lilium

lily

Lilium auratum

☐ Height 45cm-2.1m (1½-7ft)
☐ Planting distance 10-30cm (4-12in)
☐ Flowers early to late summer
☐ Well-drained, humus-rich soil
☐ Heads in sun, roots in shade
☐ Bulbs available early to late autumn
  and late winter to spring

Some lilies thrive in acid soil and some in alkaline soil; some like sun and some like partial shade. This means that every garden, provided the soil is well-drained and fertile, can grow a clump of these striking plants. Their stately habit, elegant flowers in every colour except blue, and lush green foliage covering most of the stem, combine to form a magnificent sight in summer. So plant lilies where they'll be seen – massed together in a mixed herbaceous border, among shrubs, or in tubs on a patio. The lily genus has so many species and hybrids that it's impossible to cover every one. Only those that are easily available and suitable for growing outdoors are listed here.

Popular species and hybrids

Lilium amabile has nodding Turk's cap flowers (recurved or rolled back petals) which are bright red spotted black. These appear in early to mid summer on 90cm (3ft) high stems. This is a particularly hardy species, thriving in light shade, and it will tolerate alkaline soils as long as they are well-drained. Plant the bulbs 12cm (5in) deep.

Lilium auratum, sometimes called the golden-rayed lily, has large, fragrant, bowl-shaped flowers. These appear in late summer and early autumn – a brilliant waxy

Lilium candidum

white with golden-yellow rays and crimson-purple spots inside. The plants stand 1.5-1.8m (5-6ft) high. Although easy to grow, it is a short-lived species requiring lime-free soil. A sunny, sheltered position where the lower part of the stem is kept in shade is best. Plant 10-13cm (4-5in) deep; excellent for pot culture.

Lilium bulbiferum croceum, the orange lily, has trumpet-shaped flowers of bright tangerine spotted purple. They appear in early and mid summer. It stands 90cm (3ft) high and should be planted 15-20cm (6-8in) apart. It is a vigorous variety that needs replanting every five to six years – in ordinary soil in a sunny or shaded site. Alkaline soil is tolerated.

Lilium candidum, the Madonna lily, has pure white trumpet-shaped flowers with yellow pollen. These appear in early and mid summer and are renowned for their fragrance. The plants reach 1.2-1.5m (4-5ft) high. Plant the base-rooting bulbs 23cm (9in)

apart and 5cm (2in) deep, preferably during warm, damp weather in mid to late autumn. They need a warm sunny site and will tolerate lime. Although a hardy lily, it can be difficult to establish and dislikes disturbance. So plant it in a bed where it can be left alone.

Lilium davidii bears a profusion of bright orange-red Turk's cap flowers in mid and late summer. The petals are covered with black spots and the pollen is red. This lily reaches 1.2-1.8m (4-6ft) high. Plant the bulbs 23cm (9in) apart in ordinary soil in sun or light shade. It is a short-lived species but easily raised from seed.

Lilium hansonii has pale orange-yellow Turk's cap flowers with brown spots and a waxy sheen. They appear in early and mid summer, crowded together at the top of 90cm (3ft) high stems and have a pleasant fragrance. Plant the bulbs 25cm (10in) apart in lime-free soil enriched with leaf-mould, and in light shade.

Lilium henryi has large apricot-

Lilium martagon

Lilium regale

yellow and recurved Turk's cap flowers in late summer and early autumn. It is a tall species, reaching 2m (7ft) high and usually needs staking. Plant the bulbs 30cm (1ft) apart in a lightly shaded site and in any ordinary soil; limy soil is tolerated.

Lilium martagon, the Martagon or Turk's cap lily, has nodding rose-purple Turk's cap flowers that open in mid summer. Despite the unpleasant smell of the flowers, it is a particularly popular and easy species. The 1.2m (4ft) high plants grow well in the semi-shade of a shrub border. They tolerate limy soils and are slow-growing. Plant the bulbs 22cm (9in) apart.

Lilium pumilum (syn *L. tenuifolium*) has small nodding bright red Turk's cap flowers that appear in early summer. It is one of the smaller lilies, standing only 45-60cm (1½-2ft) high. Plant the bulbs 10-15cm (4-6in) apart in ordinary garden soil in a sunny position.

Lilium pyrenaicum has tightly recurved Turk's cap flowers, appearing in loose clusters in early summer. They are bright green-yellow with purple-black spots, orange-red pollen and an unpleasant scent. It is a short lily, only 60-90cm (2-3ft) high. Plant the bulbs 23cm (9in) apart in a sunny site – alkaline soils are tolerated.

Lilium regale has fragrant white funnel-shaped flowers carried in loose clusters in mid summer. The centres of the flowers are yellow and the backs of the petals are shaded rose-purple. These popular lilies stand 1.2-1.8m (4-6ft) high. Planted 30cm (1ft) apart in ordinary soil and full sun, the bulbs will increase quickly. There is also a pure white form 'Album'.

Lilium speciosum has fragrant bowl-shaped white flowers heavily shaded crimson. These appear in late summer and early autumn on 1.2-1.5m (4-5ft) high stems. Given a winter mulch, it will grow in most districts. Plant the bulbs 30cm (12in) apart in lime-free soil.

Lilium tigrinum, the tiger lily, has strongly recurved Turk's cap flowers, which are bright orange-red spotted purple black. These are carried on 90-180cm (3-6ft) high stems in late summer and early autumn. Plant the bulbs 23cm (9in) apart in lime-free soil in full sun.

An enormous number of hybrids have been developed from the species, offering more robust plants in a wider range of colours. The hybrids are organized into groups according to flower shape.

Lilium speciosum

Asiatic hybrids have upright flowers, carried singly or in clusters, which appear in early and mid summer. They are hardy plants, and are suitable for growing in any ordinary well-drained soil in sun or partial shade. The plants reach 90-150cm (3-5ft) high and the bulbs should be set 15-23cm (6-9in) apart. Popular hybrids include 'Brandywine' (orange), 'Connecticut King' (golden-yellow), 'Electric' (orange-rose with white bands), 'Enchantment' (a warm orange-red colour),

155

Asiatic 'Exception'

Asiatic 'Red Lion'

'Exception' (pink and white), 'Red Lion' (red tipped with white), 'Sterling Star' (white) 'Syndicate' (peach-pink, yellow throat), and 'Uncle Sam' (yellow spotted with brown).

Martagon hybrids have small pendent Turk's cap flowers in early and late summer. They reach 1.2-1.8m (4-6ft) high, and the bulbs should be set 23-30cm (9-12in) apart. These hybrids are easy to grow in light shade and well-drained soil – they will tolerate alkaline soils. Popular hybrids include 'Backhouse Hybrids' (cream, buff, yellow or pink), 'Marhan' (orange) and 'Paisley hybrids' (white, yellow, orange, lilac, tangerine or mahogany).

Candidum hybrids have long pendent trumpet-shaped flowers carried singly along the 1.2-1.8m (4-6ft) high stems. These appear in early and mid summer and have an attractive scent. Plant the bulbs 23cm (9in) apart in rich soil in full sun. The most popular hybrid is *L. × testaceum* (apricot), also called the Nankeen lily.

American and Bellingham hybrids have brightly coloured

Asiatic 'Uncle Sam'

Turk's cap flowers in mid summer. They are tall hybrids, reaching 1.5-1.8m (5-6ft) high. They give the best results in light shade, in well-drained, lime-free soil enriched with leaf-mould. Plant the bulbs 23cm (9in) apart. These lilies make excellent, long-lasting cut flowers. Popular hybrids include the 'Bullwood Hybrids' (red to orange), 'Lake Tahoe' (pink-red and white) and 'Shuksan' (orange).

Trumpet and Aurelian hybrids have large trumpet-shaped fragrant flowers. They're vigorous hybrids flowering in mid and late

summer, and come in a wide range of colours on 1.2-2.1m (4-7ft) high stems. All the hybrids are lime-tolerant but their site requirements differ slightly: the white and yellow flowered varieties grow in sun or partial shade, but the pink flowered ones must have shade or their colours fade. Popular hybrids include 'African Queen' (gold-orange), 'Black Dragon' (white and purple-brown), 'Golden Clarion' (yellow), 'Green Dragon' (white and Chartreuse-green), 'Limelight' (greenish yellow), 'Pink Perfection' (pink) and 'Sunburst' (yellow).

Oriental hybrids have large strikingly coloured flowers in crimsons and pinks. The flowers appear in mid and late summer on 90cm-2.1m (3-7ft) high stems. Plant the large bulbs 30cm (1ft) apart and 10-15cm (4-6in) deep in well-drained acid soil enriched with leaf-mould. A site in dappled shade is best. Popular hybrids include 'Bonfire' (deep crimson edged silver), 'Hitparade' (rose-

Asiatic 'Enchantment'

Asiatic 'Brandywine'

pink), 'Kyoto' (pure white, spotted pink), 'Imperial Silver' (white and maroon), and 'Treasure' (rose-pink, edged white).

Cultivation

Lily bulbs should be planted in autumn or spring. Put the bulbs in the ground immediately after purchase to reduce the chance of drying out. If the bulbs are slightly shrivelled, place them in a tray of moist potting compost for a week before planting.

All lilies require well-drained soil. With heavy soils this can be achieved by digging in leaf-mould and coarse gritty sand. Poor sandy soils may need enriching with humus to make them moisture retentive. Some lilies tolerate limy soils, others prefer acid. Dig leaf-mould into all chalky soils. If you want to grow lilies that don't suit the soil in the garden, grow them in containers on the patio.

Lilies prefer their heads in the sun and roots in partial shade. They grow best with plenty of light and space around them, though they must be sheltered

Trumpet and Aurelian 'Green Dragon'

from strong winds.

For the best effect, plant in groups of at least three. Cover species bulbs and hybrids with small bulbs with 6-8cm (2½-3½in) of soil, and large-bulbed hybrids with 10-20cm (4-8in) of soil. *Lilium candidum* is an exception requiring the bulb tips to be only just below soil level. Mulch all lilies after planting, and renew mulch annually in spring.

During the growing season, water frequently. Every spring, mulch with well-rotted manure,

Trumpet and Aurelian 'Pink Perfection'

compost or leaf-mould. Stake species that are tall or heavily flowered or those with arching stems.

To grow lilies in containers, plant in pots 25cm (10in) deep and 20cm (8in) across, putting one bulb in each pot. Alternatively use pots 30cm (1ft) deep and 30cm (1ft) across and plant three bulbs in each. Place gravel over the drainage holes and add a layer of leaf-mould. Fill the container half-way up with a suitable potting compost, position the bulbs and cover

157

Muscari
grape hyacinth

Muscari armeniacum

Trumpet and Aurelian 'Sunburst'

with another 5cm (2in) of compost. Water well. Keep in a cool, frost-free position, or plunge the pot in an outdoor bed for the winter. When the lilies start to grow in spring, water to keep the compost moist. Place in their flowering position when the weather improves. Stake if necessary and feed once a month with a balanced garden fertilizer. Dead-head. When the leaves and stems die back in autumn cut them down, then return the containers to a frost-free place. Repot every two years in mid or late autumn. In the years you don't repot, give a top-dressing in early spring. Only grow varieties under 90-120cm (3-4ft) high in containers.

Propagation Division is the easiest way to increase stock. Separate and replant overcrowded clumps every three or four years between mid autumn and early spring.

Species lilies can also be increased from seed or leaf bulbils sown in early autumn and left to germinate in a cold frame. Grow the seedlings on in an outdoor nursery bed; they will reach flowering size after one to three years.

Pests and diseases Slugs may damage the plants and aphids can transmit virus diseases. Leatherjackets sometimes feed on roots and bulbs. Botrytis, a fungus, can be a problem in humid weather.

LILY-OF-THE-VALLEY – see *Convallaria*
MONTBRETIA – see *Crocosmia*

☐ Height 15-40cm (6-16in)
☐ Planting distance 7.5-10cm (3-4in)
☐ Flowers early spring to early summer
☐ Well-drained soil
☐ Full sun
☐ Bulbs available in autumn

The individual flower spikes of grape hyacinths may seem a little insignificant, but *en masse* these plants are always useful for introducing splashes of blue to rockeries, window-boxes, border edges and woodland corners in spring. They also make good long-lasting cut flowers. All the species look fairly similar, with just slight variations in height, flower colour and flowering time. They are easy to grow and colonize readily.

Popular species
Muscari armeniacum has scented cobalt-blue flowers rimmed white, that appear in mid and late spring. The plants reach 20-25cm (8-10in) high. It is a popular species to grow since it increases rapidly.
Muscari botryoides 'Album' has scented white flowers appearing from mid to late spring. It stands 15-25cm (6-10in) high.
Muscari comosum has olive green and purple flowers all on the same spike. It flowers later than other

Muscari, appearing in late spring to early summer, and it is also taller, standing 40cm (16in) high. A pretty violet-blue form, 'Plumosum', popularly called the feather or tassel hyacinth because of its feathery appearance, can also be obtained.
Muscari tubergenianum (syn. *M. aucheri*) has dark blue and pale blue flowers ('Oxford and Cambridge') all on the same spike. These appear in early spring, 20cm (8in) above ground.

Cultivation
Plant the bulbs between late summer and late autumn, setting them 7.5cm (3in) deep and 7.5-10cm (3-4in) apart, in groups or drifts. They grow in any ordinary well-drained soil, but should be planted in full sun – in shade they produce excessive leaf growth and fewer flowers.
Propagation When the leaves start to turn yellow, divide overcrowded clumps every three or four years. Replant immediately.
Pests and diseases The flowers can be affected by smut fungus.

Narcissus

daffodil, narcissus

□ Height 5-45cm (2-18in)
□ Planting distance 7.5-20cm (3-8in)
□ Flowers late winter to early summer
□ Well-drained, moist, humus-rich soil
□ Full sun or partial shade
□ Bulbs available late summer to late autumn

It's hardly surprising that narcissi are so popular among gardeners: they're cheap to buy, easy to grow, spread with little encouragement once in the ground, and provide an eye-catching display through the spring. The first narcissi flowers open in late winter, the last in early summer so, depending on the region, with a selection of different varieties, a colourful display is possible for almost five months.

Nearly all except the very short stemmed varieties are suited to growing among rough grass, where they can be left undisturbed, to colonize over the years. The large varieties grow well in groups in shrub and herbaceous borders, while the flowers of the dwarf varieties look enchanting in a rockery or sink garden. All make excellent cut flowers.

Narcissi thrive in acid and neutral soils but they will tolerate chalk. Ideally the soil should be well-drained, but moist, with plenty of humus in it.

The correct botanical name for all members of the genus is narcis-

Trumpet 'Mount Hood'

sus; those in the trumpet group are usually called daffodils.

Popular species and hybrids
The numerous narcissi hybrids developed from the species are arranged into groups according to the size of the cup or trumpet (corolla) and outer petals, and the species from which they have been developed. There are ten groups.

Trumpet daffodils (Division 1) have cups that are longer than the petals. The 20-45cm (8-18in) high stems carry only one flower which appears in late winter or early spring. They look particularly effective planted in drifts in long grass beneath trees. A vast number of varieties have been developed, offering several colour combi-

Large-cupped 'Romance'

nations: 'Golden Harvest' and 'King Alfred' (yellow), 'Mount Hood' (white), 'Queen of Bicolors' and 'Trousseau' (white and yellow).

Large-cupped narcissi (Division 2) have cup-shaped corollas a little more than one-third the length of the petals. Only one flower is held on each 32-45cm (13-18in) high stem. The flowers appear between late and mid spring, depending on variety, in a wide range of colours. Plant in mixed grass. Popular varieties include 'Carlton' and 'St Keverne' (yellow), 'Ice Follies' (pure white), 'Belisana' (white with an orange cup) and 'Duke of Windsor' (white with an apricot yellow cup).

Small-cupped narcissi (Division 3) have small cups – less than one-third the length of the petals. One flower is held on each 35-45cm (14-18in) high stem. The flowers appear in early spring and come in several colour variations. They are suitable for grow-

Large-cupped 'Duke of Windsor'

Trumpet 'Trousseau'

Large-cupped 'Carlton'

Small-cupped 'Barrett Browning'

ing in borders or for naturalizing in grass. Popular varieties include 'Birma' (yellow petals and a deep orange cup) and 'Barrett Browning' (pure white petals and an orange-red cup).

Double-flowered narcissi (Division 4) have double flowers. These are scented, and stand 30-45cm (12-18in) above ground in early and mid spring. Plant in borders. Popular varieties include 'Cheerfulness' (cream-white); 'Flower Drift' (white with an orange-yellow cup) and 'Texas' (yellow).

Triandrus narcissi (Division 5) have pendent flowers with funnel-shaped cups and back-swept petals. The 15-38cm (6-15in) high stems each carry two or three flowers in mid spring. Plant in a sunny spot, at the front of a border. Popular varieties include 'Liberty Bells' (yellow), 'Thalia' (pure white) and 'Tresamble' (white).

Cyclamineus narcissi (Division 6) have pendent flowers with long, narrow, frilled, trumpet-shaped cups and swept-back petals. They stand 15-38cm (6-15in) high and appear in late winter. Grow in fine grass or among dwarf plants in a rockery. Popular varieties include 'February Gold' (golden-yellow), 'Peeping Tom' and 'Charity May' (soft yellow).

Jonquilla narcissi (Division 7) have several small sweetly scented flowers, sometimes with swept-back petals, on stems 28-42cm (11-17in) high. These appear in mid and late spring. They grow best in a sheltered, sunny spot. Popular varieties include the tall 'Trevithian' (two or three lemon-yellow flowers on each stem), 'Suzy' (up to four flowers on each stem with bright yellow petals and an orange cup) and 'Waterperry' (ivory-white petals and pink-orange cup).

Tazetta and Poetaz narcissi (Division 8) have short cups and petals that are often frilled. In late spring, several sweetly scented flowers appear on each 45cm (18in) high stem. They grow outdoors only in very mild areas; elsewhere they are ideal for forcing to flower indoors in winter. Popular varieties include 'Cragford' (white with an orange cup), and 'Paper White' (white).

Poeticus narcissi (Division 9) have white petals with a yellow or red frilly edged cup. Only one scented flower is held on each 35-42cm (14-17in) high stem in late spring. These narcissi are best grown in borders and beds, but they can be naturalized in grass. Popular varieties include 'Actaea' (white with a red-rimmed yellow cup) and 'Old Pheasant's Eye' (white with a red cup).

Species narcissi (Division 10) have flowers in a variety of shapes and sizes. Most are dwarf plants, suitable for growing in a rock garden or naturalizing in short grass. The most popular is *Narcissus bulbocodium*, otherwise called

Small-cupped 'Birma'

Double 'Flower Drift'

Double 'Texas'

Triandrus 'Tresamble'

Jonquilla 'Trevithian'

Narcissus cyclamineus

Tazetta 'Paper White'

Tazetta 'Cragford'

'Yellow Hoop Petticoat', with a wide funnel-shaped cup and narrow insignificant petals. Its yellow flowers appear in late winter and early spring, only 5-15cm (2-6in) above ground. Plant in short grass.

Narcissus pseudonarcissus, the Lent lily, is the true wild daffodil which is sometimes found growing in English woodland and meadows. The flowers, with near-white petals and long lemon-yellow trumpets, appear in mid spring 15-30cm (6-12in) above ground. It is best grown in moist soil. An all-white form and an all-yellow form are also available.

Cultivation

Narcissi thrive in rich well-manured soil in full sun or partial shade – under trees or in the shade of a hedge or taller plants. Scatter a general fertilizer over the ground before planting. Plant as soon as the bulbs are available in late summer and early autumn.

Aim for a natural look, setting them in irregular groups rather than precise circles or rows. Scatter the bulbs on their planting site at random to decide their exact position, but ensure they are at least 10cm (4in) apart. Use a dibber to plant small bulbs and a trowel or special bulb planter for the larger ones. The bottom of the holes should be flat so the bulbs

rest on the soil. Make the holes three times the depth of the bulb in ground which can be left undisturbed; set them a few centimetres deeper in borders likely to be forked or hoed after the bulbs are planted. Space most bulbs 10-20cm (4-8in) apart; the shorter Triandrus and Cyclamineus varieties and *N. bulbocodium* should be planted 5-7.5cm (2-3in) apart.

After flowering, always let the

leaves die down completely, or at least become yellow. This allows the foliage to feed the bulbs, ensuring flowering the following year. Knotting leaves is not a good idea. It reduces the leaf surface exposed to the sun and prevents the bulbs' food reserves from building up for next year.

Propagation Lift overcrowded clumps between mid summer and early autumn, remove bulb offsets and plant out in a nursery bed. They reach flowering size in two or three years.

Pests and diseases Root rot may rot or stunt the growth of bulbs. Otherwise generally trouble free.

Poeticus 'Actaea'

Narcissus bulbocodium

Nerine
Guernsey lily

Nerine bowdenii

☐ Height 40-60cm (16-24in)
☐ Planting distance 10-15cm (4-6in)
☐ Flowers early to late autumn
☐ Well-drained soil
☐ Sheltered sunny position
☐ Bulbs available late spring to summer

From early to late autumn, when most other plants are finishing their display, the beautiful *Nerine bowdenii* from South Africa produces large heads of up to eight flowers. Each has six elegant, narrow, backward-arching petals of bright glowing pink. They are long-lasting as cut flowers.

The 45-60cm (16-24in) high stems rise from tufts of unexciting strap-shaped leaves. These start to fade in autumn so avoid planting nerines at the front of a border. *Nerine bowdenii* and its hybrids 'Pink Triumph' and 'Fenwick's Variety' are the only members of this genus that can be grown out-

doors. They must be given full sun and shelter so a protected bed at the bottom of a south-facing wall or fence is ideal.

Cultivation
Plant in late spring in any ordinary well-drained garden soil. Set the bulbs so their long necks are just covered, 10-15cm (4-6in) apart. Do not disturb for four or five years. Protect bulbs exposed on the soil surface with a 30cm (12in) layer of straw or bracken in winter. Remove faded flower heads.
Propagation Lift, divide and replant overcrowded plants every four or five years.
Pests and diseases Trouble free.

ORNAMENTAL ONION – see *Allium*

Ornithogalum
star-of-Bethlehem

Ornithogalum umbellatum

☐ Height 15-30cm (6-12in)
☐ Planting distance 10cm (4in)
☐ Flowers mid to late spring
☐ Fertile well-drained soil
☐ Sun or partial shade
☐ Bulbs available in autumn

Ornithogalum umbellatum is hardy and free-flowering. It is a small plant, up to 30cm (12in) high, with glistening white, star-shaped flowers that produce a fine show in mid and late spring. Its one disadvantage is that the flowers open flat only when the sun is out. Any fertile well-drained soil is suitable, and it tolerates partial shade, although a sunny position is preferable. Narrow borders, short grass and rockeries all make good sites.

Cultivation
Plant in mid autumn, setting the bulbs 5cm (2in) deep and 10cm (4in) apart in irregular groups. Dead-head regularly.
Propagation Left alone, star-of-Bethlehem self-seeds and colonizes readily. Crowded clumps can be lifted, divided and replanted in late summer.
Pests and diseases Trouble free.

Oxalis
wood sorrel

Oxalis acetosella 'Purpurescens'

Oxalis laciniata

☐ Height 5-10cm (2-4in)
☐ Planting distance 15-30cm (6-12in)
☐ Flowers in spring, summer or autumn
☐ Well-drained, humus-rich soil
☐ Sun or light shade
☐ Bulbs available in early autumn

Many members of the wood sorrel genus are invasive weeds, but a few of these hardy, low-growing plants make graceful additions to a rock garden or as low edgings to borders. All have neat clumps of handsome foliage comprised of several leaflets; the funnel-shaped flowers, with five petals, open wide in full sun.

Popular species
Oxalis acetosella is the well-known native wood sorrel, not a true bulbous species but it spreads to 30cm (12in) from a creeping rhizome. It has neat tufts of pale green, shamrock-like leaves, and pearl-white flowers faintly veined with pink, in early to late spring. It grows only 5cm (2in) high and is suited to a shady and moist woodland setting where it will naturalize freely. The variety 'Purpurescens' is deep rose-pink.
Oxalis adenophylla grows 7.5-10cm (3-4in) high from a bulbous rhizome and produces compact rosettes of crinkly grey foliage. The long-stemmed lilac-pink flowers are borne above the leaves from late spring to mid summer.

Oxalis enneaphylla is tuberous-rooted, hardy and only 7.5cm (3in) high. It has distinctive folded grey leaves and, in early and mid summer, large white, scented flowers. A pale rose-pink variety, 'Rosea', is sometimes available.
Oxalis laciniata also has grey-green leaves, but with wavy margins. It grows to 10cm (4in) high, with thin stems rising from fleshy rhizomes. The solitary, fragrant flowers vary in colour from deep lavender-blue to pale purple, often with darker veins. They appear from late spring to late summer.

The plants die back after flowering. *Oxalis lobata* is near-hardy and needs protection from frost with a winter mulch. It grows 10cm (4in) high, bears bright green leaves and, in early autumn, yellow flowers.

Cultivation
Plant in early autumn, 5cm (2in) deep in well-drained soil containing plenty of organic material, and in full sun or light shade. Most types die back after flowering – mark their sites to avoid damaging the rootstocks during cultivation.
Propagation Lift, divide and replant bulbs and rhizomes in late summer, before the leaves die.
Pests and diseases Trouble free.

PERUVIAN LILY – see
Alstroemeria
PINEAPPLE LILY – see
Eucomis
PLEATED LEAVES – see
Curtonus
POPPY ANEMONE – see
Anemone

Oxalis acetosella

Puschkinia
striped squill

Puschkinia scilloides

☐ Height 10-15cm (4-6in)
☐ Planting distance 5-7.5cm (2-3in)
☐ Flowers early to late spring
☐ Well-drained humus-rich soil
☐ Sun or light shade
☐ Bulbs available in autumn

Puschkinia scilloides (syn.*P. liba-notica*) is the only available member of this hardy genus from the mountains of eastern Turkey and Iran. It is a fine spring-flowering bulb that deserves to be seen more often.

Its clusters of bell-shaped, hyacinth-like flowers are an unusual pale icy blue with a creamy centre and a dark blue stripe on the inside of each petal; a white form 'Album' without blue stripes is sometimes available. Two leaves, mid-green and strap-shaped, appear at flowering time.

As the plants are only 10-15cm (4-6in) high, they look most effective at the front of a border, in a rockery, or in a sink garden or out-door container. 'Album' is best grown against a background of dark foliage to set off its discreet flowers.

Cultivation
Plant in autumn in well-drained humus-rich soil in an open position in sun or light shade. Set the bulbs 5-7.5cm (2-3in) deep and 5-7.5cm (2-3in) apart. Leave undisturbed for several years.
Propagation When the foliage dies down in summer, lift, divide and replant overcrowded clumps.
Pests and diseases Slugs sometimes eat the bulbs, stems and leaves. Disease is not usually a problem.

QUAMASH – see *Camassia*

Ranunculus
buttercup

Ranunculus asiaticus

☐ Height 30-38cm (12-15in)
☐ Planting distance 10-15cm (4-6in)
☐ Flowers early and mid summer
☐ Humus-rich, well-drained soil
☐ Sunny site
☐ Tubers available late winter to mid spring

Most species in the *Ranunculus* genus are herbaceous annuals or aquatic plants. The turban buttercup *Ranunculus asiaticus* is an exception, however, being a bulbous plant with tuberous roots. It is half-hardy in all but the mildest areas so plant the tubers in spring for summer flowering, then lift and store during the winter.

Each stem bears a semi-double or fully double peony-like flower. The flowers come in whites, pinks, apricots, oranges, reds and yellows and are usually sold as a mixed selection. The blooms last a long time when cut, making them popular with flower arrangers, though they are also useful for providing colour in borders.

Cultivation
Plant the tubers with their claw-like roots pointing downwards, placing them 5cm (2in) deep and 10-15cm (4-6in) apart. The well-drained soil should be enriched with well-rotted manure or garden compost and the site must be in full sun.

Lift the tubers when the leaves turn yellow in autumn, dry and store them in dry sand in a frost-free place over winter.
Propagation Separate clusters of tubers in autumn.
Pests and diseases Trouble free.

ST BERNARD'S LILY – see *Anthericum*

Schizostylis

kaffir lily

Scilla nutans

Scilla

squill/bluebell

☐ Height 60-90cm (2-3ft)
☐ Planting distance 15cm (6in)
☐ Flowers in autumn
☐ Moist fertile soil
☐ Sunny sheltered site
☐ Rhizomes available in spring

This splendid genus of autumn-flowering plants comes from South Africa. One species – *Schizostylis coccinea* – is relatively hardy in Britain, though it won't survive in the coldest districts of the north and east. Its flower spikes stand above the erect sword-like leaves. They bear up to ten bright scarlet flowers which are crocus-shaped at first but open into stars in bright sun.

Kaffir lilies are valuable for herbaceous borders, as they bloom from early to late autumn when most other herbaceous plants are coming to the end of their display. They also make excellent long-lasting cut flowers. Popular varieties include 'Major' (deep pink), 'Mrs Hegarty' (pale pink) and 'November Cheer' (shell pink).

Cultivation
Plant in early spring, in moist fertile soil in a sheltered sunny position. Set the rhizomes 10cm (4in) deep and 15cm (6in) apart. Mulch

Schizostylis coccinea 'Major'

every mid or late spring with forest bark or compost to keep the soil moist and encourage new growth. In summer water freely. In winter cut down any untidy growths and protect the roots with a layer of bracken or leaves.

Propagation Every two or three years, lift and divide the clumps into clusters of five or six shoots and replant in early to mid spring.

Pests and diseases Botrytis may infect the leaves and buds.

Schizostylis coccinea

☐ Height 10-45cm (4-18in)
☐ Planting distance 7.5-10cm (3-4in)
☐ Flowers from early spring to early summer
☐ Moist but well-drained soil
☐ Sun or partial shade
☐ Bulbs available late summer to late autumn

This genus includes the bluebells that form such magnificent blue carpets in woodlands from mid spring to early summer. In the garden these colonize rapidly so they are ideal for naturalizing beneath shrubs, in a wooded corner, or among grass that can be left uncut until after the leaves have died down in summer.

The other common species in this genus are smaller with similarly coloured blue blooms. They are ideal for rockeries, sink gardens and the fronts of borders. All scillas require moist but well-drained soil and, therefore, a site that is not too dry, in sun or partial shade.

Popular species
Scilla campanulata (syn. *Endymion hispanica*), the Spanish bluebell, is a robust plant with large flowers and wide glossy green leaves. It stands 30-45cm (12-18in) high. Blue, pink and white forms have been developed from this species.

Scilla nutans (syn. *Endymion non-scriptus*), the native English bluebell that grows wild in the woods, is distinguished from the Spanish bluebell by its more deli-

Sparaxis

harlequin flower

Sparaxis tricolor

- ☐ Height 30-45cm (12-18in)
- ☐ Planting distance 10cm (4in)
- ☐ Flowers late spring to early summer
- ☐ Rich well-drained soil
- ☐ Sheltered sunny position
- ☐ Corms available in autumn

Scilla campanulata

Scilla siberica 'Spring Beauty'

cate form, narrower leaves and the curved tips of its flowering stems. It stands 25-30cm (10-12in) high.
Scilla siberica has small drooping bell-like flowers of an intense blue. These appear in early spring, just 15cm (6in) above the ground. Each bulb produces several stems so only a few bulbs are needed to make an impact in a rockery, sink garden or at the base of a shrub. A white form 'Alba' and an earlier flowering sky-blue form, 'Spring Beauty', are also available.
Scilla tubergeniana is similar to *S. siberica* but it has paler blue, striped blooms that appear earlier on in spring. The plants reach 10cm (4in) high.

Cultivation

Any moist but well-drained soil will suit scilla bulbs. Plant as soon as they are available in autumn. Scatter the bulbs so they are approximately 7.5-10cm (3-4in) apart and plant with a bulb trowel or dibber. Bulbs vary in size and should be planted at a depth of three times their size.
Propagation Bluebells increase rapidly if left alone. Lift and divide established clumps in summer or autumn and replant immediately. The smaller scillas produce few offsets, but vigorous leaf growth indicate their presence. Lift and divide them as bluebells, or buy in fresh stock.
Pests and diseases Rust disease may sometimes affect the leaves.

Sparaxis tricolor is one of the few species in this South African genus available in Britain. It thrives in mild districts and elsewhere must be given a sheltered sunny location in south-facing rock gardens or at the foot of warm walls. The flowers come in an attractive array of bright colours – shades of red, purple, yellow and white and are excellent for cutting. They are usually sold as a mixture.

Cultivation

Plant the corms 7.5-10cm (3-4in) deep and 10cm (4in) apart in mid spring in rich well-drained soil in a sheltered sunny site. Mulch with shredded forest bark after planting. Keep the ground free of weeds.

Lift when the leaves die down in mid summer. The corms can be stored in a frost-free place over winter and replanted the following spring, but they often start sprouting too soon. It's easier just to plant new ones every year.
Propagation Increase stock with new bulbs.
Pests and diseases Trouble free.

SNAKE'S-HEAD FRITILLARY – see *Fritillaria*
SNAKE'S-HEAD IRIS – see *Hermodactylus*
SNOWDROP – see *Galanthus*
SNOWFLAKE – see *Leucojum*

SQUILL – see *Scilla*
STAR-OF-BETHLEHEM – see *Ornithogalum*

Sternbergia
yellow star flower

Sternbergia lutea

☐ Height 10-15cm (4-6in)
☐ Planting distance 10-15cm (4-6in)
☐ Flowers in autumn
☐ Well-drained soil
☐ Sunny sheltered site
☐ Bulbs available in summer

With their brilliant yellow goblet-shaped flowers, this genus of crocus look-alikes provides a brilliant autumn display. In the wild these small bulbous plants grow in sunny rock crevices and scorched scrubland, and in the garden they need a sheltered sunny spot.

Sternbergia lutea is the only widely available species grown outdoors. It has bright golden-yellow flowers in early and mid autumn, borne on short stems.

Cultivation
Plant the bulbs 10-15cm (4-6in) deep and 10-15cm (4-6in) apart in late summer. Set them in any well-drained soil in full sun. Do not disturb unless the plants become overcrowded.
Propagation In late summer, lift, remove any offsets, and replant separately at once.
Pests and diseases Slugs may eat flowers and mice may disturb bulbs.

STRIPED SQUILL – see
Puschkinia
SUMMER HYACINTH – see
Galtonia
SWORD LILY – see *Gladiolus*
TIGER FLOWER – see *Tigridia*

Tigridia
tiger flower

Tigridia pavonia

☐ Height 40-45cm (16-18in)
☐ Planting distance 15cm (6in)
☐ Flowers mid summer to early autumn
☐ Rich, well-drained soil
☐ Warm sheltered position
☐ Corms available in spring

The flowers of *Tigridia pavonia*, a bulbous plant from Central America, last only a few hours in the morning, but they look so exotic that it's worth finding a small space for them in the garden.

They come out in succession from mid summer to early autumn – brilliant yellows, crimsons, oranges and whites, plain or speckled, and usually sold as a mixture. Several butterfly-like flowers are carried on a central flower stem 40-45cm (16-18in) high. They are accompanied by an elegant fan of upright pleated leaves.

The tiger flower is only half-hardy so, in the British climate, a sheltered sunny spot is essential if it is to survive. Coming in such strong colours, it is best grown on its own in a small group.

Cultivation
Plant the corms in rich well-drained soil from late spring, when the soil begins to warm up. Set each corm 8-10cm (3-4in) deep and 15cm (6in) apart. During the growing season water them well and apply a liquid fertilizer every two weeks.

Lift in autumn when the leaves are dying back, before the first severe frosts, and store in dry sand or compost in a frost-free place. Keep the compost just moist enough to prevent the corms from shrivelling. Replant in late spring. In mild sheltered districts, the corms can be left in the ground where they will slowly multiply and flower more profusely.
Propagation Stock is best increased by planting new corms.
Pests and diseases Corms sometimes suffer from storage rot.

Trillium
trillium

Trillium grandiflorum

□ Height 30-45cm (12-18in)
□ Planting distance 15-20cm (6-8in)
□ Flowers mid spring to early summer
□ Rich, moist well-drained soil
□ Partial shade
□ Rhizomes available late summer and
   early autumn

Trilliums flourish under woodland conditions so they should be given a shaded spot with humus-rich soil. They are extremely hardy. All three popular species have flowers with three petals and three stamens, accompanied by three broad mid green leaves. The flowers appear from mid spring to early summer. Plant in large clumps for maximum effect.

Popular species
Trillium erectum has small wine-coloured flowers which face out-wards. The plants may reach up to 30cm (12in) high and the rhizomes should be set 20cm (8in) apart. A yellow form 'Luteum' also exists.
Trillium grandiflorum, commonly known as wake robin, is the most popular species. It has large out-ward-facing flowers, which are snow-white at first but gradually turn pale pink with age. The plants grow 40-45cm (16-18in) high and the rhizomes should be set 20cm (8in) apart.

Trillium sessile has erect, narrow, pointed flowers with a slight scent. Ranging in colour from red and maroon to a greenish-yellow, they are stemless and accompanied by marbled grey and deep green leaves. The plants stand 30-40cm (12-16in) high, and the rhizomes should be planted 15-20cm (6-8in) apart.

Cultivation
Plant the rhizomes as soon as they are available in late summer to early autumn, or at any time during the winter in mild dry weather. Trilliums must be planted in moist but well-drained soil with plenty of humus incor-porated. Ideally the site should be in partial shade, though trilliums tolerate sun if the soil is always kept moist. The rhizomes of all species should be set 7.5-10cm (3-4in) deep.
Propagation Lift and divide the rhizomes after the foliage has died down in autumn. Make sure each piece has a growing point. Only divide plants which are at least five years old. After division they may take a year or more to re-cover.
Pests and diseases Slugs attack young shoots and flower buds.

Tulipa
tulip

Triumph 'Paul Richter'

□ Height 7.5-80cm (3-32in)
□ Planting distance 7.5-20cm (3-8in)
□ Flowers early to late spring
□ Any well-drained soil
□ Sunny site
□ Bulbs available in autumn

Almost every garden and every park boasts a display of tulips in spring – a factor that's hardly sur-prising, given their availability, cheapness and the huge choice of colours and forms. The popular large-flowered garden tulips are ideal for bedding schemes – a clas-sic combination being with forget-me-nots and wallflowers. For less formal plantings, however, grow them in scattered clumps among perennials or other bulbs.

The smaller species tulips come in fewer colours than the garden tulips, but their more delicate form gives them a charm of their own. Rockeries and sink gardens, or the front of borders, tubs and containers, are the most suitable places to grow them.

All tulips have fairly specific growing requirements. During the growing season the plants need plenty of light and in the summer the bulbs have to be kept warm and dry so they can ripen. Garden tulips are best lifted and stored in a warm dry place until autumn, when they can be planted outdoors again. Species tulips and their hybrids can be left in the ground, provided they are growing in exceptionally well-drained soil – a sunny rockery, bank or border, for example.

Single early 'Bellona'

Double early 'Electra'

Popular species and varieties

The vast number of large-flowered hybrids are organized into 11 groups or divisions, according to flowering time, plant shape, flower size and form. Most have lance-shaped leaves. Species and species hybrids make up other groups. Most garden centres and some bulb catalogues sell the large-flowered garden tulips in packets of mixed colours according to group (a selection of Single early tulips, for example) or in packets of named individual varieties.

Single early tulips (Division 1) have rounded petals forming small deep cup-shaped single flowers which sometimes open flat in full sun. They are among the earliest garden tulips to flower, appearing in mid spring. The plants reach 20-38cm (8-15in) high and the stems are thick so they stand up well to wind and rain. They are excellent for bedding (plant the bulbs 10-15cm/4-6in apart), though some varieties are also suitable for forcing indoors. Popular hybrids include 'Apricot Beauty' (apricot-pink), 'Bellona' (golden-yellow), 'General de Wet' (golden-orange) and 'Keizerskroon' (scarlet and yellow).

Double early tulips (Division 2) have large double flowers resembling peonies – not to be confused with Peony-flowered tulips that flower later on (see *Double late tulips*). The long-lasting flowers appear in mid spring, soon after

the Single early tulips. They are carried on short stout stems 25-30cm (10-12in) high, and are suitable for growing in mass bedding schemes or containers. Ideally the site should be sheltered. Plant the bulbs 10-15cm (4-6in) apart. Popular varieties include 'Electra' (cherry-red), 'Mr Van de Hoef' (golden-yellow), 'Orange Nassau' (deep red), 'Peach Blossom' (rose-pink) and 'Schoonoord' (white).

Triumph tulips (Division 3), sometimes referred to as Mid Season tulips in bulb catalogues, have large, single, angular flowers in mid spring. These are long lasting and carried on sturdy stems 40-50cm (16-20in) high. They stand up well to wind and rain so you can use them for bedding schemes in exposed sites. Plant the bulbs 15-20cm (6-8in) apart. Popular varieties include 'Attila' (violet-purple), 'Dreaming Maid' (violet edged white), 'Garden Party' (white and carmine-pink), 'Keef Nellis' (pink and yellow) and 'New Design' (pink, white and yellow).

Darwin hybrids (Division 4) form one of the most popular groups with their large, round brilliantly coloured flowers. They appear in late spring on strong stems 55-70cm (22-28in) high. Their bold flowers make them use-

ful for focal planting. Set the bulbs 15-20cm (6-8in) apart. Popular hybrids include 'Apeldoorn' (orange-red), 'Big Chief' (old rose), 'Elizabeth Arden' (salmon-pink), 'Holland's Glory' (carmine-red), and 'Olympic Flame' (yellow and red).

Single late tulips (Division 5) have squared-off, oval or egg-shaped flowers that appear in late spring (in catalogues they are sometimes referred to as May-flowering tulips). They are borne on stems 60-70cm (24-26in) high. These sturdy tulips are commonly used in bedding or border schemes;

Darwin 'Olympic Flame'

Fringed 'Fringed Beauty'

Single late 'Avignon' and 'Golden Harvest'

set the bulbs 12-17cm (5-7in) apart. Popular varieties include 'Avignon' (red), 'Clara Butt' (soft pink), 'Golden Harvest' (lemon-yellow), 'Queen of Bartigons' (salmon-pink), 'Sorbet' (white and red) and 'Queen of the Night' (maroon-black). 'Georgette' (clear yellow, edged red) has several flowers on each stem.

Lily-flowered tulips (Division 6), another group of favourites, have long single flowers with pointed petals, often curving out at the tips. These appear in mid spring. They are graceful plants with strong wiry stems 50-60cm (20-24in) high. Set the bulbs 10-15cm (4-6in) apart in a sunny site. Popular varieties include 'Aladdin' (crimson and yellow), 'China Pink' (soft pink), 'Maytime' (mauve-lilac with white edges), 'Red Shine' (deep red), 'West Point' (yellow) and 'White Triumphator' (white).

Fringed tulips (Division 7) have flowers similar to those of the Single late group but with fringed petals – a feature that makes them popular among flower arrangers. The blooms appear on stems 50-65cm (20-26in) high. Plant the bulbs 15-20cm (6-8in) apart. Popular varieties include 'Burgundy Lace' (wine-red), 'Fringed Beauty'

(red and yellow) and 'Hamilton' (buttercup yellow).

Viridiflora or Green tulips (Division 8) are similar to the Single late tulips but the petals are partly green – a feature that appeals to flower arrangers. The flowers appear in late spring on 25-50cm (10-20in) tall stems. Plant the bulbs 15-20cm (6-8in) apart. Popular varieties include

'Angel' (ivory-white and green), 'Artist' (apricot-pink and green), 'Florosa' (rose, white, yellow and green), 'Greenland' (green-edged rose) and 'Spring Green' (lemon-yellow and green).

Rembrandt tulips (Division 9) have large single flowers with petals streaked or blotched with a second colour – caused by a harmless virus. The flowers appear in late spring on plants 45-75cm (1½-2½ft) high. Plant the bulbs 15-20cm (6-8in) apart. Among the varieties available are 'Insulinde' (violet and yellow), 'Lotty van Beuningen' (lilac, purple and white) and 'Union Jack' (raspberry red and ivory-white).

Parrot tulips (Division 10) have large flowers with frilled and/or twisted petals. The flowers, which open in mid and late spring, are often bicoloured. Plants reach

Triumph 'Keef Nellis'

Lily-flower 'China Pink'

Fosteriana 'Rockery Beauty'

Kaufmanniana 'Heart's Delight'

173

Parrot 'Flaming Parrot'

only 45-60cm (18-24in) high, but staking may be necessary as the stems are too weak to support the flowers. Plant the bulbs in a sheltered position 15-20cm (6-8in) apart. Popular varieties include 'Black Parrot' (purple-black), 'Fantasy' (pink), 'Flaming Parrot' (yellow flamed red) and 'Texas Flame' (buttercup-yellow, striped rose).

Double late tulips (Division 11), sometimes called Peony-flowered tulips, have large showy flowers, resembling peonies, in late spring. The plants reach 40-60cm (16-24in) high. They don't stand up well to wind and rain so, if the flowers are to last their full course, they need a sheltered position. Plant the bulbs 15cm (6in) apart. Popular hybrids include 'Allegretto' (red edged yellow), 'Angelique' (pale pink), and 'Mount Tacoma' (white).

Kaufmanniana hybrids (Division 12), otherwise known as Water-lily tulips, have long, often bicoloured, flowers. They are the first species hybrids to flower, appearing in early spring. As they stand only 10-25cm (4-10in) high, these tulips look most effective in rock gardens, containers, or along the edges of borders. Plant the bulbs 10-15cm (4-6in) apart. Popular hybrids include 'Berlioz' (uni-

Viridiflora 'Spring Green'

Double late 'Angelique'

form deep yellow), 'Heart's Delight' (carmine-red, white and yellow), 'Johann Strauss' (red and white), and 'The First' (white tinted carmine-red).

Fosteriana hybrids (Division 13) have large, long flowers in early to mid spring. They stand 20-40cm 8-16in) high and, with their brilliant strong colours, make good tulips for focal planting. Set the bulbs 15cm (6in) apart. Popular hybrids include 'Cantata' (deep scarlet), 'Orange Emperor' (pure orange), 'Rockery Beauty' (deep red) and 'White Emperor' (white).

Greigii hybrids (Division 14) have particularly colourful flowers in early to mid spring,

accompanied by maroon or purple-brown veined or spotted foliage. They reach 15-45cm (6-18in) high, though most are short so they look best in rockeries and containers. Popular hybrids include 'Cape Cod' (bronze-yellow and apricot), 'Plaisir' (creamy white with red stripes), 'Red Riding Hood' (scarlet), 'Rose d'Amour' (carmine rose, edged ivory), and 'Toronto' (salmon-orange).

Species tulips (Division 15) tend to be smaller and more delicate in form than the garden tulips, ranging from 10-45cm (4-18in) in height. Those listed are the most readily available species, though others are sometimes sold by specialist bulb growers.

Tulipa clusiana, the lady tulip, has white, pointed petals flushed red in mid spring. Its grey-green leaves are upright and exceptionally narrow. The plants reach 23-30cm (9-12in) high and the bulbs

Single late 'Sorbet'

Tulipa clusiana

should be planted 7.5cm (3in) apart. 'Cynthia' is red, tipped green.

Tulipa praestans has long red flowers with blunt petals in early and mid spring. The plants reach 30-45cm (12-18in) high. Each stem carries between two and five flowers accompanied by broad grey-green leaves. Plant the bulbs 12-15cm (5-6in) apart. 'Fusilier' is a popular multi-flowered variety; 'Unicum' has yellow-variegated leaves.

Tulipa tarda has white narrow-petalled flowers with a yellow base in mid spring. Up to five flowers are carried in a cluster on each stem, 10cm (4in) above ground. The narrow mid-green leaves form a rosette at flowering time. Plant the bulbs 7.5cm (3in) apart.

Cultivation

Plant the bulbs of garden tulips and the Fosteriana and Greigii hybrids for bedding schemes or informal group plantings in borders in early winter – if they're put in the ground any sooner, early

Kaufmanniana 'Berlioz'

growth may become frost-damaged. The soil should be well-drained and ideally alkaline; if it's acid apply lime just before planting. Set the bulbs 10-15cm (4-6in) deep depending on soil type.

Dead-head as the first petals fall, leaving the stems and leaves intact to feed the bulb. Remove any fallen petals from the ground as they may harbour disease.

It's best to lift the bulbs when the leaves start turning yellow, but if the site is needed for summer bedding, lift the tulips earlier, replant them in a spare corner, and lift again when the leaves have died down.

Place the plants in shallow boxes and store in a dry shed.

Plant the bulbs of species and Kaufmanniana hybrid tulips in early winter, in well-drained soil in a south-facing position, sheltered from strong winds. Set the bulbs 7.5cm (3in) deep.

After flowering, remove the leaves and stems as they die. Leave the bulbs in the ground.

Propagation Remove offsets when the bulbs are lifted. Store the largest ones in a dry place at 16-18°C (61-65°F). Plant them in late autumn 10-15cm (4-6in) deep and with a gap twice the width of the offsets in between. They should flower the following season.

Pests and diseases Stored bulbs may be eaten by mice, and slugs may feed on the bulbs, stems and leaves of small plants. The arabis mosaic and cucumber mosaic viruses affect tulips, blue mould may develop on damaged bulbs and tulip fire can cause scorched areas on leaves and flowers.

Greigii 'Toronto'

ACKNOWLEDGEMENTS

Photographer's credits
A-Z Botanical Collection 15(l), 28(tr), 78(tr), 83(bl), 110(r), 122(tl), 123(r), 128(r), 130(tr); Bernard Alfiera 91(b); Heather Angel 133(r); Pat Brindley 23(l), 37(r), 38, 40-41(b), 43(tl), 45(tr,br), 53(br), 54(r), 55(tr), 60, 160(bl), 161(cl), 166(r), 167(b), 169(r), 171(tr), 174(b), 175(tl,b); Brian Carter 18(tr), 20(l), 23(c), 27(r), 28(b), 30(b), 31(tl), 34(tr), 37(c), 40(tr), 48(r), 52(l), 53(tr), 66(l), 71(l,r), 72(l), 74(b), 75(tl), 85(t,bl), 87(l,c), 88(c), 108(tr), 110(l), 131(c,b), 133(l), 140(bl), 155(tl), 168(b); Michael Chinery 70(tl), 102(r); Eric Crichton front cover(tl), 14(l), 17(l), 21(l), 27(l), 46(r), 49(tr,br), 50(t), 51(l), 57(r), 61(br), 63, 64(l), 69(r), 72(r), 73(l), 78(b), 80(tr), 81(c,r), 89, 90, 91(tl,tr), 92(r), 97(r), 101(c), 103(br), 104(r), 105(r), 106, 107(t), 114, 116-7, 118, 125(br), 132(b); Arnaud Descat 11(b), 36(r), 37(l), 131(tr), 140(tl), 141(r), 167(tr); EWA (Jerry Harpur) front cover(br), 13, Philippe Ferret 15(c), 18(b), 52(r), 53(l), 59(l), 61(l), 169(l); Garden Picture Library (Lyn Brotchie) 8, (Brian Carter) 93(tl), 116, 140(tr), (Bob Challinor) front cover(bl), (Marijke Heuff) 115(t), (J Sira) front cover(bc); John Glover 112; Derek Gould 33(r), 43(bl), 56, 86(tl), 87(r), 95(b), 99(br); Diane Grenfell 124(b); Rob Herwig 155(b), 156(tr), 160(tl,tr), 161(t), 168(tr), 171(b), 172(tr), 174(c), 175(tr); Neil Holmes 34(tl), 100(b); Jacqui Hurst 137(tr), 142(l); Lamontagne 18(tl), 29(l), 31(tr,b), 44(t,b), 61(tr), 62(tl,tr), 68(b), 80(tl), 84(tl), 94(r), 107(b), 111(t), 118(tl,tr), 119, 120(tl,tr), 121, 122(tr), 126(tl,bl), 128(l), 130(b), 134(tr), 142(r), 148(tr), 150(tl,b), 152(tl,tr), 153, 154(r), 155(tr), 156(tl), 156(c,b), 157(t,br), 158(l), 162(tr), 167(tl), 168(tl), 172(b), 173(t), 174(tr); Andrew Lawson 82(l), 83(t), 84(tr), 86(b), 172(tl), 173(b); George Leveque 67(r), 129(tr); S and O Mathews 11(t), 24, 34(b), 98(l) 148(tl), 157(bl), 159(tr), 164(l); Tania Midgley 10, 12-13, 16(br), 19(r), 20(r), 36(l), 41(br), 50(b), 58(l), 74(t), 79(t), 82(r), 88(tl), 92(r), 96(l), 103(bl), 108(tl,b), 109(tl,tr), 111(b), 120(b), 124(tr), 170(l); Peter McHoy 26(r), 48(l), 72(c), back cover; Clive Nichols 2-3, 4-5; Philippe Perdereau/Brigitte Thomas 129(b); Photos Horticultural front cover(tc,tr,cl,cm,cr), 6-7, 14(r), 16(l), 21(r), 23(r), 25(r), 26(l), 28(tl), 30(l), 32, 33(l), 46(l), 47, 49(l), 51(r), 54(l), 55(l), 58(c,r), 59(r), 62(b), 64(r), 65, 66(r), 67(l), 68(t), 69(l), 75(b), 77(tl,tr), 78(tl), 79(b), 81(l), 84(b), 86(tr), 88(b), 97(l), 99(l,tr), 100(tl,r), 102(l), 109(b), 115(b), 118(b), 126(r), 132(tr), 134(tl,b), 135, 136, 137(tl,b), 138, 139(r), 143(tl), 144(tl), 145(r), 146(tl,tr), 147(l), 148(b), 149(tr,br), 150(r), 151(r), 152(b), 159(tl), 161(bl,br), 162(b), 163, 164(r), 165(tl,b), 166(l), 174(tl); Annette Schreiner 129(tl), 141(l); Harry Smith Collection 15(r), 16(tr), 17(r), 19(l), 22, 25(tl,tr), 26(c), 29(r), 30(r), 35(r), 39, 40(tl), 40-1(t), 41(tr), 42, 43(tr,br), 45(tl), 55(br), 70(tr,b), 73(r), 75(tr), 76, 77(b), 80(b), 83(br), 85(br), 92(l), 93(tr,b), 94(l), 95(tl,tr), 96(r), 98(r), 101(l,r), 103(t), 104(l), 105(l), 122(b), 124(tl), 125(l,tr), 127(b), 130(tl), 132(tl), 139(l), 143(tr,b), 144(tr,b), 145(l,c), 146(b), 147(r), 148(c), 149(l), 151(tl,b), 154(l), 165(tr), 170(r), 171(tl); Thompson and Morgan 131(tl); Don Wildridge 88(tr); D Woodland 123(r).

Illustrators
All illustrations are © Reader's Digest.

Typesetting SX COMPOSING, ESSEX; Printing & Binding PRINTER INDUSTRIA, GRÁFICA S.A. BARCELONA
Separations COLOURSCAN OVERSEAS CO PTE LTD, SINGAPORE; Paper PERIGORD-CONDAT, FRANCE

53-007-1